Practical Classroom Applications of Language Experience

Looking Back, Looking Forward

Olga G. Nelson

Eastern Michigan University

Wayne M. Linek

Texas A&M University

with **Nancy Bristol**
Editorial Assistant

Allyn and Bacon

Boston • London • Toronto • Sydney • Tokyo • Singapore

Vice President and Editor in Chief, Social Sciences and Education: *Sean W. Wakely*
Senior Editor: *Virginia C. Lanigan*
Editorial Assistant: *Bridget Keane*
Director of Education Programs: *Ellen Mann Dolberg*
Marketing Manager: *Brad Parkins*
Editorial-Production Administrator: *Annette Joseph*
Editorial-Production Coordinator: *Holly Crawford*
Editorial-Production Service: *Colophon Production Service*
Composition Buyer: *Linda Cox*
Electronic Composition: *Publishers' Design & Production Services, Inc.*
Artist: *Asterisk Group Inc.*
Manufacturing Buyer: *Suzanne Lareau*
Cover Administrator: *Jenny Hart*
Cover Designer: *Suzanne Harbison*

Library of Congress Cataloging-in-Publication Data

Practical classroom applications of language experience : looking
    back, looking forward / [edited by] Olga G. Nelson, Wayne M. Linek,
    with Nancy Bristol.
        p.   cm.
    "For the Language Experience Special Interest Group of the
International Reading Association."
    Includes bibliographical references and index.
    ISBN 0-205-26156-6
    1. Language experience approach in education.   2. Language arts.
3. Special education.   I.   Nelson, Olga G.   II.   Linek, Wayne M.
III.   Bristol, Nancy.   IV.   International Reading Association.
Language Experience Special Interest Group.
LB1576P687   1999
372.62—dc21   98–21656
                                                                               CIP

Printed in the United States of America

10   9   8   7   6   5   4   3   2   1   03   02   01   00   99   98

CONTENTS

Preface   vii

SECTION ONE   *History, Principles, and Issues*

1 The Language Experience Approach: A Framework for Learning   1
   Nancy D. Padak and Timothy V. Rasinski

2 Focus on Language Experience Learning and Teaching   12
   MaryAnne Hall

3 Language Experience Approach: A British Perspective   19
   Robin Campbell

4 The History of Language Experience: A U.S. Perspective   25
   Jane L. Davidson

5 The Language Experience Special Interest Group (LESIG) of the
   International Reading Association: An Historical Overview   37
   Bonnie C. Wilkerson

SECTION TWO   *Teaching Strategies and Classroom Applications for Early Childhood and Primary Grades*

6 Using Language Experiences in Beginning Reading: How a Language
   Experience Program Works   41
   Roach Van Allen

7 Making Written Language Learning Meaningful   48
   MaryAnne Hall

8 Approaches to Environmental Print with Young Children   53
   Bobbie Gibson Warash, Mary W. Strong, and Rachel N. Donoho

9 The Scrapbook Project   59
   Bobbie Gibson Warash and Diana J. Kingsbury

10 Developing Story Discourse: A Technique for Parents   64
    Lane Roy Gauthier and David B. Yaden, Jr.

11 Guided Imagery as Language Experience   68
Barbara J. Walker

12 Play as Story   73
Kathleen Roskos

13 Using Nursery Rhymes with Early Experience Stories: A Language/
Literature Program   82
K. Eleanor Christensen and William J. Oehlkers

14 Linking Literacy and Lyrics through Song Picture Books   87
Kathy Barclay

15 Beginning Writing: Where Does It Really Begin?   93
Kathy Barclay

16 Using LEA to Assess Literacy in the Primary Grades   102
Elizabeth Gibbons Pryor

17 Tying Assessment to Instruction: Adam Learns to Read the LEA
Way   109
Olga G. Nelson, Patricia A. Charles Kalmes, and Elizabeth Hatfield-Walsh

18 My Experience with Language Experience   123
Marilyn L. Fletcher

19 A First-Grade Whole Language Teacher Talks about the Principles That
Guide Her Practice and Decision Making   126
Janice V. Kristo and Mary H. Giard

SECTION THREE   *Teaching Strategies and Classroom*
Applications for Intermediate Grades

20 Language, Experience, and Learning: A Natural Connection for the
Middle Grades   137
Elizabeth G. Sturtevant

21 The Group Mapping Activity for Instruction in Reading
and Thinking   142
Jane L. Davidson

22 Awareness and Anticipation: Utilizing LEA and DR-TA in the Content
Classroom   148
Bonnie C. Wilkerson

23 Sorting: A Word Study Alternative   156
Jean Wallace Gillet

24 The Directed Spelling Thinking Activity (DSTA): Providing an Effective Balance in Word Study Instruction   161
Jerry Zutell

25 More than Just a Brownie: Language Experience and Edible Science for the Middle Grades   174
Ellen Lawrence Pesko

26 Wiliamsville: An Integrated Language Experience Approach to Math   183
Patty Tarrant

27 Collecting, Writing, and Telling Family Folklore Stories   189
Annette Nancy Taylor and Olga G. Nelson

28 Making History Memorable   195
Carolyn Johns

29 LEA: A Framework for Assessing Students' Higher-Level Thinking Skills   199
Mary Elizabeth Kline

30 Is Anybody Really There? Developing Voice in Student Writing   208
William J. Romeo

31 Writing Workshop: The Power of Language Experience in the Middle Years   214
N. Suzanne Standerford

SECTION FOUR   *LEA: An Approach That Includes All Learners*

32 LEA and Students with Special Needs   221
Harvetta M. Robertson

33 Empowering Students with Learning Disabilities through Language Experience   224
Sandra M. Stokes

34 ZPD + LEA = Reading for Special Needs Children: A Formula for Success   230
Rose Anne Casement

35 Variations on a Theme: Using Thematically Framed Language
       Experience Activities for English as a Second Language (ESL)
       Instruction   237
       Kathleen A. J. Mohr

36 Literacy Development of Second Language Learners with Technology
       and LEA   248
       Vicki Parsons Duling

37 Negotiated Language Experience and Content Area Instruction in the
       Bilingual Classroom   257
       Linda Lewis-White

S E C T I O N   F I V E   *Looking Forward*

38 The Language Experience Approach: Yesterday, Today,
       and Tomorrow   263
       Michael R. Sampson and Mary Beth Sampson

A P P E N D I X

A Chronology of the Language Experience Special Interest Group   269
       Bonnie C. Wilkerson

Index   275

PREFACE

As editors of this book, our purposes are threefold: to look back at language experience as an educational approach, to provide practical classroom applications, and to reconceptualize language experience as an overarching educational process. This book is divided into five major sections. In the first section, our authors attempt to conceptualize language experience by defining it as a process and examining its historical evolution. In the second section, our authors provide practical classroom applications for early childhood and primary-grade teachers and learners. In the third section, our authors provide practical classroom applications for middle-grade students. The fourth section explores sensible language experience processes and scenarios that meet the needs of special learners. In the final section, our authors step back and examine the big picture of the overriding purposes of education, consider the continually swinging pendulum of approaches, and provide insight into language experience as an enduring and evolving philosophy.

We envision language experience as a process of using experience to socially construct knowledge. The process encompasses the following concepts:

- What I *think* I can say and discuss with others.
- What I *say* can be written and shared with others.
- What I *write* can be read by myself and others.
- What we *read* can be thought about, shared, and discussed.
- We can all think, read, write, share, and discuss in order to understand each other's perceptions.
- Although our perceptions may differ, sharing and discussing with others encourages us to construct and negotiate meaning while defining our beliefs.
- As we socially negotiate and construct meaning while defining our beliefs, we come to appreciate the views of others.

The concepts in this ongoing interactive process overlap and act in concert.

We also believe that experience has two faces, actual and vicarious, and that the tools of communication provide opportunities to expand our experiential base. Thus, the language experience approach is elegant in its simplicity but takes into account previously developed content knowledge and the cultural complexities of today's society. The language experience approach values individuals, their prior experiences, knowledge that was previously recorded, social interaction, the tools of communication (reading, writing, speaking, and listening), a wide variety of thinking processes, and the concept of interactive processing.

This book attempts to expand readers' views of the purposes of language experience and how far one may take the process. The long-held view that language experience is a teaching approach that facilitates the "click" between spoken and written words for beginning readers, ESL students, and bilingual students remains valid. However, we also believe that the purpose of LEA is not only to introduce and reinforce reading during childhood, but also to socially construct knowledge at any age. Although each person's beliefs, sources of information, and questions differ, sharing and discussing them using LEA processes facilitates the construction of meaning and an appreciation of others' views. Thus, language experience appears to be the most logical vehicle for instruction and learning in a future in which change and growth are the only constants. LEA is appropriate for the twenty-first century because it can help educators conceptualize learning and literacy in a world that accepts and values diversity.

We would like to thank all of the authors, editors, reviewers (Jeri Golovin Gillin of Providence College and Barbara J. Grugel of Clarion University), university personnel, Allyn & Bacon, and members of LESIG who helped make this book a reality. We would like particularly to thank our mentors, Nancy Padak and Tim Rasinski, for encouraging us to publish this book, and Virginia Lanigan, our editor, for providing support and guidance.

Finally, we challenge you to make the connections between language experience, theory, and practice explicit to parents, politicians, colleagues, administrators, and the general public. As teachers, we often have the theory behind the practice in our heads, but we don't always explain to others the rationale behind why we do what we do in the classroom. Therefore, establishing credibility as experts on learning and learners should be a concern to all educators so that during the twenty-first century we can avoid unrelenting media and political fire. Please accept our challenge to "get political," establish our credibility as experts, and truly professionalize education.

1

The Language Experience Approach

A Framework for Learning

NANCY D. PADAK
Professor, Kent State University

TIMOTHY V. RASINSKI
Professor, Kent State University

Nowadays it's hard to pick up a journal about literacy education or to attend a professional meeting, an inservice session, or college-level course about literacy without seeing or hearing reference to whole language instruction for literacy learning. Whole language is viewed as an innovative, child-centered approach to classroom literacy instruction. That is, children learn to read in ways that build on their own knowledge, experiences, and interests.

We are certainly whole language advocates. We think the whole language philosophy and instructional practices associated with it hold great promise of having a positive impact on school reading and writing instruction. So, why, then, a separate book about the language experience approach (LEA)? After all, language experience is already incorporated in many elaborated models of whole language. Why not just drop the "language experience" banner?

Our reasons for maintaining professional attachment to LEA are pragmatic and personal. First, LEA has been around a while—it has historical value. In fact, its history precedes Dewey and the Progressive Education era (see Davidson, Chapter 4). We see this longevity as a strength. Second, LEA is a well-articulated and elegant approach to literacy education that is grounded in decades of research and professional practice. (See Preface and the following pages for complete definitions of LEA.)

LEA has been found effective in a variety of instructional settings. This variety is readily apparent to anyone who searches the professional literature for written descriptions of LEA in practice. For example, we recently ran an ERIC search using "language experience approach" as the descriptor, asking only for citations of English language journal articles. We were curious about the extent to which LEA is a topic for professional writing.

The earliest citations in the ERIC database were published in 1978. Since then, 231 have appeared, an average of about 14 per year. Although most of the articles described LEA for beginning readers, nearly 20 percent detailed LEA in non-primary classrooms (e.g., with middle school, high school, college, or adult readers). Another 10 percent focused on LEA in use with people who were learning English as a second language. And approximately 20 percent addressed LEA for learners with special needs, especially those who are deaf, hearing impaired, or learning disabled (Padak & Rasinski, 1996). Knowing the basic assumptions and procedures underlying language experience, then, teachers have a flexible set of instructional procedures that can be implemented in many classroom contexts with a wide variety of learners.

Perhaps the most important reason for our continued commitment to LEA is based on our many observations of teachers who use language experience. Not only do they provide literacy instruction in a powerful, efficient, and theoretically sound manner, but teachers who use and are committed to language experience exhibit a genuine caring for learners and respect for the experiences, interests, and motivations that they bring to the classroom that we don't always see in more traditional classrooms. When teachers accept the learners' experiences and utterances as valid and worthwhile, learners develop confidence in themselves. When a teacher orchestrates a group of children in an experience, discussion, or creation of a story, children learn how to work with one another in cooperative and responsible ways. When students work in pairs or groups of three on a language experience activity, they learn the importance of reflecting and of helping and caring for others.

To us, language experience is more than a vehicle for teaching reading. It's a vehicle for helping children develop as informed, confident, and caring human beings. It is a way to teach learners about life inside and outside the classroom.

Our intent in this chapter is to describe the essence of LEA. To do this we will first rely heavily on the words and ideas of five outstanding LEA scholars—Roach Van Allen, Jane Davidson, MaryAnne Hall, Russell Stauffer, and Jeannette Veatch—to describe the teaching–learning environment in LEA classrooms. Next we focus on critical aspects of LEA, including its similarities to whole language. To conclude, we offer several instructional guidelines based on LEA philosophy and research.

LEA Defined

Understanding the essence of LEA requires attention to several related theories: how we learn, how we read, and how others can assist us in these efforts. Hall (1985) summarizes the ways these theories interact in LEA classrooms:

> Language experience learning is based on the premises that the learner
> is an active user of language, that learning is prompted through per-

sonal involvement, that communication of meaning is the purpose and heart of language learning, and that the learner's products are valued and valid materials for literacy learning. (p. 5)

LEA advocates have developed tenets of their instructional framework or philosophy by considering, in part, the psychological foundation that supports language learning. One important aspect of this base points to conditions that make learning easy. Stauffer (1969) notes that "pupil interests, experiences, and knowledge must be used as a basic source of funds and must be extended and refined . . . . The rules of the psychology of learning must be observed . . . . [A] love of and appreciation for what reading can do for people must be fostered" (pp. 186–187). Hall (1985) echoes these notions when she describes LEA as "rooted in the elements of success, relevance, involvement, attitude, interest, and motivation" (p. 6). LEA classrooms are characterized by these psychological attributes, which facilitate learning for all students.

Another aspect of the psychological foundation of LEA centers on the nature of and relationships among thinking, problem solving, and reading. Stauffer (1969) describes reading as "a phenomenon of mental activity akin to thinking" (p. 4). To comprehend, he says, readers restructure meaning from experience and react to the meaning they create according to their purposes. He also draws parallels between this type of thinking and problem solving: "The thinker does not deal with a problem in a habitual, blind manner, but rather constructs and reconstructs a situation according to the inner relationships of the problem as a whole" (p. 20).

What, then, do we do as we read? Stauffer's seminal work (1969) is based on a conception of reading as consisting of three interrelated processes:

- Readers declare their own purposes for reading. In other words, readers must decide for themselves why they are reading a particular text. Reading for someone else's purposes just isn't as effective. Readers' purposes are often questions to be answered, which are motivating because they set up "a perplexity that demands a solution" (p. 26). Moreover, these self-set purposes allow readers to regulate their reading, to decide when they have read enough or if they have learned enough. For Stauffer, individual purpose setting is absolutely critical: "Possession of the ability to declare purposes makes the difference between an able reader and an intellectual bungler" (p. 26).
- Readers think or reason while they read. Thinking and constructing meaning are at the center of all reading. Meaning is dependent, in part, on the reader's purpose, knowledge, and experience. "[Readers manipulate] the ideas to discover logical relations, or [they rearrange] logical patterns in such a way that the conclusion can be reached" (p. 27).
- Readers judge, evaluate, and draw conclusions as they read. Good readers think backwards and forward when reading. That is, they draw conclusions about what they have read and make predictions about what they are likely to encounter. "The judgments made must be relevant to the purposes declared

as well as correct. To judge, the reader must select and weigh the facts and make decisions that are pertinent and discriminate" (p. 27).

Together these three processes—regulating reading by establishing purposes, reasoning while reading, and judging—describe what happens when we read. They are not sequential steps or stages but rather occur simultaneously. "It is apparent, therefore, that both reading and thinking start with a state of doubt or desire. It is apparent also that the process of reconstructing goes on as inquiry or discovery, until the doubt is resolved, the perplexity settled, or the pleasure attained" (Stauffer, 1969, p. 38).

LEA advocates (as well as many others) share these notions about learning, thinking, and reading. Their behaviors as teachers reflect their beliefs. Instructionally, "reading is never treated as something apart from language and thought" (Allen, 1976, p. 10). Stauffer (1969) concurs: "Reading is not only to be thought of as a communication process but is also to be taught that way. Meaning is the important thing—not saying words. Reading is a thinking process and not a parroting process" (p. 186).

As the chapters in this volume amply illustrate, LEA teachers act on these beliefs. They "operate on the assumption that if a child can acquire meaningful and communicative oral language without 'talking lessons,' that same child can relate to the printed forms of language without 'reading lessons.' Reading and writing—literacy skills—emerge as basic linguistic structures mature and interrelate" (Allen, 1976, p. 12).

To create a classroom environment that reflects these beliefs, Veatch (1986) advises teachers "no matter the grade, the subject, or the age, [to] utilize some aspect of the internal world of the pupil. There must be some kind of personal choice, some kind of individual input into the task of learning the given matter in hand. The act of instruction must be predicated upon a process that guarantees such personal choices" (p. 32). Such a classroom features student freedom and choice, to be sure, but also student responsibility.

> In sum, teaching and learning . . . is firmly grounded on order, on rigor of knowledge acquisition, on system, and on a high degree of personal commitment that comes from one's own world of thought, idea and language. With such activities in our schools, a child cannot help but feel that the world is his oyster, and his mind is a glorious instrument that makes his living vital, dramatic, and worthwhile. (Veatch, 1986, p. 34)

What Goes on in LEA Classrooms?

There is a simple answer to this question: lots. Stauffer (1969) describes LEA classrooms as busy places where students are reading, writing, using the library, talking with others (including the teacher, sometimes) about what they have read or written, engaging in group or individual inquiry, or participating in lessons designed to support their growth as literate people. Hall (1985) stresses the importance of pupil authorship. Davidson (1973) speaks of the importance of independent reading and comments that "emphasis is placed on learning and the learning process, in order to help children understand that reading isn't the only way to learn" (p. 29).

Allen (1976) describes LEA environments as providing opportunities for students to experience communication, study communication, and relate others' communication to themselves. These three major strands are realized through a variety of language experiences:

- sharing and discussing experiences—telling or illustrating something or interacting with what others say or write;
- telling or listening to stories—organizing one's thinking so that it can be shared in a clear and interesting manner or relating what others have to say to one's own experience;
- dictating—choosing from all that might be said what is most important to record for oneself or for someone else to read;
- reading texts independently for information and recreation and critically by determining the reliability and validity of information, if appropriate (also "reading" other symbols in the environment, such as clocks, calendars, charts, and so forth);
- writing independently and working to improve the style and form of one's writing; and
- improving reading and writing abilities by developing awareness of language patterns, by learning new words through reading and listening, by studying new words, by participating in comprehension activities, by integrating and assimilating new ideas through reading, listening, summarizing, outlining, and so forth.

These descriptions of LEA classrooms go well beyond the use of simply worded experience charts as part of beginning reading instruction. In fact, they could as easily portray a college classroom as a first-grade classroom; they could as easily be written about social studies instruction as reading instruction. This flexibility and versatility of the LEA framework is one of the major points we wish to make in this chapter: LEA practices work effectively in all instructional settings, with all learners, in all content areas.

LEA with Novice Readers

Of course, LEA is useful for helping children (or adolescents or adults) get off to a good start in reading. Veatch (1986), who concentrated much of her attention on beginning reading instruction, believes that "five interrelated aspects . . . weave in and out of daily classroom practice" (p. 33):

- giving attention to the alphabet, which is useful, she believes, primarily for learning letter names, which pupils can then use in their writing;
- focusing on writing that is "original as to topic by the pupil writer and includes evidence of what is known as 'invented spelling'" (p. 33);
- learning Key Vocabulary, a notion based on Sylvia Ashton-Warner's (1963) work. Pupils work with and learn the words that are important to them— their own, personal "key" words;
- generating and using experience charts; and
- reading trade books that are "CHOSEN [original emphasis] by the reader . . . read, recorded, and then brought . . . every day or two, to the teacher for an individual instructional conference" (p. 34).

Organizing for Instruction

Regardless of the age of the learners or content focus for instruction, LEA classrooms are organized to facilitate learning. The focus in LEA is on pupils and their interests and experiences. The physical setup of the classroom reflects this focus; it is a "learning laboratory . . . . No longer are desks and chairs kept in neat little rows . . . . [They are] grouped so children can interact with one another . . . . A classroom should be a center for discussions, sharing, discovering, learning, and thinking" (Davidson, 1973, p. 24).

Students sometimes work alone in LEA classrooms; other times they interact with peers in pairs, small groups, or whole-class activities. These groups are frequently initiated by students, although the teacher may convene groups as well. The "freedoms and responsibilities of self-selection" (Stauffer, 1969, p. 187) are readily apparent. Students make many decisions about how they will spend their classroom time, but teachers provide a structure or framework for the learning environment so that students will make good decisions. For example, some LEA teachers start each morning with planning periods in which students think about their plans for the day and fill out plan sheets indicating their decisions (Davidson, 1973).

Just as the organizational framework supports students' independence, so too does the availability of materials. Allen (1976) describes necessary materials as "a wide variety of books . . . trade books, books in content fields, and current publications such as newspapers and magazines are useful. Books that children produce are required . . . . Multisensory materials (and realia) are used extensively" (p. 21). All this material, print and nonprint "is naturally incorporated into the classroom environment" (Hall, 1985, p. 8).

The Role of Strategy Instruction

As the preceding descriptions make evident, strategy instruction is a part of LEA classrooms. For nearly thirty years LEA scholars have decried strategy or skills instruction in isolation or apart from meaningful use. Stauffer (1969) cautioned teachers that

> stilted artificiality must be avoided and no excuse trumped up for its use . . . . Word attack skills need to be taught as a "first-aid" to meaning . . . . Reading skills must be taught and paced in such a way that individuals are able to assimilate them and use them. (pp. 186–187)
>
> The practice of writing new words on the chalkboard so as to study them and "prepare" the reader for the reading of a story is an absurd and asinine procedure. It has no practical significance. Similar comments could be made about teaching phonetic skills in isolation, and the comment is just as applicable if the skills are taught in isolation after the reading has been done and so-called fundamental skill training is being accomplished. (p. 8)

Skills and strategies are addressed in LEA classrooms but never for their own sake and never in isolation from meaningful use.

In summary, everything that happens in LEA classrooms reflects "the premise that children react positively to those things which are relevant" (Davidson, 1973, p. 4), especially their own interests, experiences, and language. Moreover, LEA classrooms feature plentiful opportunities for children to express themselves using all the language arts. Teachers who employ language experience activities encourage children to make choices, help students establish realistic goals, and facilitate students' negotiation and construction of meaning, and in this way students learn to take responsibility for their own learning.

Language Experience and Whole Language

Those familiar with whole language (WL) educational philosophy probably see striking similarities between the LEA, as described above, and whole language principles and practices. Consider, for example, the following ideas, upon which whole language is based:

> (a) language is for making meanings, for accomplishing purposes; (b) written language is language—thus what is true for language in general is true for written language; (c) the cueing systems of language (phonology in oral, orthography in written language, morphology, syntax, semantics, pragmatics) are always simultaneously present and interacting in any instance of language use; (d) language use always occurs in a situation; (e) situations are critical to meaning-making. (Altwerger et al., 1987, p. 145)

These ideas could (and do) describe the foundations of LEA teaching and learning.

Like whole language, LEA is a perspective on language learning and teaching with classroom implications that extend far beyond reading and writing instruction. Many of these classroom applications are also similar. For example, both LEA and WL teachers insist that students engage in "real reading and writing, not exercises in reading and writing" (Altwerger et al., 1987, p. 145). Moreover, both LEA and WL teachers attempt to create classrooms that are rich in a variety of print. WL and LEA teachers also have similar dispositions regarding strategy instruction:

> What distinguishes direct instruction (and phonics) in a whole language classroom from the same lesson in a traditional classroom is purpose. A WL teacher might directly teach a child how to use semicolons (or she might draw attention to sound/letter relationships) because the student needs them for a letter she is writing . . . but not because using semicolons (or phonics) is a skill required by the curriculum guide or by the teacher's "skills" notion of literacy. (Edelsky, 1993, p. 549)

Some (e.g., Altwerger et al., 1987; McGee & Lomax, 1990) have argued that there are fundamental differences between LEA and WL. We feel they take an overly narrow view of LEA. In comparing whole language to language experience, for example, Altwerger et al. (1987) maintain that dictation often takes the place of writing in LEA classrooms and that LEA advocates endorse "fragmented exercises" and "programmed materials" for "teaching about parts of language" (p. 150).

To us, none of this describes language experience teaching and learning. Instead we agree with Yetta Goodman (1989), who values

> the language-experience approach, which stresses the significance of children having personally meaningful experiences surrounded by rich oral language opportunities prior to reading and writing and related this to integrating subject matter with the language arts through the use of thematic units. Both of these influences were supported by two principles: that the needs of the child were central to all curriculum planning, and that children needed to be actively involved in their own learning. (p. 123)

We see virtually no difference between LEA and WL as currently practiced by knowledgeable teachers. Both perspectives are child-centered and focus on curricular integration, active and purposeful involvement, intellectual commitments, and thoughtful construction of meaning in a way that values and respects learners and the social nature of learning. (See Davidson, Chapter 4, for additional information about LEA and WL.)

Does LEA Work?

The effectiveness of LEA instruction has been a focus for research since the U.S. Office of Education's massive First Grade Studies research project that was conducted in the late 1960s. Those studies provided "evidence that language experience approaches do result in good achievement" (Hall, 1985, p. 7).

In the late 1970s, the International Reading Association published a research review of LEA (Hall, 1978) that showed "very convincingly that language experience programmes work . . . . And not only that it works in the attainment of good achievement scores but that it does far more than that. It promotes learning that is pleasurable and that is congruent with how language competence flourishes" (Hall, 1985, p. 10).

More recently a research synthesis conducted by Steven Stahl and Patricia Miller (1989), which attempted to compare "whole language and language experience approaches" for beginning readers with "basal reader approaches," found clear superiority for the former at the kindergarten level. Like other research that attempts to single out and study one aspect of the instructional milieu, the Stahl and Miller study generated criticism (e.g., McGee & Lomax, 1990; Schickedanz, 1990). Critics cited some problems with definitions, such as whether instruction from the 1960s can be meaningfully compared to instruction from the late 1980s. Aspects of study design and analysis procedures were also criticized. Nevertheless, the results of the Stahl and Miller (1989) study provide further evidence of the effectiveness of LEA.

Neither LEA nor whole language is simply a set of activities. Instead, each is a theoretical perspective, and since the perspectives are complementary, classroom practices associated with them are similar. Researchers have provided us with a fair amount of evidence, spanning more than two decades, that LEA instruction is effective.

Conclusion

Although the language experience approach is widely accepted by literacy scholars and curriculum developers as an important and viable approach to teaching reading at all levels, our own experience with teachers indicates that its use may not be pervasive among practitioners. Often in our discussions with teachers in the field or in our own graduate classes, we are surprised by the number who are not familiar with LEA, the number who do not employ it in their classrooms, and the number whose depth of knowledge of LEA is limited. We believe many teachers do not take full advantage of the benefits of LEA (Rasinski & Padak, 1996).

We also believe understanding the comprehensive nature of the LEA framework may help teachers rethink and revalue LEA principles and practices. Our purpose in this chapter has been to provide a more expansive understanding of LEA. Subsequent chapters and sections of this book provide practical classroom activities and reflections of teachers' practice. Perhaps the best synthesis of LEA principles and practices comes from the Language Experience Special Interest Group (LESIG) of the International Reading Association. At LESIG's tenth annual business meeting in 1979, members decided to prepare a "statement of commitment" that captured their beliefs about LEA teaching and learning. We conclude by sharing this statement:

We believe the Language Experience Approach represents a global concept of reading instruction based on sound philosophical and psychological premises. Reading is viewed as a thinking process in which meaning from print is attained. The methodology used in the Language Experience Approach can be appropriately modified for learners at all levels of instruction.

We believe humanistic procedures permeate all levels of instruction; the dignity, integrity, and self esteem of all learners and the uniqueness of all learners' language and experiences is valued. Each learner is actively involved in affective-cognitive processes necessary for the construction of knowledge and the formulation of intellectual commitments. Holistic instruction strategies provide for the integration of the language arts rather than the isolation and fragmentation of skills and subjects. The concept of authorship is valued and nurtured.

We believe the teacher is regarded as responsible, knowledgeable, and accountable for educational decisions and for creating a rich learning environment in which there is no fear of failure. Teacher judgment is critical in the evaluation of each learner's progress based on each learner's overall performance. Therefore, the IRA Language Experience Special Interest Group is committed to continuing dialogue and dissemination of information about the theory, research, and practices of the Language Experience Approach to reading instruction. (Wilkerson, 1988, p. 25)

REFERENCES

Allen, R. (1976). *Language experiences in communication*. Boston: Houghton Mifflin.

Altwerger, B., Edelsky, C., & Flores, B. (1987). Whole language: What's new? *The Reading Teacher, 41*, 144–154.

Ashton-Warner, S. (1963). *Teacher*. New York: Simon & Schuster.

Davidson, J. L. (1973). *The language-experience approach to teaching reading*. Springfield, IL: Illinois Office of Education.

Edelsky, C. (1993). Whole language in perspective. *TESOL Quarterly, 27*, 548–550.

Goodman, Y. (1989). Roots of the whole language movement. *Elementary School Journal, 90*, 113–127.

Hall, M. (1978). *The language experience approach for teaching reading: A research perspective*. Newark, DE: International Reading Association.

Hall, M. (1985). Focus on language experience learning and teaching. *Reading, 19*, 5–12.

McGee, L., & Lomax, R. (1990). On combining apples and oranges: A response to Stahl and Miller. *Review of Educational Research, 60*, 133–140.

Padak, N., & Rasinski, T. (1996). LEA in ERIC. *Language Experience Forum, 26*(2), 4–5.

Rasinski, T., & Padak, N. (1996). An examination of language experience in reading methods texts. *Language Experience Forum, 26*(2), 6–8.

Schickedanz, J. (1990). The jury is still out on the effects of whole language and language experience approaches for beginning reading: A critique of Stahl and Miller's study. *Review of Educational Research, 60*, 127–131.

Stahl, S., & Miller, P. (1989). Whole language and language experience approaches for beginning reading: A quantitative research synthesis. *Review of Educational Research, 59,* 87–116.
Stauffer, R. G. (1969). *Directing reading maturity as a cognitive process.* New York: Harper & Row.
Veatch, J. (1986). Teaching without texts. *Journal of Clinical Reading, 2,* 32–35.
Wilkerson, B. (1988). The Language Experience Special Interest Group of the International Reading Association: An historical overview. *Journal of Language Experience, 9,* 17–25.

2 Focus on Language Experience Learning and Teaching

MARYANNE HALL
Retired Professor of Education, Georgia State University

Developing reading and writing programs from the learner's language and thinking is the core of language experience learning and teaching. The term "language experience approach" is a common one, yet the designation of the term "approach" may put the focus on methodology and may signal a reaction of comparisons of LEA with other approaches. Language experience is more than an approach. It is a perspective and a philosophy about language learning and about language teaching.

Since much of the material written about language experience does include the word "approach," that term will be used occasionally in this article in reviewing ideas and research on language experience even though the intent here is to present a broader perspective. In this chapter a description and rationale for language experience learning are presented first. A historical perspective is next, followed by an explanation of current developments and factors influencing the implementation of language experience programs.

A Description of Language Experience Learning and Teaching

Language, meaning, experience, thinking, and individuality—all are central in language experience learning and teaching. Language experience learning is based on the premises that the learner is an active user of language, that learning is promoted through personal involvement, that communication of meaning is the purpose and heart of language learning, and that the learner's products are valued and valid materials for literacy learning. Language experience learning is based on a view of reading and writing as language processing. Language experience is then a whole language approach as the language learner draws on information from the syntactic, semantic, and graphophonic cueing systems simultaneously to construct meaning from print. Even in the beginning stages, the vocabulary is uncontrolled (other than by learners' oral language). Reading and writing are integrated with the other language arts, and the materials are composed by the learners.

Language experience learning comes from the learners—their language, their experiences, their lives, their uniqueness. The psychological base for language experience is rooted in the elements of success, relevance, involvement, attitude, interest, and motivation that promote learning. Carl Rogers observes that "human beings have a natural potential for learning" (1969, p. 157). He has elaborated the features of experiential learning, and these elements certainly relate to language experience learning:

> It has a quality of personal involvement—the whole person in both his feelings and cognitive aspects being in the learning event. It is self-initiated. Even when the impetus or stimulus comes from the outside, the sense of discovery, of reaching out, of grasping and comprehending, comes from within. It is pervasive. It makes a difference in the behavior, the attitudes, perhaps even the personality of the learner. It is evaluated by the learner. He knows whether it is meeting his need, whether it leads toward what he wants to know, whether it illuminates the dark area of ignorance he is experiencing. The focus of evaluation, we might say, resides definitely in the learner. Its essence is meaning. When such learning takes place, the element of meaning to the learner is built into the whole experience. (p. 5)

Rogers conveys so well that it is the learner who does the learning. Unfortunately, reading programs sometimes seem to put too much focus on teaching and materials and not enough emphasis on the learner.

Sylvia Ashton-Warner has probably described the language experience idea best. In her book *Spearpoint* she says, "The professional formula—Release the native imagery of our child and use it for working material—remains timeless, changeless, and axiomatic, but the application of it needs constant variation" (1972, p. 17). In her book *Teacher* she says, "I reach a hand into the mind of the child, bring out a handful of the stuff I find there, and use that as our first working material. Whether it is good or bad stuff, violent or placid stuff, coloured or dun . . ." (1963, p. 34).

Language experience programs traditionally have been and still are most evident for prereaders and beginning readers and for children in the primary grades. Language experience instruction is frequently employed with remedial readers, adult illiterates, and in other special education settings. Many teachers who offer an integrated language arts program will rely heavily on having students use language in creative ways and will feature extensive pupil authorship.

The procedures for developing language experience materials by providing opportunities for experiences and talk leading to dictation, to the teacher, to reading, and to follow-up activities appear to be well known. The books by Allen (1976), Allen and Allen (1982), Hall (1981), and Stauffer (1980) provide detailed descriptions of teaching procedures.

A Historical Perspective

With the focus on large units of meaningful language, language experience beginnings have some early roots in the sentence and story methods of the 1800s. It was, however, the pioneering work of the gifted New Zealand teacher, Sylvia Ashton-Warner, who moved many educators to examine her views of "organic teaching." *Teacher* (1963) has become an educational classic and certainly essential reading for a definitive view of learning that is truly learner-centered.

As the interest in language experience grew in the United States through the progressive education movement of the 1930s, experience charts became quite common in primary classrooms. Such experience materials were often viewed as only a supplement to a formal beginning reading program, and language experience learning was not generally considered to be a major way of organizing a reading program.

In the United States language experience programs seemed to come of age in the early 1960s when language experience was included as one of the major approaches to beginning reading in the U.S. Office of Education's First Grade Studies research project (Bond & Dykstra, 1967). Roach Van Allen's work in developing language experience programs in California and Arizona in the 1960s and 70s attracted much national attention and interest. At the same time, the noted American reading educator, Russell Stauffer, was also expanding and promoting language experience instruction and research on the east coast.

Since the time of the First Grade Studies, research and knowledge in reading and language have moved beyond the question "Which method is best?" to explore the nature of the reading process and to study children's reading and writing behaviors. Work of psycholinguists since the 1960s continues to support language experience learning and teaching. Although the rationale for language experience is strong, actual use of language experience is spotty throughout the states since there are so many pressures on teachers and school systems to standardize their programs and to use commercially produced reading materials.

It is important to note that the informal education and open classroom movements of British schools contributed considerably to the concepts of the language experience approach. British educators believed that language experience should be an integral part of the total school experience and that learners could be actively involved with the creation of materials about their lives as expressed in their own language (see Campbell, Chapter 3).

Current Development in Language Experience Learning and Teaching

The basic tenets of language experience learning and teaching remain viable as new information on the nature of the reading and writing processes and on literacy acquisition has accumulated in recent years. Of particular interest to language experience advocates are the detailed examination of the emergent literacy stage, the interrelationship of reading and writing, and the explosion of attention to writing. These influences as well as diagnostic opportunities with language experience, including its status today, are considered later in this chapter.

Recently, educators have noted a change in the view of prereading and beginning reading from skill-oriented instruction to an increased awareness and appreciation of the emergent literacy learning exhibited by young children. Holdaway (1979) observes that emergent literacy development is evident in children's book behaviors and responses when books are read aloud to them. He comments further, "Going hand in hand with the practice of reading-like behaviour is an equally spontaneous involvement in writing-like behaviour" (p. 61). Studies have revealed that writing precedes reading for the early literacy learners (Durkin, 1966; Hall, Moretz, & Statom, 1976). Harste, Burke, and Woodward (1982) and Goodman and Goodman's (1979) examination of early writing and awareness of environmental print document that children learn much about written language before formal instruction is initiated.

Language experience advocates have long extolled the benefits of having large amounts of written language available to the novice reader. Language experience materials develop the understanding that print makes sense. Knowledge of the conventions of written language is acquired through repeated experiences with the dictated accounts. Knowledge of word boundaries, left-to-right sequence, capitalization, and punctuation are not learned as rules but are understood when shown functionally. The language experience activities avoid the artificiality of readiness workbooks—usually devoid of much print—and eliminate the sharp division between prereading and beginning reading so evident in many commercial materials. One particular significant point about language experience activities in preschool and kindergarten settings is that these activities use considerable print in conjunction with the ongoing curriculum. Cooking, participating in creative dramatics, caring for pets, maintaining weather records, creating art projects, and going on trips are natural situations for presenting meaningful experiences with print. The point is that the print is naturally incorporated into the classroom environment. Taylor, Blum, Logsdon, and Moeller (1982) reported that "high-implementing" teachers in a language-based program for kindergarten children had far more print available in the classroom and used in the daily activities than did the "low-implementing" teachers. Their findings also indicated that the students of the "high-implementers" outperformed students of the "low-implementers" on tests of written language awareness and conventional measures of readiness.

Not only are reading and writing closely intertwined in the emergent literacy of quite young children but the reading and writing processes are interrelated throughout the school experiences. Language experience programs have always stressed pupil authorship and the integration of all the language processes. One of the well-known findings of the First Grade Studies (Bond & Dykstra, 1967; Dykstra, 1968) was that when a writing component was added to a reading program, reading achievement improved.

Reading–writing connections are now being probed extensively by researchers and acknowledged by teachers. The possible connections between writing and comprehension are particularly intriguing. The "sense-of-story" (Applebee, 1978) that children acquire from being read to and by reading themselves is reflected in their writing. Extensive writing should strengthen learners' application of such features as plot structures, dialogue, and characterization. The degree of personal involvement in writing certainly would contribute to the impact of their learning.

Donald Graves (1983) recommended that writing receive greater emphasis in the curriculum. Today we see teachers integrating the writing process into their curriculum. At all levels students are engaged in producing pieces that reflect their knowledge of particular incidents, observations, and reflections. The focus is on the writing process and the writer's involvement in that process. Like the language experience philosophy, the writing process programs value the individual and the individual's unique repertoire of experiences, thoughts, and language from which the personal narratives spring.

One of the hallmarks of effective teachers is their careful observation and perceptive interpretation of children's reading and writing behavior. Language experience teachers who put a premium on individual responses and ideas are often quite attuned to children's efforts to master reading and writing. Diagnostically, teachers can learn much about children's reading patterns through careful observation.

Clay's (1979) account of reading behavior helps teachers interpret and guide children's reading and writing progress. There is a wealth of diagnostic information that can be observed and noted starting in the emergent literacy stage. Children match word cards to experience stories, cut a sentence apart into words to illustrate knowledge of word boundaries, point to show directional orientation and the match between spoken and written language, and make miscues. Additional rich sources of diagnostic information are children's invented spelling, their individual progress in writing over a period of time, the number and pattern of words in their word banks, and their oral expression in formulating ideas for the dictated stories. This sort of evaluation is based on children's everyday responses in actual reading and writing situations rather than test scores (see Pryor, Chapter 16 and Nelson, Kalmes, & Hatfield-Walsh, Chapter 17).

Language experience has merit because creativity, extensive writing, literature, and drama experiences benefit and appeal to all students including special education, gifted/talented, and students with other specific needs who struggle with reading (see Section 4). Language experience is most appropriate because the approach and materials stress success, positive self-concept, and individual pacing.

A number of forces mitigate against the implementation and acceptance of language experience instruction. Too many administrators seem to want a clearly delineated curriculum that can be followed exactly by all teachers and that can be explained matter-of-factly to parents. Some administrators believe that a carefully structured commercial program will correspond with the content of standardized tests. More recently, state-mandated tests in the United States are influencing curriculum because many teachers feel pressured to spend an inordinate amount of time preparing students to take the tests. Such pressures have resulted in rigid adherence to programs adopted by school systems with little encouragement for teachers to provide instructional experiences other than those associated with the commercial materials adopted by their school system.

A research review published by the International Reading Association (Hall, 1978) shows very convincingly that language experience programs work and have a positive impact on reading achievement. Proponents of language experience need to share and publicize this information, as well as how it promotes learning that is pleasurable and congruent with how language competency flourishes.

Key school personnel—classroom, master, resource, and special education teachers, supervisors, and administrators—can all be change agents because implementation of language experience is modest in terms of budgetary considerations, yet high in terms of freedom and independence on the part of teachers and students. The basic requirements for effective language experience instructional programs are: accepting teachers, students who are free to express themselves, and classrooms rich in experiences, in talk, in drama, in art, in literature—in short, in functional, expressive communication.

To enrich and improve reading and language instruction, strong teacher education programs are essential. These programs must be strong in the knowledge base provided about language development, in reading and language arts across the curriculum, and in children's literature. The attention to language experience in teacher education has increased considerably in recent years and that attention needs to continue.

Conclusion

The rationale for, the interest in, and the implementation of language experience programs have grown tremendously since 1960. We have theoretical and research evidence that language experience learning is indeed effective. However, since language experience programs cannot be conveniently packaged commercially, there is the danger that language experience is not considered feasible by many. It will be the efforts of committed teachers who keep language experience alive and thriving.

Postscript

The years since the original publication of this article in 1985 have seen tremendous growth of the whole language movement. The theoretical foundations and instructional programs of whole language along with the attention to diversity of learners and to appropriate assessment and evaluation related to holistic learning are encouraging indeed. Language experience learning can be compatible with whole language when the premises of language experience are basic to the instruction offered. Both whole language and language experience are inclusive with wide choices for adaptation of instruction according to the individuality of learners and teachers.

REFERENCES

Allen, R. V. (1976). *Language experiences in communication*. Boston: Houghton Mifflin.

Allen, R. V., & Allen, C. (1982). *Language experience activities* (2nd ed.). Boston: Houghton Mifflin.

Applebee, A. N. (1978). *The child's concept of story*. Chicago: University of Chicago Press.

Ashton-Warner, S. (1963). *Teacher*. New York: Simon & Schuster.

Ashton-Warner, S. (1972). *Spearpoint*. New York: Alfred A. Knopf.

Bond, G. L., & Dykstra, R. (1967). The cooperative program in first grade reading instruction. *Reading Research Quarterly, 2,* 5–142.

Clay, M. M. (1976). *What did I write*? Auckland, New Zealand: Heinemann.

Clay, M. M. (1979). *Reading: The patternings of complex behavior* (2nd ed.). Auckland, New Zealand: Heinemann.

Durkin, D. (1966). *Children who read early*. New York: Teachers College Press.

Dykstra, R. (1968). Summary of the second-grade phase of the cooperative research program in primary reading instruction. *Reading Research Quarterly, 4,* 49–70.

Goodman, K. S., & Goodman, Y. M. (1979). Learning to read is natural. In L. B. Weaver, & P. A. Weaver (Eds.), *Theory and practice of early reading: Vol. 1* (pp. 137–186). Hillsdale, NJ: Erlbaum.

Graves, D. H. (1983). *Writing: Teachers and children at work*. Portsmouth, NH: Heinemann.

Hall, M. (1978). *The language experience approach for teaching reading: A research perspective*. Newark, DE: International Reading Association.

Hall, M. (1981). *Teaching reading as a language experience* (3rd ed.). Columbus, OH: Merrill.

Hall, M., Moretz, S., & Statom, J. (1976). Writing before grade one—A study of early writers. *Elementary English, 53,* 582–584.

Harste, J., Burke, C. L., & Woodward, V. A. (1982). Children's language and world: Initial encounters with print. In J. A. Langer, & M. T. Smith-Burke (Eds.), *Reader meets author: Bridging the gap* (pp. 105–131). Newark, DE: International Reading Association.

Holdaway, D. (1979). *The foundations of literacy*. Portsmouth, NH: Heinemann.

Rogers, C. (1969). *Freedom to learn*. Columbus, OH: Merrill.

Stauffer, R. G. (1980). *The language experience approach to the teaching of reading* (2nd ed.). New York: Harper & Row.

Taylor, N. E., Blum, I. M., Logsdon, D. M., & Moeller, G. D. (1982). *The development of written language awareness: Environment aspects and program characteristics*. Paper presented at the meeting of the American Educational Research Association, New York.

3 Language Experience Approach

A British Perspective

ROBIN CAMPBELL
Professor Emeritus, University of Hertfordshire, UK

This chapter presents some of the historical and theoretical foundations upon which the British primary school curriculum is based. The investigations that impacted the shift from a more traditionally driven curriculum to one that is predicated on an interactive view of learning that builds on children's experiences and language are highlighted and discussed.

At the same time that educators in the United States (Bruner, 1960; Dewey, 1916, 1938; Lee & Allen, 1963; Stauffer, 1970) were exploring how children learn, British educators who studied children in primary settings were developing parallel theories (Gardner, 1966; Goddard, 1958; Isaacs, 1930, 1932; Marshall, 1963). These theories were derived from examining children's experiences at home, in the classroom, and in other daily activities. Results of these formal and action research studies had an impact on curriculum. Curriculum began to shift from an emphasis on knowledge acquisition to a concept that valued what children already knew and how they assimilated new knowledge.

At about the same time that these grassroots investigations were being conducted, the British government initiated several studies to investigate all aspects of primary education. These reports included recommendations for the most effective teaching in the classroom (Department of Education and Science, 1967, 1975; British Board of Education, 1931). Results of these studies indicated similar conclusions to those conducted by classroom teachers; that is, children learn best through activity and experiences and that those experience are the critical basis for language and literacy learning. These foundations that were developed fifty years ago remain a cornerstone of British primary education today.

Grassroots Investigations

Nora Goddard (1958) wrote about her own classroom practice: "In approaching reading through interest the natural sequence is: first, that the child has something he wants to say, second, that we write it down for him, and last, that he reads it, and wants to read it because it tells of something that is of real interest to him" (p. 12). Goddard placed a strong emphasis upon using children's interests as a basis for learning to read and subsequently for extending that reading. Although she did not use the term "language experience approach," the sequence that she suggested is a very succinct statement of what is recognized as the essence of language experience.

Subsequently in 1974, Nora Goddard published her book *Literacy: Language-Experience Approaches*. This book was based on Goddard's work, first as an infant school teacher and head teacher teaching 5–7 year old children, then as an inspector of infants' education in London. Goddard emphasized using children's feelings, interests, and experiences to help them with both spoken and written language. In particular, Goddard suggested that teachers needed to learn about children's preschool experiences and integrate new experiences in school with those prior experiences. She advocated that these rich experiences were important in order to encourage literacy learning, and that the way for teachers to incorporate the experiences in the classroom was to act as scribes by writing down what children say. Goddard also stated that it is important to include story reading and nursery rhymes in the classroom.

Goddard recognized the historical background of language experience approaches: Rousseau (Foxley, 1911), who emphasized firsthand learning; Froebel (Lilley, 1967), who noted the value of play in early childhood; and Dewey (1916, 1938), who advocated natural ways of learning and teaching. Goddard also cited contemporary writers such as Sylvia Ashton-Warner (1963) and her work with Maori children in New Zealand. Ashton-Warner also advocated employing children's language about their loves, hates, and fears, as well as their interests and life experiences. This theory of teaching children indicated a clear connection to language experience.

In addition to those worldwide connections, other British influences appeared to impact Goddard's perspective, such as the widely accepted practice of the language experience approach in the United Kingdom. Goddard's work (1974) was seen as a representation, in many respects, of what numerous primary school teachers were developing in their classrooms as common practice.

Classroom practitioners were also reporting on their practice and demonstrating how language experience approaches were being used in their classrooms during the same forty-year period (1931–1975) that government studies were being conducted. For example, Sybil Marshall (1963) gave an account of her teaching in a Cambridgeshire village school over an eighteen-year period. The village school was so small that children had to be grouped into one multiage classroom. As a result, she developed a curriculum based on education through the arts. Literacy learning was very much based on the experiences that children brought to school and the many experiences that the school provided. Marshall suggested that

language, in general, had to be "felt or experienced" (p. 170) and that the arts provided the appropriate opportunities to connect language with life experiences.

Marshall even encouraged five-year-old children to write, illustrate, and produce their own stories and books on various topics. The process required that the
teacher serve as a scribe to take down the children's dictations. "When the picture
was finished, each one [child] told me what it was about, and I wrote for them a
few words about their picture" (p. 140). Because the children were actively involved
with the printed words, Marshall believed that this was a substantial aid to learning to read. The books produced through this learning process engaged children's
interests and became their reading materials.

Susan Isaacs's work (1930) in the experimental Malting House School in the
County of Cambridgeshire described how children were encouraged to read and
write about their interests and experiences as part of their play activities; children
also wrote letters to meet specific purposes and real needs. Her later work (Isaacs,
1932) emphasized using children's interests and experiences in order to facilitate
their development. As Head of the Department of Child Development at the University of London's Institute of Education, Isaacs shared and disseminated this philosophy and practice with others.

Isaacs was succeeded in that post by Dorothy Gardner, who continued to
research and teach about progressive education in infant and junior (7–11 years of
age) schools based on a knowledge of child development. In particular, her extensive studies of progressive and traditional schools indicated that using children's
interests and experiences as a basis for literacy learning supported children's
development (Gardner, 1966).

Government Initiatives

A feature of the British educational system has been the frequent creation of committees to explore aspects of the structure, curriculum, teaching, and learning in
schools. One such committee was established in 1928 to inquire and report about
the courses of study suitable for children up to the age of eleven. The report from
that committee (British Board of Education, 1931) is widely known as *The Hadow
Report*, named after the chairman of the committee. That report considerably influenced subsequent teacher preparation programs and classroom practices in British
primary schools. In particular, the committee concluded that the best way to
structure studies in the primary school was not to have distinct and separate subjects but rather to have the curriculum arranged to meet the needs of young children. The next problem facing the committee was to find such an appropriate
curriculum.

The answer was found in a child-centered language experience approach. The
British primary school at that time employed methods that started with and built
on children's experiences, their inquisitive natures, their interests, and their developing talents and abilities. Therefore, it was recommended that children's experiences and interests serve as the starting point for the teaching and learning that
was to take place. Most important, since the children's experiences were to be used

as the basis for teaching, the language experience approach became the natural foundation for learning. *The Hadow Report* concluded that: "Applying these considerations to the problem before us, we see that the curriculum is to be thought of in terms of activity and experience rather than knowledge to be acquired and facts to be stored" (British Board of Education, 1931, p. 75). Thus, activity and experience became a standard for British primary school teachers as they developed their classroom practice.

In 1963 the Minister of Education asked the Central Advisory Council for Education "to consider primary education in all its aspects." The report that followed became known as *The Plowden Report* (Department of Education and Science, 1967), after the chairperson, Bridget Plowden. This extensive report indirectly recommended the use of language experience approaches. The report specifically stated that "it is quite common for writing to begin side by side with the learning of reading, for children to dictate to their teachers and gradually to copy and then to expand and write for themselves accounts of their experiences at home and at school" (p. 218). Although the report did not specifically use the term "language experience approach," the philosophical foundations and instructional practices embraced and followed in the primary schools in England during the early 1960s were basically identical to the principles and philosophy of the language experience approach to teaching and learning.

The publication of *The Bullock Report* (Department of Education and Science, 1975) clearly indicated a movement to support both the principles and philosophical foundations of the language experience approach as well as the use of the term "language experience." Since the main purpose for the Bullock committee had been to consider "all aspects of teaching the use of English, including reading, writing, and speech," (p. xxxi) the report included an extensive statement on the teaching and learning of literacy. Essentially, the report suggested that a language experience approach be employed as the basis for primary school teaching. The influence of James Britton, a member of the committee, is apparent in many parts of the report. For example, the report suggested that writing in infant schools begins with the making of books. "The teacher writes beneath a child's drawing or painting the caption he dictates to her. The child may be asked to trace over the writing, and later to copy it underneath. By degrees, beginning with the words he already knows, the child will take over the writing until the whole caption is his own work" (p. 63). The report suggested that the source for children's writing should be the day-to-day experiences that children bring to school about their homes, families, pets, other animals, and, of course, the experiences that are provided in school.

Theory into Practice

Over a period of about forty-four years, from *The Hadow Report* (British Board of Education, 1931) until *The Bullock Report* (Department of Education and Science, 1975), governmental committees and agencies suggested employing, in essence, language experience in early literacy teaching. Although that term itself was not used in the earlier reports, it is interesting to note that all the reports were influenced by theoretical perspectives and classroom practice consistent with the language experience approach. As noted earlier, educators such as Nora Goddard, Sylvia Ashton-Warner, Sybil Marshall, Susan Isaacs, Dorothy Gardner, James Britton, and others provided the theoretical basis for such language-based approaches. At the same time, classroom teachers in the United Kingdom who had professional autonomy developed their own classroom practice based on their understanding of child development, literacy learning, and classroom management. Thus, it appears that the theoretical perspectives developed and promoted by many educators, government reports, and initiatives happened concurrently and sometimes independently of each other. Yet each influenced the findings and conclusions of others and, more important, were influential in establishing the foundations for a language experience approach to teaching and learning.

Conclusion

Such language experience practices continue to be a part of the curriculum in primary schools in the United Kingdom today (Campbell, 1992, 1995). However, some aspects of the approach have created considerable debate, such as the recent practice of encouraging children to use invented spelling rather than taking children's dictations and using correct spelling. The tradition of learning through experience and using children's experiences as a basis for literacy learning, however, has been upheld by the most recent version of the National Curriculum (Department for Education, 1995): "They should write in response to a wide range of stimuli, including stories, plays and poems, their interests and experiences, and the activities of the classroom" (p. 15).

Some of the National Curriculum's recommended literacy assessment practices, however, have met with resistance from teachers. For example, teachers have felt a loss of autonomy even though the recommended literacy assessment practices include holistic testing, such as assessing a seven-year-old child's reading and writing abilities by using a classroom library book and analyzing a child's writing sample/story. Teachers believe in the philosophical foundations that align themselves with a language experience approach, but feel constrained and restricted by the proscribed and enforced directives. Teachers feel pressured by time to complete all the proscribed activities and paperwork and still maintain their own curricular agendas, topics, and schedules. In conclusion, although philosophical conflicts still exist, the belief that children learn through activity and experience and that experience forms a basis for language and literacy learning remains a cornerstone of British primary education today.

REFERENCES

Ashton-Warner, S. (1963). *Teacher*. London: Secker & Warburg.
British Board of Education (1931). *The primary school (The Hadow Report)*. London: Her Majesty's Stationery Office.

Bruner, J. S. (1960). *The process of education*. Cambridge, MA: Harvard University Press.

Campbell, R. (1992). *Reading real books*. Buckingham, England: Open University Press.

Campbell, R. (1995). *Reading in the early years handbook*. Buckingham, England: Open University Press.

Department for Education. (1995). *English in the national curriculum*. London: Her Majesty's Stationery Office.

Department of Education and Science. (1967). *Children and their primary schools (The Plowden Report)*. London: Her Majesty's Stationery Office.

Department of Education and Science. (1975). *A language for life (The Bullock Report)*. London: Her Majesty's Stationery Office.

Dewey, J. (1916). *Democracy and education*. New York: Macmillan.

Dewey, J. (1938). *Experience and education*. New York: Macmillan.

Gardner, D. (1966). *Experiment and tradition in primary schools*. London: Methuen.

Goddard, N. (1958). *Reading in the modem infants' school*. London: University of London Press.

Goddard, N. (1974). *Literacy: Language-Experience approaches*. London: Macmillan Educational.

Isaacs, S. (1930). *Intellectual growth in young children*. London: Routledge.

Isaacs, S. (1932). *The children we teach*. London: University of London Press.

Lee, D. M., & Allen, R. V. (1963). *Learning to read through experience*. New York: Appleton-Century-Crofts.

Lilley, I. (Ed.) (1967). *Froebel: A selection of his writing, 1822–1843*. Cambridge, England: Cambridge University Press.

Marshall, S. (1963). *An experiment in education*. Cambridge, England: Cambridge University Press.

Rousseau, J. J. (1911). *Emile*. (B. Foxley, Trans.) London: Dent. (Original work published in 1776.)

Stauffer, R. G. (1970). *The Language-Experience approach to the teaching of reading*. New York: Harper & Row.

4 The History of Language Experience

A U.S. Perspective

JANE L. DAVIDSON

Professor Emerita, Northern Illinois University

More than twenty-five years have passed since Russell G. Stauffer's (1970) first book on the Language Experience Approach (LEA) was published, and ninety years have passed since Huey (1908) described concepts relevant to the origins of LEA. Through the years, LEA methods have been adapted, modified, explored, refined, researched, and reaffirmed. LEA continues to be widely used by educators, and it is altogether fitting to examine its heritage.

The beginnings of LEA are easily traced to Huey (1908). The origins of LEA are defined in Huey's discussion of the impact of John Dewey and the work of Miss Flora Cooke. At the Chicago Institute where Miss Cooke taught at the Francis W. Parker School, children learned to read as they learned to talk in order to "find out or tell something" (p. 297). The children gathered together to talk about something they had done or observed. As they talked, the teacher wrote their statements on the board. These statements were read aloud, corrected, and then returned to the children in printed form for the children to read. They took the printed accounts or stories and read them to themselves, to other children, and to their parents. They drew illustrations to make their accounts clear to others.

Huey stated that children's vocabularies grew with their experiences. New words that emerged in discussions were written on the board and pointed out so that the children could see the words visually and could use them at later times. Miss Cooke also found that children could read those words when they appeared in other printed materials. In addition, she would stop in discussions and indicate to the children that they could find out more information in printed leaflets. Huey quoted Miss Cooke as writing:

> I can vouch, after nearly twenty years' experience, that the method is a success when carried out by a thoughtful teacher . . . I think the third grade children are good testimony on the subject, as they read, with

ease, fluency, and pleasure, almost anything one can put into their hands. (p. 300)

Huey was adamant that children's reading should be as natural as possible. He stated that the child "should always know what the whole sentence means or is likely to mean before attempting to say it, or should at least be *trying* [original emphasis] to get or express a whole thought" (p. 318) when reading. Parent help in working with preschool children was advocated—help in making signs, labels, illustrations, and messages or letters. In addition, Huey recommended such help in reading, writing, and drawing as early and as fast as children were interested. Finally, Huey urged that activities should be based on children's personal interests and experiences. He described the entire process as a natural method of learning to read.

In the history of reading instruction in the United States, the alphabet method seemed to be the first instructional approach: children memorized the names of the letters; identified upper- and lowercase letters; spelled and pronounced two-letter combinations, then three-letter combinations, and, finally, words. Oral reading was stressed.

The word method followed. However, when children couldn't identify the names of the letters, the phonic method was used. Use of the phonic method resulted in poor comprehension of reading material and problems in spelling. Next came a swing in the 1920s back to the word method, which was expanded to phrase, sentence, and story methods with an emphasis on comprehension (West, 1964). Because there were so many new words to learn in the early readers, in the 1930s vocabulary was controlled. Controlling the vocabulary of the content resulted in less interesting content.

A variety of basals were developed, all dealing with vocabulary control. Series of books dealt with instruction from the preprimer level through the sixth- or eighth-grade level (West, 1964), and, finally, ability grouping was advocated to meet the needs of individuals in the classroom. Generally, three ability groups—low, average, above average—were formed in each classroom. Sometimes each group might have a different basal program; sometimes each group might work through the same basal but at a different pace. Children moved through the stories and activities in sequential order.

During these years, two philosophies emerged regarding the teaching of reading (Smith, 1965). From 1925 to 1935, one group advocated methods giving children practice in learning sequential skills; the other group believed that the children's learning was best served by allowing the children to set their own purposes and involving them in problem-solving activities based on their own experiences and needs. This latter group's philosophy became expressed through what was called the Activity Movement. During this period, basal readers were predominately used throughout the United States. Reading instruction, however, was generally correlated with numerous activities during the school day, and it was not integrated into the curriculum. The Activity Movement, at the same time, was growing. In 1933 The National Society for the Study of Education Yearbook, Part

II (Judd & Buswell, 1934), presented discussions of the movement. Descriptions of curriculum showed that children were involved in inquiry-type reading; experience charts were used, as were written accounts, reports, and booklets. There were schools in which no basals were used, and their entire curricula stemmed from the Activity Movement.

Both groups representing the two philosophies made use of experience charts with children. Smith (1965) reported that the use of experience charts for beginning readers during that time was considered a radical departure from commercial materials. Lamoreaux and Lee's (1943) book on the use of experience charts was widely used throughout the next decade. However, purposes and practices showed a range of differences. The basic purpose for experience charts in many classrooms was to get children "ready to read" the controlled vocabulary of the preprimers in basal reading programs. Experience charts were generally written after a field trip or, in many instances, as a result of discussion about a particular concept that the children had experienced. The children talked about what had happened and the teacher recorded their dictation on a chart, which they then read. Follow-up activities provided additional practice, such as rereading the chart to each other or having the account cut into sentence strips to be read and then placed in sequential order or having the sentences cut up into words and using the word cards for word drill.

In other classrooms, experience charts were used to give children practice with words and sentences that dealt with familiar concepts. Children moved on to other easy materials as they gained reading proficiency.

Practices differed concerning how children's divergent language patterns were treated. Most teachers changed children's language to standard English for the purposes of recording on the chart. Some teachers made radical changes by shortening the children's sentences so that each sentence began and ended on one line. The result was not unlike "See Spot run." And there were some teachers who simply recorded children's language exactly as it was dictated. Differences in charts reflected the teachers' philosophies about what they thought was appropriate.

While most reading instruction was still based solely on the use of basal readers, the period of the 1950s and early 1960s was marked by the emergence of Individualized Reading. Smith (1965) reported that the

> concept of individualized instruction in reading as it evolved during the present period extends far beyond the earlier plans of permitting children to progress at their own rates. It is primarily concerned with reading as it meshes into and promotes child development in its many aspects—physical, mental, social, emotional, linguistic, and experiential. It is interested not only in a child's reading achievement but also in his interest in reading, and his personal self-esteem and satisfaction on being able to read. (p. 378)

In addition, Smith reported that Individualized Reading appeared to have gained impetus as dissatisfaction with basals arose. The so-called lockstep approach stifled children's interest in reading. Educators became aware that basal instruction was not meeting the needs of many children, particularly those children who had a problem in reading. Ability grouping appeared to create a caste system in the classroom that led to poor self-esteem for children who were in "low" groups. Surveys also showed that among the people in the survey who could read, few did so.

In Individualized Reading programs children selected their own books, read them, conferenced with teachers, and received individualized or small-group instruction based on their own needs. Teachers recorded strengths and weaknesses and provided instruction accordingly. Classrooms had interest centers, such as book, art, and science centers. In these centers, children could carry out additional activities, including personal inquiry. The power of these programs resulted in children who read more books and who were more interested in reading/learning, as well as teachers who were more enthusiastic about teaching.

Writing was an integral part of some Individualized Reading programs. Children wrote reports, poems, and stories, and they kept their own reading and writing records. In many classrooms children kept logs of their own progress and met with their teachers to discuss them. Word recognition activities were taught during writing activities.

As stated earlier, experience charts were used in beginning reading programs to assist children in developing a sight vocabulary that was adequate for reading easy materials and for developing reading skills. In some instances, children moved from experience charts to preprimers, based on the premise that children would know most of the words encountered in the preprimers and would feel successful at onset (Vite, 1958). However, in many Individualized Reading classrooms, the progression began with experience charts, moved to easy materials, and then continued with more challenging children's literature.

Advocates of Individualized Reading programs observed the strong relationship between reading and writing. Groff (1967) commented that language experience had been "overlooked in some discussions of individualized reading" (p. 43). He pointed out a need for language experience in beginning reading and also throughout the middle grades, indicating that the "possibility of maintaining language arts as a truly integrated program seems much more likely if the language-experience activities become an integral part of the individualized reading program at all grade levels" (p. 43).

Critics of the Language Experience Approach and Individualized Reading, many of whom were associated with basal reader programs, lamented the lack of vocabulary control and what appeared to them as a haphazard instructional program due to the abandonment of sequential skills development. However, Groff (1967) pointed out that the assumption of the importance of vocabulary control might not be a valid one; there appeared to be no harm in omitting vocabulary control "since children in their language practices do, of course, use all the so-called high frequency words found in various word lists" (p. 39).

A variety of professional books, mimeographed booklets and leaflets, and other kinds of professional materials served as resources for teachers who wanted to implement Individualized Reading, including Lazar's (1960) classic work, *A Practical Guide to Individualized Reading*, and professional books written by Barbe (1961), Meil (1958), Brogan and Fox (1961), Stauffer (1957), and Veatch (1959). It was not uncommon to find teachers using basal reader workbooks and tests to make certain they were "covering skills" that basal programs had singled out as important. Russell G. Stauffer, an advocate of Individualized Reading, as well as the Language-Experience Approach (Stauffer, 1965b) worked with Alvina Treut Burrows, another advocate of Individualized Reading, and others (Burrows, Jackson, and Saunder, 1964) to develop a basal reader series, *The Winston Basic Readers Communication Program* (Stauffer et al., 1962), which was published in the early 1960s. Stauffer and Burrows presented a modified approach that combined individualized reading with group instruction by means of the Directed Reading-Thinking Activity (DR-TA) in the readers. The Language-Experience Approach was used for beginning reading, along with readiness books, preprimers, and primers. The series was short-lived because the publishers decided to promote another series of books.

At about that same time, Lee and Allen (1963), who disagreed with the notion that children must progress through a system of predetermined skills and materials in learning how to read, developed a conceptual framework that identified a sequence of concept development:

- What a child thinks about he can talk about.
- What he can talk about can be expressed in painting, writing, or some other form.
- Anything he writes can be read.
- He can read what he writes and what other people write.
- As he represents his speech sounds with symbols, he uses the same symbols (letters) over and over.
- Each letter in the alphabet stands for one or more sounds that he makes when he talks.
- Every word begins with a sound that he can write down.
- Most words have an ending sound.
- Many words have something in between.
- Some words are used over and over in our language and some words are not used very often.
- What a child has to say and write is as important to him as what other people have written for him to read.
- Most of the words he uses are the same ones that are used by other people who write for him to read (pp. 5–8).

Lee and Allen believed that children would develop more mature concepts about reading as they progressed from kindergarten onward. Children dictated individually or in small groups to the teacher. Several kinds of experience charts were recommended. Personal language charts were written, which contained records of children's own language recorded on chalkboards or newsprint. Teachers were advised never to require children to read what they said. Work charts, written to organize and give guidance to classroom activities, were developed by the teacher with the children. Narrative charts, which were records of shared group experiences, were used to summarize learning and provide for follow-up activities that ranged from skill development to additional practice in reading.

In addition, children made books of words, stories, and poems. Emphasis was placed on silent reading. Lee and Allen also stressed that word recognition skills that needed to be developed must emerge as a natural language experience.

The Lee and Allen version of LEA, while deeply involving children in reading and writing processes, lacked a strong rationale and foundation and appeared to be more concerned with what the children were doing than with why the children were doing what they were doing. They seemed to provide more assistance to teachers for use with children who were already reading. Much attention was given to writing and the writing process.

Allen (1976) provided more detail and suggestions for teachers in a later work. His major contribution to language experience was in helping teachers (1) integrate the language arts along with art, music, and dance, and (2) develop interest, enthusiasm, and awareness of the power and value of children's writing. He was firm about accepting children's divergent language patterns when they dictated and/or wrote. He presented numerous recommendations to help involve children in editing and preparing final manuscripts.

Stauffer contributed the major refinement of language experience by providing a strong foundation that was solidly grounded in theory, research, and pedagogy. Reading and the reading process were carefully defined. He presented a step-by-step program for teachers to use as an instructional guide when teaching beginning readers. Stauffer (1965a) provided support for his version of language experience when he described the child as a language user who could deal with symbols and concepts. He described the development of the habit of credulity within children as they sort out their experiences, make distinctions and compare them with others, and generalize. In addition, he described children learning to perform as thinking readers who must also learn to do their own thinking.

Reading was defined as a thinking process by Stauffer (1969a), who acknowledged the contributions of Gray (1937), Horn (1937), and Betts (1946) along with contributions from semanticists (Ogden & Richards, 1946), psychologists (Dewey, 1910, 1933; Vinacke, 1952; Wertheimer, 1959; Russell, 1956; Guilford, 1959; Getzels & Jackson, 1962; Johnson, 1955), and others. He built a strong framework (1969b) for holistic instruction in the Language-Experience Approach, which showed the influences of the work of Piaget (Flavell, 1963), Bruner (1960), Dewey (1910, 1933), and others.

Stauffer (1970) referred to the "Language Arts Experience Approach" to show the integration of the language arts with a learner's experience, encompassing "an individual's perceptual and conceptual world, his interests, curiosities, and creativity, his culture, and his capacity to adjust, learn, and use" (p. 21). He was firm about the need to place a hyphen between the words *language* and *experience* to show the dynamic interplay between the two as a communication concept.

Stauffer (1970) stated that writing a basal series helped him to learn why children who were learning to read should never be put in readiness books, preprimers, and primers. He suggested that the tremendous wealth of vocabulary possessed by children went far beyond the vocabulary of these early readers—that, in fact, the language of the basals was so controlled that it became substandard for children who, as a result, had difficulty reading them.

Eleven conditions were presented in Stauffer's approach:

1. If reading instruction is to be paced even in part on ability grouping, the range and frequency of pupil distribution has to be determined and considered. (He pointed out the average range of individual differences among six-year-olds is at least five years.)
2. Reading is to be thought about as a communication process and taught that way. Meaning is the important thing. Reading is a thinking process.
3. Individualized reading procedures and group reading procedures are to be used.
4. Stilted reading materials must be avoided—written materials must convey meaning.
5. The vocabulary, concepts, and cognitive processes that children have developed for oral communication purposes must be utilized to the fullest by linking written words as the stimulus to trigger the same concepts.
6. Word-attack skills must be taught as a first-aid to meaning. Words should be introduced in a communication context; meaning clues to word recognition should be the first functional source of help. Phonic elements must be taught in a pronunciation unit or in context, not in isolation.
7. Pupil interests, experiences, and knowledge must be used as a basic source of funds and must be extended and refined.
8. Reading skills must be taught and paced in such a way that individuals are able to assimilate and use them.
9. The rules of the psychology of learning must be observed.
10. The freedom and responsibilities of self-selection must be initiated from the beginning.
11. A love and appreciation for what reading can do for people must be fostered (Stauffer, 1970, pp. 21–22).

Stauffer presented a structured program for beginning reading, combining the use of group- and individually dictated accounts based on children's actual experiences, combined with writing, inquiry activities, and individual and group instruction. Children's language was taken verbatim in dictations, not only to give them ownership of the process, but as a means to accept language patterns regardless of how divergent they were from standard English.

Stauffer urged the use of his procedure, the Directed Reading-Thinking Activity (1969b), to guide group instruction in reading, because it emphasized the reading–thinking process through the use of problem-solving techniques. Instruction in word identification was tailored to fit the needs of individuals.

As learners progressed to greater maturity in reading and writing, inquiry activities became more complex and in-depth. Individualized reading and self-selection continued. Activities were based on curricular units and projects, many of which called for integration of the overall curriculum.

Stauffer also made certain that his program could be modified to fit in with a basal reading program. However, in his later years he told me that he was convinced that the key to learning was in inquiry reading.

On the surface, ideas advocated by Lee and Allen and by Stauffer have similar characteristics: each places emphasis on reading as a thinking process; each places emphasis on individualized reading and self-selection; each makes use of experience charts and writing; and each focuses on integration of the language arts. Stauffer's detailed recommendations for inquiry reading, combined the reading and writing processes, targeted instruction for learners who were beginning to read and continued with goals for grade three and beyond. Detailed recommendations were also included for work with the writing process. His step-by-step suggestions for the DR-TA provided teachers with a means for assessment and evaluation of learners' progress in reading and writing.

Stauffer defined reading as a thinking process—a cognitive process leading to concept attainment and an active process in which the learner questions, tests, invents, and then processes and generates information (Stauffer, 1967). He urged that learners should read to learn at onset, in contrast to those who advocated learning to read first. He further advocated that learners must have ownership of their own learning. He recommended strongly that the learner should be an active problem solver and that learning should take place in a setting requiring social interaction—that learning was, in fact, a social process. It was no accident that his DR-TA procedure involved problem solving within a group setting where all learners were active in working together to solve problems and the teacher's role was to serve as a facilitator to the group. He was strongly influenced by the work of Abercrombie (1960), Bruner (1960), and others who dealt with problem solving. He succinctly stated that children must be permitted to do their own learning:

> Teachers must present children with situations in which the children experiment by trying things out to see what happens, by manipulating things, by posing questions and seeking answers, by reconciling what they find at one time with what they find at another, and by comparing their own findings with one another. (Stauffer, 1967, p. 10)

Stauffer formed the International Reading Association's first special interest group in 1970, called the Language Experience Special Interest Group (LESIG). The special interest group brought together reading educators from all over the world. More unity between different philosophies and practices was achieved as educators shared research, writing, and practices concerning language experience.

At the end of the 1960s and throughout the 1970s, a wealth of new thinking and research was published that had a strong impact on reading educators.

Goodman's (1969) and Smith's (1971) works dealt with applied psycholinguistics and its influence on the reader and the reading process. Chomsky's (1971) research dealt with the relationship between reading and writing, and suggested that children need ownership in learning about reading and writing by constructing their own rules. Clay's (1975) work marked conceptual thinking about the process of emerging literacy, as did Holdaway's (1979) work. Halliday (1977, 1978) presented new insights in language and meaning. Rosenblatt's (1978) work dealt with the process in gaining meaning. And Vygotsky's (1978) "Zone of Proximal Development" added to the knowledge concerning learning as a social process.

Reading educators began to further refine and expand the overall theoretical notions of language-experience, defined by Stauffer, to encompass the new thinking. The LESIG wrote a statement of commitment in 1980 to express the basic principles and practices that they thought more adequately described the direction they had taken (see Padak & Rasinski, Chapter 1).

The Language Experience Approach was soon a major aspect of the overall curricula of many schools. In addition, adaptations were made for working with the hearing impaired and other special education students. Additional adaptations were made for working with bilingual children and in English as a Second Language programs. Finally, LEA was adapted for use with adult literacy programs.

In the 1970s another group was formed and advocated a program they called "whole language." Edelsky, Altwerger, and Flores (1991) stated that the perspective of whole language was developed from research into the reading process by Goodman (1968, 1969) and Smith (1971). Goodman summarized whole language as follows:

- Whole language learning builds around whole learners learning whole language in whole situations.
- Whole language learning assumes respect for language, for the learner, and for the teacher.
- The focus is on meaning and not on language itself, in authentic speech and literacy events.
- Learners are encouraged to take risks and invited to use language, in all varieties, for their own purposes.
- In a whole language classroom, all the varied functions of oral and written language are appropriate and encouraged (p. 40).

Edelsky, Altwerger, and Flores (1991) acknowledged language experience as a whole language historical predecessor and thought that the approach could be divided into two parts: teaching reading to beginners in early grades and individualizing reading for later literacy instruction. However, in their description of language experience in the 1970s, they limited their discussion to Allen's (1964) perspective and ignored much of the writings of Stauffer as well as the work and writings of the LESIG. Consideration was also not given to the adaptation of language-experience for use with special groups and populations.

A careful examination of the Language-Experience Approach and whole language indicates that there is no philosophical difference between them. Differences that appear to exist may be merely political in nature.

The Language Experience Approach has evolved as a powerful force for the 1990s high-technology challenge. The movement in schools toward more emphasis on relevant problem solving and inquiry has been a critical element of the Language Experience Approach for more than twenty-five years. The Davidson, Padak, and Wilkerson studies (Davidson & Wilkerson, 1988) over more than a decade show that learners are (1) learning how to learn, (2) deeply involved in problem solving, and (3) making maximum use of social interaction as they learn. Moreover, learners have more control and ownership of their learning, and they care about doing quality work.

Language experience classrooms of the 1990s are centers for inquiry. The best practices in many schools show total integration of the language arts with inquiry activities. Kindergarten children begin their involvement with writing and the writing process. Inquiry activities are undertaken at every grade level. Children participate in literature circles and study groups. They have considerable ownership in assisting with the curriculum process. Children using computers carry on in-depth projects and communicate with other children around the world via the Internet.

Districts have developed statements of philosophy, statements of purpose, and standards for achievement. Groups of teachers and specialists create curriculum within districts. Teachers and children work cooperatively in planning how to meet curriculum goals and maintain high standards. Teachers provide mini-lessons, small-group, large-group, and one-on-one instruction, to meet the needs of each child, including those with special needs.

Many districts have established ongoing professional development activities to assist teachers in the acquisition and maintenance of professional currency in their areas of expertise and in their strivings toward excellence in education. Communities have established adult literacy programs that make strong use of language experience as adult educators find that LEA provides a means of meeting the unique needs and interests of their adult learners.

Education, and literacy education in particular, continues to be a political issue at the levels of state and federal government. There are persons who fail to recognize that phonics instruction for those who are becoming literate is included in almost all language experience instructional programs. They continue to perpetuate a senseless battle of advocating phonics instruction, while ignoring and sidetracking the need for strong professional development programs in literacy instruction for preservice and inservice teachers. However, there are teachers and educators who continue to use their common sense and forge ahead in the never-ending struggle for excellence in education. History shows that our heritage of language experience will continue to grow and thrive.

REFERENCES

Abercrombie, M. L. Johnson (1960). *The anatomy of judgment*. New York: Basic Books.

Allen, R. V. (1964). The language experience approach. In W. G. Cutts (Ed.), *Teaching young children to read*. Washington, DC: U. S. Office of Education.

Allen, R. V. (1976). *Language experiences in communication*. Boston: Houghton Mifflin.

Barbe, W. B. (1961). *Educator's guide to personalized reading instruction*. Englewood Cliffs, NJ: Prentice Hall.

Betts, E. A. (1946). *Foundations of reading instruction*. New York: American Book Co.

Brogan, P., & Fox, L. K. (1961). *Helping children read*. New York: Holt, Rinehart & Winston.

Bruner, J. S. (1960). *The process of education*. Cambridge, MA: Harvard University Press.

Burrows, A. V., Jackson, D. C., & Saunder, D. O. (1964). *They all want to write* (3rd ed.). New York: Holt, Rinehart & Winston.

Chomsky, C. (1971). Write first, read later. *Childhood Education, 47*, 269–299.

Clay, M. (1975). *What did I write*? Auckland, New Zealand: Heinemann.

Davidson, J. L., & Wilkerson, B. C. (1988) *Directed reading-thinking activities*. Monroe, NY: Trillium Press.

Dewey, J. (1910). *How we think*. Boston: Heath.

Dewey, J. (1933). *How we think*. Boston: Heath.

Edelsky, C., Altwerger, B., & Flores, B. (1991). *Whole language—what's the difference*? Portsmouth, NH: Heinemann.

Flavell, J. H. (1963). *The developmental psychology of Jean Piaget*. Princeton, NJ: Van Nostrand.

Getzels, J. B., & Jackson, P. W. (1962). *Creativity and intelligence: Explorations with gifted students*. New York: Wiley.

Goodman, K. (1968). The psycholinguistic nature of the reading process. In K. Goodman (Ed.), *The psycholinguistic nature of the reading process* (pp. 13–260). Detroit, MI: Wayne State University Press.

Goodman, K. (1969). Analysis of oral miscues: Applied psycholinguistics. *Reading Research Quarterly, 5*, 9–30.

Gray, W. S. (Ed.) (1937). *The teaching of reading: A second report. Thirty-sixth Yearbook of the National Society for the Study of Education, Part I*. Bloomington, IL: Public Schools.

Groff, P. (1967). Individualized reading and creative writing. In L. C. Hunt, Jr. (Ed.), *The individualized reading program: A guide for classroom teaching: Proceedings of the 11th annual (IRA) convention*, Vol. 11, Part 3, (pp. 36–43). Newark, DE: International Reading Association.

Guilford, J. P. (1959). Three faces of intellect. *American Psychologist, 14*, 469–479.

Halliday, M. A. K. (1977). *Learning how to mean*. New York: Elsevier North-Holland.

Halliday, M. A. K. (1978). *Language as a social semiotic: The social interpretation of language and meaning*. Baltimore, MD: University Park Press.

Holdaway, D. (1979). *Foundations of literacy*. Portsmouth, NH: Heinemann.

Horn, E. V. (1937). *Methods of instruction in the social studies*. New York: Scribner.

Huey, E. B. (1908). *The psychology and pedagogy of reading*. New York: Macmillan.

Johnson, D. M. (1955). *The psychology of thought and judgment*. New York: Macmillan.

Judd, C. H., & Buswell, G. T. (Eds.) (1934). *The thirty-third yearbook, Part II., of the National Society for the Study of Education*. Chicago: University of Chicago.

Lamoreaux, L., and Lee, D. (1943). *Learning to read through experience*. New York: Appleton-Century-Crofts.

Lazar, M. (Ed.) (1960). *A practical guide to individualized reading*. Board of Education, City of New York, Bureau of Educational Research, Publication No. 40.

Lee, D. M., & Allen, R. V. (1963). *Learning to read through experience*. New York: Appleton-Century-Crofts.

Meil, A. (Ed.) (1958). *Individualizing reading practices: Practical suggestions for teaching*. New York: Bureau of Publications, Teachers College, Columbia University.

Ogden, C. K., & Richards, I. A. (1946). *The meanings of meaning*. New York: Harcourt, Brace & World.

Rosenblatt. L. (1978). *The reader, the text, the poem.* Carbondale, IL: Southern Illinois University Press.

Russell, D. H. (1956). *Children's thinking.* Boston: Ginn.

Smith, F. (1971). *Understanding reading.* New York: Holt, Rinehart & Winston.

Smith, N. B. (1965). *American reading instruction.* Newark, DE: International Reading Association.

Stauffer, R. G. (Ed.) (1957). *Individualized reading instruction.* Proceedings of the 39th annual education conference, Vol. 6. Newark, DE: University of Delaware.

Stauffer, R. G. (1962). *The Winston basic readers communication program.* New York: Winston.

Stauffer, R. G. (1965a). Language and the credulity. In R. G. Stauffer (Ed.), *Language and the higher thought process* (pp. 1–8). Champaign, IL: National Council of Teachers of English.

Stauffer, R. G. (1965b). A language experience approach. In J. F. Kerfoot (Ed.), *Perspectives in reading, No. 5, First grade reading programs* (pp. 86–117). Newark, DE: International Reading Association.

Stauffer, R. G. (1967). Reading and cognition. In R. G. Stauffer (Ed.), *Highlights of the 1966 pre-convention institutes: Reading and the cognitive process* (pp. 3–11). Newark, DE: International Reading Association.

Stauffer, R. G. (1969a). *Directing reading maturity as a cognitive process.* New York: Harper & Row.

Stauffer, R. G. (1969b). *Teaching reading as a thinking process.* New York: Harper & Row.

Stauffer, R. G. (1970). *The language-experience approach to the teaching of reading.* New York: Harper & Row.

Veatch, J. (1959). *Individualizing your reading program.* New York: G. P. Putnam.

Vinacke, W. E. (1952). *The psychology of thinking.* New York: McGraw Hill.

Vite, I. (1958). A primary teacher's experience. In A. Meil (Ed.), *Individualizing reading practices: Practical suggestions for teaching* (pp. 18–43). New York: Bureau of Publications, Teachers College, Columbia University.

Vygotsky, L. (1978). *Mind in society.* M. Cole, V. John-Steiner, S. Scribner, and E. Souberman (Eds.). Cambridge, MA: Harvard University Press.

Wertheimer, M. (1959). *Productive thinking.* New York: Harper & Row.

West, R. (1964). *Individualized reading instruction.* Port Washington, NY: Kennikat Press.

Wilkerson, B. C. (1988). The language experience special interest group of the international reading association: An historical overview. *Journal of Language Experience, 9*(1), 17–25.

5 The Language Experience Special Interest Group (LESIG) of the International Reading Association

An Historical Overview

BONNIE C. WILKERSON

Director of Research, Evaluation and Assessment, Elgin, IL

The Language Experience Special Interest Group (LESIG), organized by Russell G. Stauffer in 1969, was the first special interest group of the International Reading Association (IRA). The group was described as "experimental" when announced to the membership of IRA in its membership newsletter, *Reading Today*, in March 1970. Guidelines developed by the IRA Board of Directors in response to the request from the "experimental" group became the foundation for the organization of subsequent special interest groups of IRA.

Beginnings

In the year 1969 reading educators were examining the U.S. Office of Education's cooperative reading studies, exploring and debating various theories of learning to read. They were debating the Initial Teaching Alphabet (i/t/a) and examining its effects on spelling competence. They were writing about the relationships between oral language and beginning reading and debating the effectiveness of code- and meaning-emphasis beginning reading programs. They were exploring issues of disadvantaged children and the teaching of reading, examining correlations of reading readiness among children of varying backgrounds. Articles published in Volume

22, 1968–69 of *The Reading Teacher* reflect these and many more issues of importance and intensity, many deserving continuing attention and debate.

That same year, a group led by Russell Stauffer and united in beliefs about teaching and learning organized the first special interest group of the International Reading Association. The group was formed to provide a forum for sharing ideas and raising questions about the Language Experience Approach (LEA). Ten years later Richard T. Vacca, first Editor of the *Journal of Language Experience* (JLE), describing the types of manuscripts that were desired by the JLE, succinctly described the interests and purpose of LESIG, which functioned "to see important contributions on all aspects of language centered instruction, . . . to have balanced critiques of language experience," and to examine practices "that dignify children and teachers and place language and cognition at the core of learning to read and learning to learn" (Vacca, 1980, p. 2).

For more than twenty-five years, LESIG has functioned to provide a forum for educators to explore, debate, and extend educational practices. Through the years, LESIG has brought together educators who share an interest and a passion for the concepts of language experience and its underpinnings of belief in students, teachers, and the power of experience and language. Believing that knowledge is extended and refined through sharing experiences, the group set an organizational format for itself, which included annual forums for the purpose of examining and debating new ideas and concepts, and Preconvention Institutes and Business Meeting programs at the annual International Reading Association conventions for the purpose of spreading knowledge of the beliefs, strategies and the power of language experience to a broad audience of teachers. The group initially focused on the medium of people-to-people interactions, but by 1976 it was ready to move into print media and it published its first newsletter. The newsletter was extended to a journal format with the publication of *The Journal of Language Experience* in 1979.

A Look Back

The first annual meeting of LESIG was held in Anaheim, California, in 1970. The founding members included, among others, Russell Stauffer, MaryAnne Hall, R. Van Allen, John Downing, Harry Hahn, Ed Henderson, and Eleanor Roberts. Russell Stauffer and MaryAnne Hall were LESIG's first officers. Stauffer served as president while Hall served as secretary/treasurer. Hall, Allen, Downing, Hahn, Henderson, and Roberts formed a Steering Committee, the predecessor of the Executive Board. True to their purpose, the founders planned the early programs as forums for sharing current research and practice and environments for discussion and debate.

Historically, Business Meeting programs focused on topics of broad interest that provided theoretical perspectives for the application of language experience principles. Topics included research perspectives on beginning reading, spelling, early literacy in the home and school, writing, and children's literature. Preconvention Institutes, with their longer formats, were implemented to tie research to practice for application in the classroom. Broad conceptual themes were addressed in terms of both theoretical grounding and practical application. Themes included, among others, an examination of language experience at all levels; language experience for students of diverse cultural backgrounds; language experience and the integrated curriculum; thinking, language and reading; and psycholinguistic theory and language experiences. The forum of LESIG served as an environment for sharing new ideas and research. Attended by students, theorists, and practitioners of language experience from all levels, the forum provided a format for the presentation of new research and ideas with subsequent debate and discussion. Through its forum, the Language Experience Special Interest Group provided its members with opportunities to hear current research presented by its creators, followed by rich dialogue and debate. Presentations included the writing research of Donald Graves as it was being developed at the University of New Hampshire; the early work out of The Center for the Study of Reading at the University of Illinois; cross-national and cross-lingual research; and emerging research in early literacy, presented by individuals both within and outside the membership of LESIG. The forums, through the years, presented an opportunity for members of the special interest group to share their own research and interests with others.

In May of 1996, LESIG met in Atlanta. The Business Meeting in Atlanta during IRA that year included a program of small-group presentations on the topic of the integration of language and experience for a lifetime of learning, prekindergarten through advanced university levels. Presenters came from England, Texas, Ohio, Maine, Michigan, and Arkansas. As they have throughout the history of LESIG, the presenters and participants came from across the United States and beyond. The vision of the founders of LESIG to expand knowledge about language experience is being realized. Creating discussion and debate and contributing to the growth of knowledge about language experience continues to be the important work of the group. Through the years, group membership has waxed and waned, to the point that the group once seriously considered disbanding. The Executive Board in 1992 asked the critical question, "Should we disband or go on?" Issues included a debate regarding whole language and whether LESIG was any longer important or even separate as an instructional philosophy. The question led to discussion that continues to give renewed life to the group. That discussion involves a renewed analysis of what language experience is, a renewal of the analysis of language experience as a global learning concept and of its instructional techniques as valid and critical. At one point members questioned the existence of the group due, in part, to their inability to agree on all points. Looking back to LESIG's founders, the opportunity to give life to important ideas through debate was one of the purposes of the group's foundation.

A Look Forward

Some of our founders are no longer with us. Among them, Russell Stauffer, founder and first chairperson of LESIG, died in 1994 at the age of eighty-three.

Edmund Henderson, second chairperson of LESIG, died in 1989. John Downing, third chairperson of LESIG, died in 1988. The second-, third-, fourth-, and even fifth-generation students of the founders are evidence of their influence, the success of their ideas, the importance of the group identity, and the importance of the forum for asking questions and sharing ideas that they created. Throughout the history of LESIG, the power and influence of these and other founding members is evident when one analyzes the roots of those who are now doing the work of the organization and carrying its vision forward.

On the twenty-fifth anniversary of LESIG, Olga Nelson and Wayne Linek, coeditors of this book, announced its acceptance for publication. The book is another step in fulfilling LESIG's mission to extend knowledge about language experience theory and practice.

LESIG has served as a forum for the discussion of ideas and issues and as an organizational structure for bringing programs and research to members. The group, in addition to addressing and accomplishing the goals of its founding, also greatly influenced the structure of the International Reading Association by providing the foundation for the organization's special interest groups. In 1997 there were forty-five IRA special interest groups, providing education and services to the ninety-five thousand members of IRA in ninety-nine countries. No longer an experimental concept, special interest groups function to provide forums of thought and action for reading educators who share concerns, interests, and advocacies in common. LESIG has an important and rich history. It has served and continues to serve as a dynamic environment for promoting the continuing growth of the theory and practice of language experience. (See Appendix for a chronology of the Language Experience Special Interest Group.)

REFERENCE

Vacca, R. T. (1980). Editorial: Spread the word. *Journal of Language Experience, 2*(1), 2.

attitudes that result from repeated success are viewed as being as significant as any method or material that might be employed.

The classroom is operated as a language laboratory that extends throughout the day. Language skills are extended and ideas are refined as children listen to stories and recordings, view films and filmstrips, make individual and class books, dictate stories to each other, study words, develop flexibility in using the letters of the alphabet to serve their spelling needs, and begin to record their ideas in writing independently. They view filmstrips and provide the commentary before listening to the accompanying recording. They view motion picture films with the sound track turned off and discuss their own meanings and interpretations prior to hearing the commentary. They build confidence in their own ability to use language at the same time that they are making progress in recognizing the language of other people—people who are not present but whose ideas have been recorded with writing.

Children have frequent opportunities to read their own writing to the entire class, to small groups within the class, and to other groups in the school. The child who is reading his own writing (the meaning of which he already knows) can devote his energies in oral reading to clarity of expression, effectiveness of presentation, interpretation of punctuation, and other necessary details that make listening to oral reading a pleasure.

Motivation for improving language form and usage comes as children's writing is read by others. Pride in "published" work stimulates the young authors to seek language forms that will be understood by others. They are also influenced by what they read and what they hear read to them from hundreds of authors.

As children study the English language—its alphabet, its spelling, its sentence patterns, and the flexibility of meaning in English words—they come to realize that other people use words very much like their own to express ideas. The study of words of high frequency in English to the point of mastering them at sight, correctly spelled, becomes a meaningful experience.

As children express their own ideas, they are interested in finding out, through reading, what other people think and say about topics of interest to them. Wide reading, in turn, stimulates individual authorship, which is handled in the classroom through a variety of publishing procedures.

Understanding the nature and flexibility of the English language to a degree that one can look at printed symbols and reproduce the language of another person is considered to be a lifelong process. Understanding does not always result from "exercises" in reworking other people's language; it is more likely to develop as a child works with and reworks his own language. As he writes to say something important or interesting, he is dealing with the language letter-by-letter, word-by-word, and sentence-by-sentence. It is when he has been helped to improve his own language that he makes significant gains in understanding the strengths and weaknesses of that language. Repeated success in this process of writing and refining language gives the child confidence to view reading materials as another person's language. He can approach the act of reading with an attitude of *being able to reproduce the talk of someone who is not present.*

Teachers Select Activities that Extend Learning

Through numerous studies, including the San Diego County Reading Study Project (1958–1967), researchers have identified twenty language experiences that contribute to the balanced development of language skills, including reading skills. These twenty language experiences are grouped in three categories as an aid in helping teachers select activities and materials. In well-planned programs some activities are selected from each category each day. During the progress of several weeks, the teacher is careful to choose activities that are related to all twenty experiences.

The three major categories with their emphases are listed below:

Group One. Extending experiences to include words—through oral and written sharing of personal experiences, discussing selected topics, listening to and telling stories, writing independently, and making and reading individual books.

Group Two. Studying the English language—through developing an understanding of speaking, writing, and reading relationships, expanding vocabularies, improving personal expression, studying words, and gaining some awareness of the nature of the use of high frequency words and sentence patterns.

Group Three. Relating ideas of authors to personal experiences—through reading whole stories and books, learning to use a variety of printed resources, summarizing, outlining, reading for specific purposes, and determining the validity and reliability of statements found in print.

Resource books for teachers, which insure that all three categories are dealt with frequently and that all twenty language experiences are extended through the elementary grades, are now available.

Flexible Organization Is Vital

Learning situations must be designed so that each child can view himself as worthy and able to succeed in reading tasks of increasing difficulty. How a child feels about himself and his relations to others—his family, his teacher, and other members of the class—will determine to a great extent what he is able to say, write, and read.

School practices that make reading achievement the measure of success in the early grades, such as grouping techniques that highlight lack of this success, may destroy the child's self-image rather than improve his reading skills. Ability grouping for daily reading instruction can negate any positive attitudes that may be developed in other language experiences. Since every child individualizes his reading whether the teacher wants him to or not, the sensible attitude toward building good learning situations is one that emphasizes each child's success and provides for flexible groupings.

A language experience approach allows great flexibility in organization and scheduling. The activities are selected to help the teacher use three basic patterns of classroom organization, singly or in combination, depending upon the nature of the work of the day.

The Role of the Teacher

The teacher works with the entire class. This arrangement works well for the following:

- reading aloud to children;
- permitting children to read their stories or compositions aloud;
- encouraging children to compose stories orally;
- directing class discussions on topics of interest;
- extending experiences through films, filmstrips, and field trips;
- introducing and playing games;
- singing and making rhythms;
- conducting seminars on the development of various skills.

The teacher works with small groups:

- completing activities initiated in the large group;
- taking dictation from one while others observe;
- letting children read their own books as well as those of others;
- giving special instruction in skills to some children identified as needing them;
- playing games to practice skills;
- practicing effective oral reading;
- choosing appropriate books.

The teacher serves as a resource person for individual and independent activities:

- suggesting ideas for individual books;
- helping with spelling;
- furnishing words for independent readers;
- helping children choose and organize an independent activity;
- conferring about reading and writing progress.

Language Experience Approaches
Have Advantages

Whether a language experience approach is used as the major reading program or whether it is used in conjunction with other programs, it has inherent in it certain advantages.

A language experience approach does not require standard English as a basis for success in the beginning stages. Children who use language greatly divergent from standard English are not placed at a severe disadvantage. Children with great fluency in language do not experience, when they enter school, a period of language regression while they take time to develop a small sight vocabulary and learn a few word-recognition skills.

The approach does not require, nor does it recommend, ability grouping in the class. Teachers can proceed without administering readiness tests or using valuable time to place children in ability groups. This type of grouping serves a questionable purpose in overall language development.

Materials already available can be used effectively. There is no need for large expenditures for special materials for children with reading problems. Basal readers, supplementary readers, recordings, films, filmstrips, trade books, picture sets, children's newspapers, reference materials, and word-study programs can be used to advantage within the basic framework.

Children can begin to read using a sight vocabulary that has been developing in the home and community environment. Brand names, labels, signs, and other words are seen often on television. To this vocabulary can be added words of high frequency that most children do not acquire independently. Children learn to spell the words of highest frequency at the same time that they learn to recognize them as sight words.

The method allows for the effective use of aides to the teacher. Semiprofessionals, older children in the school, interested parents, and other volunteers are examples of teacher aides.

Team teaching arrangements can be used to great advantage. A division of activities into large and small groups can continue through most of the day, thus making maximum use of all team members and their ideas.

The language experience approach is ungraded in the sense that much of the direct language teaching is done with material produced by the children. Each child produces at a level that he can understand and thus learns to recognize words at his own level. Frustration is avoided. Also, children are helped to choose their own stories and books for independent reading from the beginning. They spend little, if any, time keeping the place while another child reads something that might be too easy or too challenging.

Phonics is an integral part of the daily program. Children learn about the relationships between sounds they make when they talk and the symbols used to represent the sounds in writing. They view phonics as a natural, normal language experience. The flexibility of sound-symbol relationships in English becomes a challenge in self-expression. Teachers who wish to reinforce and extend phonics learning with a more structured program can do so and still use a language experience approach.

Children develop a level of independence in making choices in the daily program. This is seldom observed among those who study with highly structured reading programs.

The program requires that all children participate in a variety of expressive activities. What appears to be additional time scheduled for language study includes art, music, dramatization, and rhythmic activities. These are media for the expression of ideas that might later be written and used for reading development.

Children choose writing as an independent recreational activity as often as they choose reading. Self-expression is as important to them as is contact with the ideas and language of other people.

Children who live in a classroom with these major emphases in language development do have an advantage! They develop desire and resources for self-expression; they learn how to study the English language as a lifelong pursuit; they are influenced in their own thinking and their own language by the ideas and language of many authors whom they view as friends.

7 Making Written Language Learning Meaningful

MARYANNE HALL

Retired Professor of Education, Georgia State University

The phrase "learning how to mean," which is the title of one of Michael Halliday's (1975) books, is an apt expression for educators concerned with making literacy learning successful for children. Halliday believes that learning how to mean is the key to oral language acquisition. He also believes that it is the functional use of language in the "context of situation" that results in learning language. Learning how to mean should also be the central focus in learning written language, and classrooms must provide situational contexts for the functional use of written language. The knowledge and understanding young children need to learn about written language along with suggestions for activities and experiences to develop those language concepts are discussed here.

One explanation for the difficulty some children encounter in the complex task of learning to read is their lack of understanding the purpose or function of the task. Much instruction focuses on teaching children the forms of written language, but in a number of reading instructional programs little focus is placed on function. Children learn oral language by being immersed in a language-rich environment, and they discover the intricacies of language in attempts to mean, to communicate. Instructional environments for children need to provide an environment rich in written language. The print-laden environment, though, must be coupled with opportunities to use and interact with print in attempts to mean with written language.

What Children Need To Learn about Written Language

The broad generalization that print represents meaning is the cornerstone for all the additional understandings that children need to develop in order to be successful in their efforts to read and write. In addition to the foundational realization that written language—just as oral language—is a code for meaning, knowledge of other concepts also helps ease the task of learning to read. Among these are awareness of conventions of written language, such as the directional order of top-to-bottom and left-to-right, word boundaries, and concepts of letter, word, and sentence. Another concept that may also contribute to the ability to make sense of print is the acquisition and refinement of a story schema. The research of Evans, Taylor, and Blum (1979) reveals that written language awareness is significantly related to readiness for reading.

Downing (1979) draws on the investigations of Fitts and Posner (1967) to conclude that the first phase in learning any complex skill is the cognitive phase in which the learner is aware of the functions of the task to be performed. Downing points out that the learning-to-read process requires that learners develop an awareness of the functions of written language. The first essential learning then is not that of naming separate letters, discriminating between sounds at the beginning of words, or learning a few basic words. Instead the true basis for reading is the understanding that print represents meaning. Written language exposure must be part of the preschool and kindergarten experience, and the experiences with written language should demonstrate that the function of written language is to convey meaning.

The conventions of written language may present obstacles to beginners unfamiliar with print. Following print from left to right must be learned and eventually should be automatic. Clay (1979) provides illuminating examples of young children's confusion in sorting out directional order and their difficulty in distinguishing between letters and words. As she has observed children's pointing as they read aloud, she has found examples of children pointing to four letters in the first word while saying the words of a four-word sentence. In another example, she reported children often paced their pointing by saying a syllable while pointing to a word only to come to the end of a line with more words to say than were left to point to.

One convention of print often taken for granted that is not clear to novice readers is that of word boundaries. It was the work of Reid (1966) and Downing (1969) that called attention to young children's confusion about the concept of word, letter, and sentence. The research of Meltzer and Herse (1969) showed that a number of first graders did not clearly attend to the spaces between words when directed to cut a sentence into words and to circle each word on another strip with a ten-word sentence. Some children cut or circled after three or four letters and often said that a word ended before or after a letter such as *t, l, p,* or *y* that extended above or below the smaller letters.

Even though children need to solve their confusion about print and even though the point of view expressed here is that children need considerable exposure to written language before the beginning reading instruction, it is not drill with letters and words that is advocated. Instead, many, many encounters with print in the supportive framework of preschool and kindergarten programs rich in experiential learning, in language development, and in ways congruent with knowledge of how young children learn are essential.

Still another dimension of children's understanding that reading is functional and meaningful is their "sense-of-story" (Applebee, 1978). The acquisition of the sense of story is developmental as children gradually intuit knowledge about story features and structure. Hansche (1981) found that good readers had more fully developed story schema knowledge than did poor readers at the end of first grade. Expectations about story structure can foster the use of prediction as a comprehension strategy. It seems logical to assume that the development of a schema for story is directly influenced by hearing stories both read and told.

Integrating Written Language Awareness with Worthwhile Curriculum Experiences

There are countless children who have seen print in the real world prior to formal instruction in reading and who can read significant signs and labels around them but who do not make the connection between their prior experience and initial reading instruction. The point here is that prereading and beginning reading instruction needs to build a bridge from the early meaningful experiences with print to instructional experiences with print that are also meaningful. Reading should be introduced as a search for meaning, and the search for meaning continues as the central focus beyond the beginning stages.

The understanding that print makes sense must be transferred to the first experience stories and the beginning reading books or else the early experience with print is rendered useless in the efforts to master the complexities of written language. Instruction that focuses on features of print without regard for using reading and writing "to mean" ignores one crucial basis for reading success.

In one school, the kindergarten and first-grade teachers decided to use environmental print examples to show children that indeed they could read many things. In one corner of the room they posted wrappers of candy bars and soap along with the distinctive print cut from McDonald's bags and cups, cereal box panels, and other familiar products. The display was captioned with "We know what these things say." Children were encouraged to bring other items they knew, and a chart was constructed for each child with the printed items from familiar products.

After the success of the product examples, the teachers decided to continue to build children's awareness that they could read many things. The next experience was one of discussing signs that they could read and why the signs were important. The teachers again charted the language from familiar items. The first listing and sign construction by children was the reproduction of signs from the school. After the display of school signs was completed, the students were asked to think about the road signs that they knew and that drivers used.

There are any number of other examples of environmental print with products such as crayons and paint, children's lunch boxes, toys, and puzzles that can demonstrate the use of print to label and to communicate. In addition to the reading that results from these examples, writing also occurs since children often incorporate these familiar examples in their experimentation with print through writing.

Firsthand experiences that show print is meaningful can include print naturally as part of the experience—not as an artificial, thinly disguised readiness lesson. Cooking experiences, common in school programs for young children, are excellent for showing the use of print in a real situation as directions and ingredients are charted. Directions for mixing paint, for caring for classroom pets, and for storing supplies are other relevant examples for using print naturally. A child's name is usually the first word he or she wants to learn to write. When children's names are displayed on cubbyholes, lockers, artwork, mailboxes, roll charts, and in experience stories, the names of classmates will be learned quickly and easily.

In addition to the display of print incorporated into the local classroom environment, there will be meaningful print displayed on experience charts that are developed about events and topics of interest to the children. Children can dictate their ideas and have those recorded by the teacher, who will then read those ideas to and with the children. Children's artwork is an excellent stimulus for encouraging dictation. Children will profit from these kinds of activities that demonstrate how written language represents meaning. From participation in a number of language experience activities, children will gradually become aware of word boundaries and will sharpen their understanding of left-to-right direction, and of the concepts of word, letter, and sentence. These concepts cannot be internalized by children through isolated exercises but must be developed through interaction with print in the context of meaningful written language.

Still another significant element in young children's experience with written language is experimentation with writing. Learning to write often precedes learning to read for preschool children (Durkin, 1966, 1974–1975; Chomsky, 1971; Hall, Moretz, and Statom, 1976). Involvement with writing leads children to ask questions about print that then leads naturally to reading. Invented or spontaneous spellings in early writing efforts should be encouraged. Many discoveries about the patterns of the writing system are learned as children continue to write and to refine their spelling.

The initial exposure to written language occurs long before the formal introduction to reading and writing. Extending children's awareness of the functions of written language requires that preschool and kindergarten environments include print in natural and meaningful situations. Preschool, kindergarten, and primary teachers can use functional situations to develop and extend children's awareness that print conveys meaning.

REFERENCES

Applebee, A. N. (1978). *The child's concept of story: Ages two to seventeen.* Chicago: University of Chicago Press.

Chomsky, C. (1971). Write first, read later. *Childhood Education, 47,* 296–299.

Clay, M. M. (1979). *Reading: The patterning of complex behavior.* Auckland, New Zealand: Heinemann.

Downing, J. (1969). How children think about reading. *The Reading Teacher, 23,* 217–230.

Downing, J. (1979). *Reading and reasoning.* New York: Springer-Verlag.

Durkin, D. (1966). *Children who read early.* New York: Teachers College Press.

Durkin, D. (1974–1975). A six-year study of children who learned to read in school at the age of four. *Reading Research Quarterly, 10,* 9–61.

Evans, M., Taylor, N., & Blum, I. (1979). Children's written language awareness and its relation to reading acquisition. *Journal of Reading Behavior, 11,* 7–19.

Fitts, P. M., & Posner, M. I. (1967). *Human Performance.* Belmont, CA: Brooks-Cole.

Hall, M. A., Moretz, S., & Statom, J. (1976). Writing before grade one: A study of early writers. *Language Arts, 53,* 582–585.

Halliday, M. A. K. (1975). *Learning how to mean: Explorations in the development of language.* New York: Elsevier.

Hansche, L. N. (1981). *An examination of the relationship between reading ability and story schema of first graders.* Unpublished doctoral dissertation. Georgia State University, Atlanta, GA.

Meltzer, N. S., & Herse, R. (1969). The boundaries of written words as seen by first graders. *Journal of Reading Behavior, 1,* 3–14.

Reid, J. F. (1966). Learning to think about reading. *Educational Research, 9,* 56–62.

8 Approaches to Environmental Print with Young Children

BOBBIE GIBSON WARASH

Professor, West Virginia University

MARY W. STRONG

Assistant Professor, Iowa State University

RACHEL N. DONOHO

Child Care Director

Literacy development is a continuous process that begins early in life, long before young children enter school (Hall, 1987). It begins at home and extends into other environments. Print is a part of our natural environment that children experience. They respond to the signs, notices, and advertisements that they see. As children encounter and become aware of print they try to make sense of their world, and this awareness helps them become literate. Just as children learn to talk by using language in a purposeful manner, they can learn about written language in an environment enriched with meaningful messages and functional print. Although the formal teaching of reading and writing should not occur in preschools, the environment can be prepared and activities planned to expose children to language in various forms. Such a context facilitates learning about reading and writing through environmental print (Heibert, 1986).

Children have individual differences in learning styles, pace, and understanding the functions of reading and writing (Moxley & Warash, 1990–1991). To be effective, therefore, an early literacy program must provide an environment that is suitable for the child who reads labels on products as well as the child who shows little apparent interest in print.

When is it appropriate to intervene with a child? A teacher can help interest a child by creating an environment rich with opportunities that include some appropriate teacher-directed activities. Learning when and how to intervene is the key. Some children initiate their own involvement in literacy; it is very easy to encourage these precocious children to read notes on the bulletin board or messages on the chalkboard. But what about the child who doesn't show an obvious interest? Direct instruction in emergent literacy is sometimes viewed as a way of applying pressure to children in developmentally inappropriate ways. However, this does not have to be the case if the children participate because they choose to and because they enjoy the activities.

Creating an Environment for Early Literacy with Preschoolers

Although reading and writing develop concurrently for young children (Teale & Sulzby, 1989), this concurrence may not always be obvious. Some young children appear to have a more inherent interest in trying to read print while others enjoy marking, drawing, and writing. Even so, one fosters the growth and development of the other.

With so many individual differences it is a challenge for the teacher to construct a developmentally appropriate atmosphere for all children. For example, offering stimulating projects that are teacher-directed in a print-enriched environment was implemented in the West Virginia University (WVU) Child Development Laboratory. Teachers and researchers in this lab have explored variations in language experience for several years. The afternoon class enrolls eleven to fifteen children ranging in age from four to five years old. In 1988 it was decided that a concerted effort would be made to offer an environment rich in print. While LEA would continue, there would also be more involvement with environmental print.

To begin, the Lab School offers a wide range of materials that are always available for children to use. All sizes of crayons and pencils are readily available, as are stencils, stamps, stamp pads, various sizes of paper, scissors, and materials for collages. Adding machines, typewriters, and computers are also excellent resources for children. They create high interest and give children mechanisms for further exploration of print.

The daily classroom has a routine structured to include ways that children can self-chart information and take responsibility in keeping records. For example, the children sign their names on a large sheet of paper when they get to school, which eliminates the teacher's need to take roll. Any mark, picture, or letter information is acceptable. Activities of this nature have helped children see that print is functional. Sometimes to add variation, a typewriter is substituted at the sign-in table so that the children can type their names when they arrive.

Children can self-chart other activities throughout the day by marking next to their names when they complete tasks. Children at the Lab School participate in a photography unit in which they take one Polaroid picture for their album each week. After the pictures are developed they tape them in the album, then write or dictate messages about their snapshots. Each child then places a mark by his/her name on the master chart that is kept in the classroom. This record indicates who has taken their Polaroid picture for the week.

A desk calendar with big, blank letters for each date is placed on the wall in the classroom to relay information. Each "Helper of the Day" is printed by a date for the entire month. This gives the children the opportunity to read who is "Helper of the Day" and to count how many days until it is their turn. Other information that is important to children such as birthdays, holidays, and field trips is also included on the calendar.

As often as possible, children chart information so they can see relationships and comparisons. Charting shows children that their choices are important and that each person is represented. Most charting experiences involve each child printing his or her name in a column. The content of the charting experiences varies but the idea remains the same: "What is your favorite TV show?" "What is your favorite food?" "Pets that I have at home" and "Times I go to bed." Charting such content gives children the experience of reading print for information.

Charting is a graphic representation that shows individual preference and provides a means to communicate ideas and observations. This same technique can be used to organize information from any curriculum area. Charting weather and plant growth are also appropriate activities. Children chart preferences for upcoming events such as what party foods to have, color of balloons to use, field trips to take, etc. These graphs are hung at the children's eye level so that they can be reviewed at any time. Parents also enjoy reading the charts with their children.

To create an environment where children can write in a meaningful context for authentic purposes, the Lab School uses theme writing centers. The writing centers are changed weekly to add freshness to the program. These situations give children a purpose for writing because there is a role to play (Juliebo & Edwards, 1989). For example, a post office is a pertinent situation for Valentine's Day. Children can make valentines for family and friends and drop them in the class mailbox. To further enhance literacy development each child at the Lab has his or her own mailbox. Every day each child receives a piece of mail. Sometimes it is a cutout shape of an animal or object pertaining to an upcoming holiday. The mail always contains some printed information. Children enjoy receiving mail and sorting through it. Several parents have reported that their children collect the mail in a safe place at home and then review it at a future time.

A store, restaurant, pizza shop, beauty parlor, gas station, etc., include many experiences for children to role-play what they have observed in their own environment. A class store offers plenty of opportunities for printing and reading. For example, empty food boxes and cans are read as children stock the shelves and "clerks" write grocery lists and use the adding machine to sum totals. Children's interest in these centers is clearly demonstrated through their own self-direction of the activity. Reading and writing can easily be incorporated into these role-playing centers. The teacher just needs to set the scene by providing the props (Teale & Sulzby, 1989). Many businesses (local pizza shops, McDonald's, and so on) are excellent sources for free supplies.

Teachers show that print is functional by capitalizing on all occurrences that are part of the daily routine. When the children do cooking projects, the teacher makes large recipes that include rebus pictures. These are read as children cook. The children also enjoy reading the birthday train to see upon which cargo car their birthday falls. They enjoy reading the "message of the day" the teacher places on the chalkboard. This usually includes a message about a child in the Lab School. Any way that print can be integrated into the environment is helpful and useful for exploring concepts that are critical to early literacy development.

Some researchers believe that personal writing is appropriate for young children (Lamme & Childers, 1983). Each child at the Lab School, therefore, is given a theme book for personal, private writing that is kept in his or her locker. These books are outlets for children to draw, scribble, print, etc. at any time. Some children have their own diaries that they keep in a secret place at school.

Appropriate Teacher-Directed Activities with Preschoolers

Not all children take advantage of the opportunities in the environment without encouragement. Therefore, three to four teacher-directed activities are planned each day that will give all children the opportunity to participate. Teachers need to plan stimulating experiences for children that lead to discussion and writing (Karnowski, 1989). These activities help to motivate children and bring out their interest, but are by no means forceful attempts to get children to produce results beyond their capabilities.

Some teacher-directed activities are planned using children's literature, and an adult is always available to read to children at any time. The books are changed in the library area on a weekly basis. Children's magazines and other types of reading materials are also placed on the shelves. Children may check out the books by signing the enclosed library card in the front of the book. Children can also use the listening station to hear tapes and follow along in the books. In addition to contributing to a child's understanding about the many functions of print, these activities motivate children to become interested in books.

The teacher-directed activities are always conducted with small groups of children in a time span of five to ten minutes. For example, once a week, the teacher distributes predictable readers to small groups of the children. The children are instructed to read their books by looking at the pictures or the words. The first books contain a picture with one word so the children catch on very easily. Children feel a great deal of accomplishment after they have read a book on their own.

Big Books are also an appealing method of exposing children to literature. When used with small groups of children, they approximate the close feeling of being read to on a one-to-one basis. Big Books offer a wealth of opportunities for extending children's understanding of print, such as identifying common word patterns that are repeated, role playing the plot, publishing their own Big Book, or illustrating a familiar Big Book.

Using literature webs to provide a guided reading lesson with predictable books has been found to improve comprehension (Reutzel & Fawson, 1989). A simplified version of a literature web using predictable books is another teacher-directed activity that is used to stimulate conversation. The teacher makes eight to ten illustrations from a predictable book and shows them to the children in random order. The children predict the sequence of the story by placing the illustrations in clockwise order on the wall before the teacher reads the book. The children may alter the sequence of the pictures after listening to the book

Computers also serve as an excellent source of learning about print. Children have access to the computers throughout the day, and they can choose various teacher- or commercially produced programs. These same programs are used twice a week as a teacher-directed activity in order to give all children the opportunity to use computers. Although some children will not initiate using the computer, when they are placed in a group situation where several other children are working on a computer, they also want to participate. The program that is most widely used is "Vanishing Word Pictures" (Moxley & Warash, 1990–1991), an open-ended program that allows children to type words or stories that are accompanied by pictures. Children retain printouts of their stories and drawings. This picture and story from the computer language experience program is integrated with some scrapbook activities (see Warash & Kingsbury, Chapter 9). For example, the children use the computer pictures from the printouts to make rebus stories in their scrapbooks.

Conclusion

The children at the WVU Child Development Laboratory benefit from an environment rich in print that includes open-ended, teacher-directed activities. The environment at the school has helped children to view literacy in a natural way. Functional reading and writing has been integrated into the classroom curriculum as well as in the environment. The child is viewed as a purposeful user of print, no matter what his or her level of functioning. Goals are determined by the child's capability and interest. The teacher intervenes by setting up the environment for the children to play, and by planning appropriate teacher-directed activities in order that all children have the opportunity to expand their knowledge.

REFERENCES

Hall, N. (1987). *The emergence of literacy*. Portsmouth, NH: Heinemann.

Hiebert, E. H. (1986). Using environmental print in beginning reading instruction. In M. Sampson (Ed.), *The pursuit of literacy: Early reading and writing*, pp. 145–158. Dubuque, IA: Kendall/Hunt.

Juliebo, M., & Edwards, J. (1989). Encouraging meaning-making in young writers. *Young Children, 44,* 22–27.

Karnowski, L. (1989). Using LEA with process writing. *The Reading Teacher, 42,* 462–465.

Lamme, L. L. (1983). The composing process of three young children. *Research in the Teaching of English, 17,* 31–50.

Moxley, R. A., & Warash, B. (1990–1991). Spelling strategies of three prekindergarten children on the microcomputer. *Journal of Computing in Childhood Education, 2*(2), 47–61.

Reutzel, D. R., & Fawson, P. C. (1989). Using a literature webbing strategy lesson with predictable books. *The Reading Teacher, 42,* 208–215.

Teale, W. H., & Sulzby, E. (1989). Emergent literacy: New perspectives. In D. S. Strickland & L. M. Morrow (Eds.), *Emergent literacy: Young children learn to read and write,* pp. 1–15. Newark, DE: International Reading Association.

Warash, B., & Kingsbury, D. (1988). The scrapbook project: A journal activity for young children. *Journal of Language Experience, 9*(1), 12–16.

9

The Scrapbook Project

BOBBIE GIBSON WARASH
Professor, West Virginia University

DIANA J. KINGSBURY
Teacher, West Virginia University

Collecting things seems to be a favorite pastime for young children because they like to gather items and sort through them. As part of the daily routine at our nursery school, teachers create mail for each child by printing messages on construction paper cutouts. All the children have milk carton mailboxes. Children enjoy gathering and reading their mail, and then storing the messages in some other container. Some time ago, we decided that scrapbooks might appeal to children and provide an ideal place to keep memorabilia, dictations, and artwork.

Over the past four years, teachers and researchers at the West Virginia University Nursery School have been exploring variations of the Language Experience Approach (LEA) with four-year-olds. The scrapbook project is one exciting variation that encourages children to participate at their own levels—to scribble, draw, dictate, or write, and to retell or read their entries. In this manner, children interact meaningfully with the concepts of letter, word, and sentence. Working in scrapbooks helps children begin to understand the relationship between written and oral language and introduces directionality, the spacing of words, and punctuation.

The Scrapbooks

The scrapbooks measure 14½ inches by 11 inches with hardbound covers in various colors. They are always accessible, so children can draw or write new entries or read old ones. In addition, teachers conduct small-group activities with the scrapbooks two times each week. These activities often provide children with ideas for their own creations.

A variety of writing instruments are provided for children's use. Pencils, crayons, pens, erasers, and markers are always available. In addition, sometimes printed and plain stickers, stamps and stamp pads, envelopes, and other props for teacher-planned activities are used.

Overall, the children tend to dictate longer and more involved stories when they first interact with a stimulus. Sometimes they make or find pictures to cut out and paste into their scrapbooks. Other times they make rebus pictures for their scrapbooks or use stickers to tell a story.

Scrapbook Activities

Children often tell a teacher that they want to work in their scrapbooks. Their self-initiated activities usually consist of a combination of drawings and printing. They draw a picture and then ask the teacher to print their dictations or to help them spell words.

Some children prefer combining a few stickers with their drawings. Stickers are recognizable forms that often produce more dialogue from children and enhance their dictations. This may be because stickers are small pictures of objects or scenes that convey obvious messages to the child, whereas the child's drawing of an object may cover the entire page and may not be so obvious in content. The children use stickers in two ways. Sometimes they compose a story with stickers by arranging them on a page and then dictating (see Figure 9.1). Other times they draw and then find a sticker to add that fits their content.

Teacher-planned lessons usually involve discussions to stimulate ideas. For example, we may read the beginning of a story and ask children to draw what they think the ending will be. Children always have the option to dictate their stories to the teacher, who will print them, or to print the stories themselves. And, of course, each child's work is accepted and valued, from scribbles, to letterlike characters, to actual printing (see Figure 9.2). Any marks on the page are encouraged and reinforced.

When children compose lengthy stories, they seem to prefer dictation over writing. It's as if they're on a "roll" and don't want to take the time to print. Dictations are read back to the children, and they are encouraged to read their dictated and written entries. We have found that children enjoy reading their stories to each other.

Because printing by four-year-olds can be time-consuming and tedious, some activities encourage lesser amounts of printing so that children can be successful. For example, the children especially enjoy writing secret messages. The teacher reads a set of words on index cards to the children. Children then select the words they want for their secret messages. They write the messages on adding machine paper that is then taped into their scrapbooks. Using the horizontal strips seems to reinforce the concept of left-to-right directionality for children.

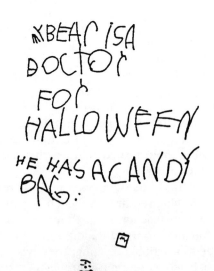

my BEAR ISA
DOCTOR
FOR
HALLOWEEN
HE HAS A CANDY
BAG.

FIGURE 9.1 A Story about a Sticker

Benefits

The children keep track of the number of times they work in their scrapbooks. Each time a page is completed, the child places a green circle sticker on a chart on the front page of the scrapbook, and the teacher dates it. Since the scrapbook contains so many dictations and writing pieces, the teacher can easily flip through the pages and observe and record children's progress.

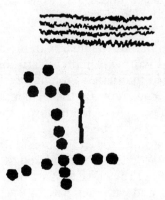

FIGURE 9.2 A Story Using Scribble

The scrapbooks provide permanent records of children's progress as literacy learners. The indicators of progress we use include the number of words dictated, the number of words printed, the number of words read, and the incorporation of story elements. We also examine children's manuscript writing for signs of growth. For example, scribbles that represent words, spaces between scribbles, letters within scribbles, and signs of left-to-right direction are indicators of progress for children whose writing did not demonstrate these aspects at an earlier time. For some children, printing their names or a few letters in left-to-right direction is an achievement. More sophisticated goals, such as printing and reading words, are more appropriate for other children.

The academic benefits of the scrapbook project are numerous. Because their entries are meaningful, children are motivated to write without looking at the word cards provided by the teacher. Thus, they are encouraged to invent spellings and are applauded for their efforts. In addition, their printing improves tremendously. Very few children scribble for long; they want to print actual letters and words. Over time their letters become more legible, and spaces appear between words. Children also begin to hold pencils properly rather than gripping them with their fists. Children who scribble at the beginning of the project can generally print their names at the end.

When children first begin to work in their scrapbooks, their dictations are short. Most children dictate under twenty words, and many simply list the objects they have drawn. Subsequent dictations become longer; many of our children's stories exceed one hundred words. We find that a few children even like to edit their stories, usually by adding content.

Children's dictations quickly become storylike. Their stories frequently contain beginnings, middles, ends, and even some dialogue. For example, Amanda's first story consisted of a picture of her family members and a short sentence about each person. After a few weeks in the project, she dictated this story:

> My closet door suddenly opened. I wondered what was going on. I got out of my bed. Then I opened the door. I looked in the closet. Something was wrong. I didn't know what was going on. It was my imagination. Then I closed the closet door. Then I got back in my bed. Then I went back to sleep.

The scrapbook project helps children become familiar with the components of print and the processes of reading and writing. Children learn that they can convey messages through print. They learn that letters are put together to form words that people can read. They show their awareness of the relationship between the written and the spoken word when they begin dictating slowly and enunciating carefully so that the teacher can keep up with their ideas.

Children also learn that writing is an outlet for creativity and that they can share what they've written or dictated. In fact, most of the children can read some of their dictated stories and their own writing. They love to share their stories and pictures with each other, with the teachers, and with their parents (see Figure 9.3).

The 🐷 planted a ⭕
pig   seed..

The   rose up
       sun

The 〰️ came out.

then a beautiful 🌸

FIGURE 9.3   Rebus Pictures Using Scribbles

For all these reasons, the scrapbooks have become an important part of our nursery school curriculum. They fit the program's philosophy of emphasizing developmentally appropriate preschool literacy activities. Children enjoy working with them and maintain this enthusiasm for the project. Lastly, the scrapbooks become wonderful keepsakes of children's nursery school experiences.

10 Developing Story Discourse

A Technique for Parents

LANE ROY GAUTHIER
Professor, University of Houston

DAVID B. YADEN, JR.
Professor, University of Southern California

Over the years, much has been written about the importance of parents reading to their preschool children. Jett-Simpson (1979) refers to the lap technique as one of the most powerful techniques available to parents. Mountain (1981) offers advice to preschoolers' parents about developing their children's reading skills; Butler and Clay (1982) provide a list of book selections for children through age six.

Researchers have explored the benefits gained from listening to stories. Both Snow (1983) and Donaldson (1978) have suggested that the talk surrounding a storybook reading provides an opportunity for children to develop the use of decontextualized language, subsequently important in understanding school lessons.

Another benefit is the acquisition of an interactional scaffold through which the child gradually internalizes a variety of strategies for discussion about a wide range of topics (Ninio & Bruner, 1978). It has been observed that children ask specific questions about print in storybooks (Morrow, 1988; Smolkin, Conlon, & Yaden, 1988) in addition to using book language in their everyday conversation at home and in school (Purcell-Gates, 1987).

Development of a sense of story is another important benefit derived from reading and sharing books with children (Applebee, 1978). Pappas and Brown (1987) have shown that as a result of read-aloud sessions, story elements such as initiating events, sequence events, and finales are increasingly incorporated into children's retellings. Recently, Wells (1986, 1987) has gone as far as to state that it

[From "Developing Story Discourse: A Technique for Parents," by L. R. Gauthier and D. B. Yaden, 1988, *Journal of Language Experience, 9*(1), pp. 54–58. Copyright 1988 by Language Experience Special Interest Group. Reprinted with permission.]

is this development of "inner storying" that accounts for the robust correlation between story reading and subsequent school achievement.

Although much of the current research has focused on the development of story discourse in school-aged children, the authors of this chapter suggest using wordless picture books with preschoolers to enhance the development of story discourse. The development and internalizing of story structures begins very early (Holdaway, 1979; Wells, 1986). The suggestions for parents provided in this chapter incorporate two important elements for developing narrative structures: use of high quality children's books and repeated exposures to the same story. In addition, the procedure fosters discussion about stories and provides opportunities for children to become authors.

Selecting and Using Wordless Picture Books

There are five simple steps to selecting and using wordless picture books to enhance literacy development.

Step 1: Select a Wordless Picture Book

The parent should select a rich, stimulating, wordless picture book, preferably one that has clear, colorful illustrations and an observable progression of events. Several wordless picture books that meet this criteria include:

Aliki (1974). *Go tell Aunt Rhody*. New York: Macmillan.

dePaola, T. (1981). *The hunter and the animals*. New York: Holiday House.

Mayer, M. (1967). *A boy, a dog, and a frog*. New York: Dial Press.

Spier, P. (1977). *Noah's ark*. New York: Doubleday.

Van Soelen, P. (1981). *A cricket in the grass*. New York: Scribners.

Step 2: Share a Wordless Picture Book

The parent should share the book with the child and talk about its contents. Discussion might focus on the aesthetic qualities of the pictures, the interesting appearance of the characters, actions and events, or anything else that might capture the child's imagination. This discussion should resemble an informal conversation. Together, the parent and child can explore the story by talking about the characters and what they are doing: "What's happening on this page? What is the character doing now?" Discussion should focus on the child's ideas, not the parent's.

Step 3: Ask the Child to Tell a Story about the Book

While discussing the pictures, the child or the adult may note that there are no words in the story. This is a good time to suggest telling and writing a story to go along with the pictures. Of course, the child should be encouraged to tell the story in his or her own words. If more than one child in involved, they can take turns telling the story or tell the story together. One child may tell his or her interpretation of one page, and another child might continue the story by telling about the next page. Turn-taking can continue until the story is completed. The dictated version of the story should be tape recorded.

Step 4: Make a Book

The parent can encourage the child to draw his or her own version of the events in the story. After the drawings are completed the parent and child can play back the dictated version of the story. The parent should transcribe the dictated story from the audio tape and place the child's words under the appropriate illustrations or on separate pages interspersed within the illustrations. Next, a lap book or a big book can be made. A cover for the book may be made of cardboard covered with contact paper. The child's drawings can be stapled securely inside the cardboard cover. A title page that includes the child's name and the date can be added, as can an about the author page.

Step 5: Read and Discuss the Child's Book

At this point, the child and parent may follow along in the child's own book while listening to the dictated version of the story. They can also discuss the story again. A discussion that is upbeat and positive and avoids remarks about the plausibility or coherence of the story is best. Parents should remember that children's versions of stories may differ considerably from their own. Children will be more likely to experiment with language and story-making when their efforts are encouraged and appreciated.

Discussion

In addition to the well-known benefits of language experience activities, such as children learning that their thoughts and language can be written and read, these procedures engage children directly in the creative act of story-making and involve them in playful language use. The wordless picture books provide an already existing scaffold for children, since they may tailor their stories to the illustrations. Thus, children's "storying" efforts are well-supported, both by the book itself and by the adult who guides and facilitates the child's exploration of the sequence of the pictures.

Even infants and toddlers can benefit from procedures like those described here. Young children may lose interest quickly, but parents should accept and receive children's varied, creative interpretations eagerly and feel encouraged and satisfied with the results. With time and maturity the child's interest and attention span will lengthen, and new versions of the wordless picture books can be created.

The primary goal with very young children is to share an enjoyable reading-related experience. The process is more important than product.

The adult's commitment, understanding, patience, and perseverance play major roles in the effectiveness of these activities. Young children's experiences with stories and print are too important to be ignored. Engaging in the activities discussed here is one way parents who recognize the value of providing rich reading and language environments can encourage and nurture literate behavior.

REFERENCES

Applebee, A. N. (1978). *The child's concept of story*. Chicago, IL: The University of Chicago Press.

Butler, D., & Clay, M. (1982). *Reading begins at home*. Portsmouth, NH: Heinemann.

Donaldson, M. (1978). *Children's minds*. New York: W. W. Norton.

Holdaway, D. (1979). *The foundations of literacy*. New York: Ashton Scholastic.

Jett-Simpson, M. (1979). Parents and teachers share books with young children. In D. L. Monson & D. K. McClenathan (Eds.), *Developing active readers: Ideas for parents, teachers, and librarians*. Newark, DE: International Reading Association, 73–81.

Morrow L. M. (1988). Young children's responses to one-to-one story readings in school settings. *Reading Research Quarterly 23*, 90–107.

Mountain, L. (1981). *Early reading instruction: How to teach reading before first grade*. Providence, RI: Jamestown.

Ninio, A., & Bruner, J. (1978). The achievement and antecedents of labeling. *Journal of Child Language, 5*, 1–15.

Pappas, C. C., & Brown, E. (1987). Young children learning story discourse: Three case studies. *The Elementary School Journal, 87*, 455–466.

Purcell-Gates, V. (1987, April). *Lexical and syntactic knowledge of written narrative held by well-read to kindergartners and second graders*. Paper presented at the annual meeting of the American Educational Research Association, Washington, DC.

Smolkin, L. B., Conlon, A., & Yaden, D. B. (1988). Print-salient illustrations in children's picture books: The emergence of written language awareness. In J. E. Readence, R. S. Baldwin, (Eds.) *Dialogues in Literacy Research*. Thirty-seventh Yearbook of the National Reading Conference, pp. 59–68. Chicago, IL: National Reading Conference.

Snow, C. E. (1983). Literacy and language: Relationships during the preschool years. *Harvard Educational Review, 53*, 165–189.

Wells, G. (1986). *The meaning makers*. Portsmouth, NH: Heinemann.

Wells, G. (1987). Apprenticeship in literacy. *Interchange, 18*, 109–123.

CHAPTER

11

Guided Imagery as Language Experience

BARBARA J. WALKER

Professor, Montana State University, Billings

Designed for use with emergent readers, guided imagery experience is a technique for teaching literacy using the procedures of language experience. The experience, however, is based on a guided imagery that encourages young children to use their imagination to create a story. Many young children learn to read by listening as an adult repeatedly reads stories to them. They experience the story as a whole rather than recognizing individual words. They do not understand where words begin and end (word boundaries) nor do they focus on the distinctive letters and features of words. The young reader thinks that the phrase "drink of water" is one word "drinkawater." Thus, one of the major challenges of young children is to learn that what they say can be written down in individual words that form a story. The Language Experience Approach (LEA) is an effective way for a young child to authentically engage in this challenge. As children describe their experiences, the teacher writes these experiences on a large tablet. The children use their experiences to form a story that they read along with the teacher. As they reread their story, the children begin to notice that once the words are written down, they stay the same. Each time the story is read, the words are in the same order; the words do not change as often happens in spoken language. The language experience activity helps children learn the concept that spoken language can be written down in words to form a story.

Another characteristic of young children's learning is that they engage in make-believe play and as they do this, they construct new ways to use oral language. Young children's cognitive development moves from this imaginary world of make-believe and image-associations to more formal, linguistic thinking. Stauffer (1970) characterizes young children's thinking as involving private, noncodified symbols. Young children remember their make-believe playing not in words but in private symbols or images. The Guided Imagery/Language Experience technique parallels the natural development of young children by leading the child's thinking from private and personal images to written words.

Not only do young children move naturally from using images to using words, but some children are more inclined to use what they have experienced as a basis for what they learn. They tend to process their experience directly without using words to label the experience (Das, Kirby, & Jarman, 1979). These children experience difficulty when asked to define a word that represents their experience. For instance, these young children might have difficulty explaining what a "princess" is, but they will have worn crowns and dressed up like royalty. Their make-believe play remains a direct experience represented in images rather than words.

Additionally, Paivio's dual coding theory indicates that both verbal and nonverbal information are represented and processed in distinct, but interlinking systems (Paivio, 1986). The imaginal system deals predominately with nonverbal information that includes the images constructed from personal experiences. On the other hand, the verbal system processes information using linguistic units that represent abstract ideas in words. Even though these systems are separate, they are also interconnected (Sadoski, Paivio, & Goetz, 1991). Thus, information can be changed from the imaginal to the verbal system as well as the verbal to the imaginal system.

The Guided Imagery/Language Experience Activity relies on creating sensory images related to a particular event and then asking children to retell their images (Walker, 1988). This moves literacy learning from an imaginal system to the verbal system. Young children are asked to imagine the whole story in one setting before connecting the meaning with oral language or common linguistic symbols (Walker, 1978). Thus, Guided Imagery/Language Experience begins with the students' closing their eyes as the teacher leads them on an imaginary journey designed to elicit vivid images. After the journey is complete and the students open their eyes, they share their imaginary journeys in pairs, allowing them to verbalize their images immediately. The children are reminded that their retelling represents the images and feelings they had when their eyes were closed. Then, the students dictate a story that represents their imaginary experience. After the teacher records the story, the children read and reread the story so that it is learned as a whole. Then, the students use the language patterns and their personal images to predict and figure out the words in the story.

Steps of the Guided Imagery Language Experience

Guided Imagery Experience is easy to incorporate into any classroom program. The only resources needed are the creative minds of the students and teacher.

The following Flower Imagery experience begins by creating an atmosphere for the multisensory experience. By using other senses, children can draw upon their imagination more readily. Phrases such as "listen to the sounds" or "feel the room getting colder" help focus the children's thinking on various senses and, thus, increases images. Having students close their eyes also decreases reliance on visual stimuli. Next, in the guided imagery, the students are directed to create the setting and characterize the traveler in the journey. If certain vocabulary words (e.g., *flower, gold, day,* and *meadow*) are targeted, these can be used as a basis for the Guided Imagery Experience. The beginning needs to engage the rich imaginations of young children, as in the following example:

> Close your eyes and sit comfortably in your chair . . . . Make sure you are comfortable . . . . Now listen to the noises in the room [sensory awareness statement] . . . . Can you hear them? . . . Feel the temperature of the room . . . . Is it hot or cold? . . . Now turn the sounds of this room into the sounds of the meadow [setting statement]. . . . Listen to the sounds of the meadow . . . . What kind of a day is it? . . . Sunny? . . . Cloudy? . . . Hot? . . . Cold? . . . Imagine that you are a golden flower in a large meadow [character statement].

Once the imagery and setting have been evoked, some type of calming action should be presented. This calming statement allows the imagery of the setting to unfold naturally according to the personal experiences of the student.

> . . . The wind is blowing gently on the warm, soft meadow . . . and you sway back and forth in the breeze [calming statement].

When the student is in a relatively relaxed state, the action of the adventure is suggested. Unusual and strange actions are more often effective for the young child. The various actions need to be interwoven with calming statements and pauses. The journey continues by combining the action of the journey with words that create a deepening of the relaxed, image-making dream-state.

> . . . A large bird flutters by . . . reaches down and picks you up . . . . You travel in the mouth of the bird over hills and meadows [action statement] . . . . The bird spreads his long wings and soars effortlessly through the clear, blue sky [calming statement] . . . . As you are soaring through the skies, the bird opens his mouth and you begin to float down . . . down . . . down . . . slowly to the ground [deepening statement].

Lastly, the guided imagery is left incomplete so that students can finish the journey on their own. This personalizes the story for each student. After finishing the journey, students are instructed to return to the classroom. Returning to the classroom connects the imaginary journey with classroom life.

> . . . As you reach the ground . . . notice that the air is cool . . . evening is approaching . . . I will leave you here [separation statement] . . . . You can finish the journey in your mind . . . . When you have finished your journey . . . you may return to the classroom and open your eyes [closing statement].

After the guided imagery is written, the teacher sets the stage for the imagery experience. The following steps can increase imagery flow and spontaneity of imaging.

1. If possible, dim the lights so the child can close his eyes more readily.
2. Eliminate visual stimuli.
3. Read the guided imagery experience in a calm, serene voice.
4. Use many pauses so the child has time to develop images.

When the journey is finished and students have opened their eyes, the students share the imagery experience in pairs. Then the teacher takes down the imagery experience as the students retell the story. The students are reminded that the dictated language experience needs to represent what happened in their imaginations just like a published story represents an author's images. The teacher and students chorally read the story. Any unclear statements are revised. When the story is finalized, the students and teacher repeatedly read the story. Most students quickly learn the words in the story. However, if more repetition is needed, the teacher can create chunk cards (cards with phrases from the story). Chunk cards are made by dividing the entire story into meaningful phrases and writing these phrases on cards. The chunk cards are presented to the students in the order they appeared in the story. This allows the students to use their images and the language experience to figure out words (Walker, 1996). In this technique, young children connect their images to the oral language used to describe the experience, and then to the written story that they retold.

Although language experience has been used for many years, it has been at the heart of very few literacy programs. One of the major concerns about language experience is that the topics and the vocabulary are often uncontrolled. Children's experiences take the LEA stories in many directions, and therefore they often do not repeat the same words in their stories. Using a series of guided imagery experiences around a particular theme such as meadows, including other ideas such as butterflies emerging in the spring and fireflies dancing in the moonlight, the teacher can create the numerous word repetitions while at the same time expanding the imagination and creativity of the young child. The goal of this instructional method is to develop flexible word recognition strategies by using the targeted words within the guided imagery so that the students will use these words to retell their imaginary experiences. Thus, for the child whose processing strategies are imaginal, simultaneous, and creative, teachers can use those strengths at the onset of literacy instruction.

Guided Imagery Experience allows reading to flow from a dreamlike experience into meaningful written communication. In this approach, reading moves from a holistic activity, leading the cognitive development of the child from global, experiential processing to abstract, linguistic processing. Using the Guided Imagery/Language Experience technique, learning to read can be a fascinating discovery of the magical imagery associated with the printed word.

REFERENCES

Cummings, J., & Das, J. P. (1978). Simultaneous and successive synthesis and linguistic processes. *International Journal of Psychology, 13*, 129–138.

Das, J. P., Kirby, J. R., & Jarman, R. F. (1979). *Simultaneous and successive and cognitive processes.* New York: Academic Press.

Paivio, A. (1986). *Mental representations: A dual coding approach.* New York: Oxford University Press.

Sadoski, M, Paivio, A., & Goetz, E. (1991). Commentary: A critique of schema theory in reading and a dual coding alternative. *Reading Research Quarterly, 26,* 463–484.

Stauffer, R. (1970). *The language experience approach to the teaching of reading.* New York: Harper & Row.

Walker, B. (1978, Fall). *Language experience: Synthesis of intuition and rationality.* Paper presented to Southwest Regional IRA Convention, Little Rock, AR.

Walker, B. (1988). *Diagnostic teaching of reading: Techniques for instruction and assessment.* Columbus, OH: Merrill.

Walker, B. (1996). *Diagnostic teaching of reading: Techniques for instruction and assessment* (3rd ed.). Englewood Cliffs, NJ: Prentice-Hall/Merrill.

12 Play as Story

KATHLEEN ROSKOS

Professor/Chairperson, John Carroll University (OH)

> *G*randmother to teacher: Alex just loves all books about animals. He loves the Three Little Pigs, 'cause I'll go—I'll HUFF and I'll PUFF and I'll BLOW YOUR HOUSE DOWN! And Alex will look at me, and he'll say, "Let's play!"

To travel the distance from "let's pretend" to "once upon a time" for the young child is not all that far. Both play and stories in books are invitations to leave the here and now, to explore new worlds, and to use language to create new possibilities. These early encounters with "story," whether made up in Play Time or enjoyed during Storybook Time, immerse children in the rhythms, sounds, and forms of written language. Repeated often across the early childhood years, such encounters are the wellspring of a lifelong process of learning to read and write.

In this chapter, I focus on the fundamental connections between the world of play and the world of stories and their significance for literacy development. I then describe how children's spontaneous play episodes can be shaped into written stories that may serve as the basis for early reading experiences. Finally, I highlight how teachers may facilitate play-literacy connections in early childhood settings.

Connections between Play and Story

Studies have demonstrated the many parallels between children's play and stories (see Pellegrini & Galda, 1993, for a review). At the heart of both activities lies children's developing narrative ability. Play episodes and stories have similar organizational structures (Garvey, 1977; Pellegrini, 1985a), which invite children to take roles, create settings and action sequences in order to keep events going (Sachs,

[From "Using Play Stories As Literacy Experiences," by Kathleen Roskos, 1988, *Journal of Language Experience, 9*(1), pp. 8–11. Copyright 1988 by the Language Experience Special Interest Group. Reprinted and revised with permission.]

Goldman, & Chaille, 1985). Some research suggests that it is through play that children begin to develop the "building blocks" of story—an emerging sense of setting, character, and plot (Eckler & Weininger, 1989; Wolf & Pusch, 1985).

That both play and story have narrative elements in common is evident in play's apparent influence on children's story comprehension, recall, and sequencing (Williamson & Silvern, 1991). As in the case of Alex, who wanted to re-enact *The Three Little Pigs*, play can serve as an effective means of recalling stories. A number of studies, for example, suggest that playlike dramatics after storybook reading enhance children's developing comprehension and sense of story. The common narrative structures between play and story seem to support children's thinking and help them to remember story content, such as character and sequence of events (Pellegrini & Galda, 1982; Silvern et al., 1986; Williamson & Silvern, 1990).

Play and story also rely on the imaginative uses of language. To become involved in either, the child must use and interpret language that is independent of the actual physical situation. This ability to use words in decontextualized form is central to dramatic play and literacy activity (Heath, 1983; Pellegrini et al., 1991; Snow, 1983). When children make up stories, take on roles, retell favorite fairy tales, invent spellings, they use language as a symbol system to make sense of their experience. This ability to understand language without immediate sensory cues and to create images, scenes, and meanings with it are essential strategies for handling written language. Indeed these mental manipulations with words are the very foundations of literacy (Holdaway, 1979).

Finally, although different in form, both play and storybook reading encourage social interaction and active participation that "teaches" literacy-related concepts. Play invites children to use their narrative competence and language to re-present the known and invent new situations and scenarios. To play together well, children must use the language they know, but they are also pressed to adapt and stretch it if they are to "play." And in shared storybook reading with loving adults and friends, children begin to learn how books work, how print and speech might be related, and how to construct meaning with story events through informal conversations and their own curiosities about print and books.

Thus, play and story cross paths in several ways that support literacy development in the early years. Cognitively, these activities afford rich opportunities for young children to use narrative as a way of thinking about their experience. Practically, they provide children with pleasurable and informative social opportunities to interpret and enlarge their own understandings of language as a means of oral and written expression.

From Play to Story

How can teachers capitalize on play–story connections to further children's literacy? How can they make the important links between play and story visible in the literacy curriculum of preschool and kindergarten? With some adaptation, the

Language Experience Approach (LEA) offers an excellent choice, for it draws on children's interests and life experience as the "stuff" of early reading texts (Nessel & Jones, 1981). Play becomes the stimulus for the dictated story cycle, and is translated from action to print through recall and oral discussion.

Let's take the example of some sand table play between two four-year-olds, Sara and Sheona, as an illustration of the LEA cycle in action in which play is the source of an experience story. We begin with a transcript of the play itself, which then serves as the basis for oral discussion and eventually story dictation.

The Play Experience

Sheona and Sara are standing on opposite sides of the sand table. They are mounding up sand in the middle of the table and occasionally sprinkling sand on the pile, sifting it between their fingers. They are speaking in their nasty, mean voices as if witches mixing a brew.

> **SHEONA (in an especially snarly tone):** When he licks his fingers, he'll say, "Thick! Yuk!" We put syrup on it. He hates syrup.
>
> **SARA (equally nasty):** Yeah. The syrup is on the bottom.
>
> **SHEONA:** Good. We need sprinkles.
>
> **SARA:** Lots of sprinkles. Pretend we have to put eggs in it. Not too much. Right?
>
> **SHEONA:** Plwerk! Plwerk! Two eggs. We'll put everythin' he doesn't like. Huh?
>
> **SARA:** Then we'll tickle him. Right?
>
> **SHEONA:** Then he'll get sick or somethin'. Then he'll get terrible. He hates popcorn!
>
> **SARA:** So, we should put popcorn on. Right? Because we want him to get sick. And he hates sprinkles, so we put sprinkles.
>
> **SHEONA:** Like he hates mushy, we already put that in. And he hates soda. Let's put some chocolate milk on it. He hates chocolate.
>
> **SARA:** Yeah!
>
> **SHEONA:** This cake will be so yukky! This cake will be so icky! It's icky and picky and oh so yukky!
>
> **SARA:** Yeah. [then somewhat wistfully] I wish we was bakin' a real cake.

The Oral Discussion

In the early childhood program Sheona and Sara attend, children regularly participate in Recall Time after Play Time, where they talk about their play activity and draw pictures or write to represent their play experiences. As they do, the teacher and her assistant mingle with the children, catching snatches of conversation and picking up on ideas that might become the basis of more extended language experiences. On this day, the teacher was listening as the two girls talked and drew about their play at the sand table, describing their desire to make the "icky, picky, and oh so yukky cake" for the mysterious "he." As they began to tell about their play, she recorded key words and ideas with rebuslike sketches on chart paper nearby. These brief notes served as a means to remember the gist of the play and the girls' own words (see Figure 12.1).

The Experience Story

Shortly after the girls related their play experience, the teacher met with them at the Writer's Table and suggested that they might like to make a story about it. They enthusiastically agreed. The teacher then asked what they thought might make a good title for their story. With little hesitation, the girls chimed, "The icky, picky and oh so yukky cake." And from there the two players turned authors, producing (with some assistance from the teacher) the play-based story in Figure 12.2.

Certainly the girls' dictated story did not capture the full measure of their language while playing, for example, their witchlike voices and snarly tones, the syntax and rhythm of the sentence strings, and the implied meanings of their word choices. But it did represent their ideas phrased to a large extent in their own language. In this respect, the story offered an authentic source of written text for further literacy experiences and instruction. After reading the story several times

FIGURE 12.1 Recorded Play Experience Using Rebuslike Drawings

The Icky, Picky, and Oh So Yukky Cake
by Sheona and Sara

We made a icky, picky, yukky cake. First, we
put syrup on, because he hates syrup. Then we put
sprinkles on it, because he hates sprinkles! And we
put eggs in it. Then we put popcorn on it, because he
hates popcorn! Finally we put chocolate milk on it,
because he hates chocolate milk. It's a icky and picky
and yukky cake. And he won't like it. Not at all!

The End

FIGURE 12.2   Sheona and Sara's Dictated, Play-Based Story

themselves, the girls shared the story with their peers, who also genuinely enjoyed
the words and theme. Seeing this, the teacher decided to use the story in a variety of instructional ways:

- Several children transformed the story into a big book with a sentence and
  matching picture on each page. The teacher used this resource for shared
  reading, guiding the preschoolers' attention to the orientation of print and
  framing high interest words.
- Children constructed word cards of their favorite words, which they then
  added to their Word Banks. Sometimes the teacher had the children hunt for
  these words, encouraging them to look for beginning letters and other word
  clues.
- Several mini-lessons were conducted to explore rhyming words (*icky, picky,
  sticky, Mickey, Ricky*), sound–symbol relationships, and sentence structures in
  the context of the story. The teacher pointed out, for example, the word
  because and asked the children to count how many times it appeared in the
  story. She talked with the children about this word as a way of explaining
  what we do and answering "why?"

Following these activities, the story was saved in the children's very big collection of dictated stories available to all for reading whenever anybody wanted to,
just for the sheer joy of it.

Play–Literacy Connections beyond LEA

When first considered, play and literacy may seem unlikely partners. Play is highly
active, spontaneous, unpredictable, and often boisterous while literacy is far less
so. Yet, contrary to outward appearances, both demand similar mental processes

that advance children's language and problem solving (Pellegrini, 1985b). Daily opportunities for play–literacy connections are important because, as they play and build stories, children fashion possible new worlds, create problems, invent solutions, all through the use of symbols. Teachers can support young children's meaning-making with language through play by providing them with time, choices, and opportunities for response. Moreover, they can expand their teaching role by participating in children's play and literacy-related play activity.

Time

One of the oldest and time-honored ways of sharing stories with children is reading to them. But, in addition to being read to, children need time on their own to read (even before they can conventionally read), to play around with books, to share their experiences with one another so that reading becomes a part of their lives. Margaret Meek (1981) once said that, "if children saw reading as play, they would begin to take it seriously" (p. 20). Providing time for children to engage in literacy-related play areas, like a Cozy Corner Library, in all early childhood classrooms provides access to books, generates interest, and conveys the importance of child-initiated literacy activity.

Choice

Another way to facilitate play-literacy connections is to provide young children with choice—different ways to explore, discover, and manipulate literacy concepts. Having a choice implies having a voice so as to say and do on one's own. Play areas, then, should allow for making choices. Good library corners, for example, not only include a large selection of books that reflect many different tastes. In many cases, they also involve other activities in the form of special events, such as a "reading" or a performance. Libraries also include multimedia equipment, such as a listening area with headphones, an area for young artists to display their favorite depictions of a story, a computer, a little puppet theater, flannel board activities, and notices about current community events. Introducing new materials and events encourages children to return often and to try new activities. The abundance and sheer variety of literacy resources in the play area suggest to the child that there are many ways to share and interact with stories.

Response

As Sheona's and Sara's experience story demonstrates, children often enjoy recalling their play experiences and casting them into written stories for sharing. In addition to LEA-like learning experiences, children can become involved in responsive activities after play in other ways too. Teachers and aides in one program, for example, always meet with small groups of children following play time. As they chat with the children about various play experiences, teachers often interject references to books such as, "Doesn't that remind you of Max in *Where the Wild Things*

Are" (Sendak, 1963) or "That drawing looks a lot like Richard Scarry's figures in the *Best Ever Word Book"* (1963). Sometimes, the teachers will read a particular selection that seems to capture the mood of the day. Later, the book will be placed in the library area for children to share together on their own. Other response activities may involve small-group share sessions or journal writing. In fact, some teachers have found that the best time for personal writing in the early primary years is after free-choice time. Daily journals, dialogue journal entries, activity logs, and diaries seem to take on new meaning following children's playlike activities. For the young child, writing about a puppet show just performed is likely much easier and more enjoyable than writing about yesterday's after-school experience.

Participation

Studies suggest that well-timed, sensitive teacher interaction can enhance play–literacy connections (Enz & Christie, 1993; Roskos & Neuman, 1993). However, becoming a participant in children's play may be the teacher's most challenging role. On the one hand, "entering" children's play world provides an opportunity for teachers to model literacy behaviors as well as engage in enjoyable interactions with children. On the other, it demands that teachers remain responsive to children's agendas—to listen to their intentions and hear what they are trying to say. Vivian Paley (1986) captures the difficulties of this challenge when she writes:

> I became a kindergarten teacher and in my haste to supply the children with my own bits and pieces of neatly labeled reality, the appearance of a correct answer gave me the surest feeling I was teaching. I wanted most of all to keep things moving with a minimum of distraction. It did not occur to me that the distractions might be the sounds of children's thinking. (p. 122)

It is these "distractions," so often clear indicators of the child's point of view, that we are trying to enter when assuming the role of play participant: children's attempts to construct a plot for a puppet show (which may never be produced); their frantic efforts to publish a book so it looks "just like John's" (and doesn't); the quiet murmur of mumble reading (from a book held upside-down); the excitement while scribble-writing a love note to Dana (who rejects it). To participate playfully is difficult for teachers, who by inclination and training are driven to "teach." Nevertheless, research and experience suggest that appropriate involvement in children's play can spark literacy ideas, interactions, and collaboration among children even while the play agenda remains in their hands.

Time, choice, response, and participation: these are ways teachers can facilitate play–literacy connections that support and extend the use of LEA in the early childhood classroom. Making time for play, providing appealing choices and opportunities for children to respond about their play experiences, and actively participating to enhance literacy in play can influence children's knowledge and attitudes toward literacy and books in lasting ways.

Closing Remarks

Many years ago, Lev Vygotsky (1967) proposed that "play is a zone of proximal development" where children perform as if "a head taller than themselves." In play, children transform their world by giving things, places, and people temporary identities, pretending they are something they are not. Play is an imaginary zone where the world of meaning is separated from the objects, places, and events that embody it. Similarly, when children listen to storybooks and when they read and write stories themselves, they use symbols (speech, pictures, and print) to represent meaning.

Consequently, there are important links between play and children's developing sense of narrative in written language. In fact, many children make up their first stories in the context of pretend play, creating and enacting their own dramatic narratives. Expressed in fleeting actions, these are children's first compositions. Through LEA, some of the richness, drama, and excitement of these play experiences can be captured and can profitably serve children's early literacy learning. Rooted in the intentions and desires of young children, play as story provides an authenticity that inspires children to take on the challenge of learning to read and write even as it delights them. Taken further, play itself provides a learning environment thick with opportunities for young children to see, hear, touch, wonder, and think about writing and reading on their own terms. Play is a rich literacy resource indeed.

REFERENCES

Eckler, J., & Weininger, O. (1989). Structural parallels between play and narratives. *Developmental Psychology, 25,* 736–743.

Enz, B. J., & Christie, J. (1993). *Teacher play interaction styles and their impact on children's oral language and literacy play.* Paper given at the National Reading Conference. Charleston, SC.

Garvey, C. (1977). *Play.* Cambridge, MA: Harvard University Press.

Heath, S. B. (1983). *Ways with words: Language, life, and work in communities and classrooms.* Cambridge, MA: Cambridge University Press.

Holdaway, D. (1979). *The foundations of literacy.* Portsmouth, NH: Heinemann.

Meek, M. (1981). *Learning to read.* London: Heinemann.

Nessel, D., & Jones, M. (1981). *The language experience approach to reading: a handbook for teachers.* New York: Teachers College Press.

Paley, V. (1986). On listening to what children say. *Harvard Educational Review, 56,* 122–131.

Pellegrini, A. D. (1985a). The narrative organization of children's fantasy play. *Educational Psychology, 5,* 17–25.

Pellegrini, A. D. (1985b). The relations between symbolic play and literate behavior: A review and critique of the empirical literature. *Review of Educational Research, 55,* 107–121.

Pellegrini, A. D., & Galda, L. (1982). The effects of thematic-fantasy play training on the development of children's story comprehension. *American Educational Research Journal, 19,* 443–452.

Pellegrini, A. D., & Galda, L. (1993). Ten years after: A re-examination of symbolic play and literacy research. *Reading Research Quarterly, 28,* 162–177.

Pellegrini, A. D., Galda, L., Dresden, J., & Cox, S. (1991). A longitudinal study of the predictive relations among symbolic play. *Research in the Teaching of English, 25,* 219–235.

Roskos, K., & Neuman, S. B. (1993). Descriptive observations of adults' facilitation of literacy in young children's play. *Early Childhood Research Quarterly, 8*, 77–98.

Sachs, J., Goldman, J., & Chaille, C. (1985). Narratives in preschoolers' sociodramatic play. In L. Galda & A. D. Pellegrini (Eds.), *Play, language, and stories*, pp. 45–62. Norwood, NJ: Ablex.

Scarry, R. (1963). *The best word book ever*. New York: Golden Books.

Sendak, M. (1963). *Where the wild things are*. New York: Harper-Collins.

Silvern, S., Taylor, A., Williamson, P., Surbeck, E., & Kelley, P. (1986). Young children's story recall as a product of play. *Merrill-Palmer Quarterly, 32*, 73–86.

Snow, C. (1983). Literacy and language: Relationships during the preschool years. *Harvard Educational Review, 53*, 165–189.

Vygotsky, L. (1967). Play and its role in the mental development of the child. *Soviet Psychology, 12*, 62–76.

Williamson, P. A., & Silvern, S. B. (1990). The effects of play training on the story comprehension of upper primary children. *Journal of Research in Childhood Education, 4*, 130–136.

Williamson, P. A. & Silvern, S. (1991). Thematic-fantasy play and story comprehension. In J. Christie (Ed.), *Play and early literacy development*, pp. 69–90. Albany, NY: SUNY Press.

Wolf, D., & Pusch, J. (1985). The origins of autonomous text in play boundaries. In L. Galda & A. D. Pellegrini (Eds.), *Play, language, and stories*, pp. 63–78. Norwood, NJ: Ablex.

13 Using Nursery Rhymes with Early Experience Stories

A Language/Literature Program

K. ELEANOR CHRISTENSEN
Professor Emeritus, West Chester State College

WILLIAM J. OEHLKERS
Professor, Rhode Island College

When someone says "Language Experience," what's the first image that comes to mind? Is it a group of children led in a discussion about a stimulus who then dictate an account to the teacher? This is the familiar picture—a group or an individual creating a text on the spot. Another group, another time may bring forth a very different story. However, whole language advocates (Altwerger, Edelsky, & Flores, 1987) argue that research suggests children can also learn effectively by reading directly from written language without the need to go through their oral language (i.e., dictation). In other words, they don't always need to dictate orally, then have this language transcribed into a written form and then read. They can read from text that is already prepared, preferably text that is highly predictable. Prepared text offers the following advantages to both learners and teachers:

1. Students can become acquainted with story or written language structure from the beginning of reading instruction, acquiring early rich experiences with literature and print.
2. Children can enjoy positive shared reading experiences, and they can learn by doing.

3. Teachers can make use of high-interest children's literature. They can use "real" reading material from the outset, implementing a wide range of styles from prose to nursery rhymes, riddles, and poetry.

4. Teachers can monitor children's growing language abilities either through informal observation or through more structured techniques such as echo reading or voice pointing (Gillet & Temple, 1986).

5. Since the text to be read is already prepared, time is saved—an important consideration in today's busy classroom.

Using prepared written material can have many of the advantages of dictation. Both can provide students with motivating, high-interest reading material from which they can develop a meaningful sight vocabulary. In addition, both foster success and make reading easy because students can rely on their background knowledge to predict the text.

Nursery Rhymes as a Language Experience

Big Books and predictable stories have been recommended for use in beginning programs, but we have found that nursery rhymes are also useful for getting students on the road to reading. The text is already prepared, the content has the potential to arouse interest and to motivate, and many of the procedures associated with language experience can be employed.

One practical reason for using nursery rhymes is that they are already written; their prepared text saves precious instructional time. They also bring time-tested literary pleasures to today's children, some of whom may not often hear nursery rhymes at home. We believe that children benefit from all opportunities to interact meaningfully with print, so we alternate the usual group language experience stories with nursery rhymes in beginning reading programs. Our use of nursery rhymes might best be described as a language–literature program, since we rely upon many traditional language–experience activities. Here is a procedure for incorporating nursery rhymes in a beginning reading program.

Procedures for Incorporating Nursery Rhymes in Beginning Reading Programs

1. Select a nursery rhyme with the potential for an attention-getting story. Here's one of our favorites:

> *Dr. Foster went to Gloucester*
> *In a shower of rain;*
> *He stepped in a puddle,*
> *Right up to his middle,*
> *And never went there again.*

Consider the number of high-frequency early vocabulary words in the various nursery rhymes and choose rhymes such as "Dr. Foster" or "Little Boy Blue," which contain many common beginning reading words. "Little Boy Blue," for example, includes such words as *little, boy, blue, go, your, the,* and *in.*

2. Tell the story of the rhyme to the children in contemporary language. Do not read them the original verse at this time. Do not hesitate to embellish the rhyme with your own dramatically presented creative interpretation. Here, for example, is an enhanced version of Dr. Foster:

> One day, a doctor named Dr. Foster had a phone call from a woman down the street. She said, "Dr. Foster, I'm sick. My head hurts, my stomach hurts, and my feet hurt. I need help right away. Can you come down now?" Dr. Foster looked out the window and saw that it was raining hard. He really didn't want to go out in all that rain, but because he was a good doctor, he put on his boots, raincoat, and hat and started off for the lady's house.
>
> Now the streets in town were not paved, and as it rained they became very muddy. They were so muddy that Dr. Foster began to sink in the mud, almost up to his waist.
>
> Fortunately, a farmer came along with a team of horses and pulled Dr. Foster out of the mud. He walked to the lady's house, gave her some medicine and returned home again. When he got home, he said, "I hope that I don't have to go out on a rainy day like that again."

3. Integrate the story with the children's own experiences by acting out the rhyme using nonverbal creative dramatics. Children could take the part of the horses and pull on imaginary ropes to free Dr. Foster from the mud. Other students could play the role of Dr. Foster as he struggled to free himself.

4. Next, use verbal dramatics. Create a situation in which Dr. Foster is talking on the phone to the sick woman. Allow children to put puppets on their hands as they take their respective roles. At first, it is helpful if the teacher takes the role of Dr. Foster. Improvise an imaginary conversation between the doctor and his patient:

Patient: Dr. Foster, I'm sick. Come over and help me.

Dr. Foster: What's the problem?

Patient: I have a headache.

Dr. Foster: Have you taken any medicine for it yet?

5. Help students memorize the rhyme. One way to do this is to say the rhyme and then on each subsequent recitation, drop one word from the end of each line until the students are saying the rhyme by themselves. Another way is to set the lines to appropriate finger play movements.

6. After students know the rhyme, ask them to dictate it as you write it on lined chart paper in manuscript lettering.

7. Read the rhyme to them. Read it chorally with them. Ask one or two students to stand alongside you and read it together with you while the class watches.

8. Ask students to find words they can read in the rhyme. Underline the words that they can identify.

9. Write a few of the known words at the side of the chart, on the chalkboard. Ask students what these words are. If there is a word they do not know, ask them to find it in the rhyme itself.
10. Close the lesson by reading the rhyme with the students. The class reads all the underlined words. You read all the other words.
11. Begin the next session by repeating some of the procedures from the first day. Read the rhyme to the students, have them read it with you as you point to the words, let individuals read with you, underline words that were not previously marked, and mark previously underlined words a second time. Let children again act out the drama.
12. On the third day, prepare a set of large cards on which the underlined words have been written. Cards should be on oak tag or heavy card stock and measure about four by twelve inches. Hold up the cards one at a time and ask students to identify them. Ask students to find the words in the rhyme.

Additional Activities with Nursery Rhymes

Children should have access to the rhymes they've learned. Words can be placed in envelopes and kept with the rhymes. If the rhymes are attached to skirt hangers and hung on a low dowel rod, children can easily lift off the rhymes, lay them on a table or the floor, and review the rhymes and the words selected from them.

Another time you can copy the rhyme into a teacher-made Big Book that children can illustrate. Or you can transfer a rhyme onto transparencies, have the children illustrate it, model the use of the transparencies as a shared reading experience, and then make them available to small groups of children. The rhymes with accompanying word cards can also be placed into a box for the children to use as an activity center. Reviewing old rhymes will become increasingly more important as students accumulate additional rhymes.

As children develop a basic understanding of reading, the word cards can be used for phonic activities. For example, give children word cards and ask them to match each word card with a picture that has the same beginning sound.

Trade books containing nursery rhymes should be available at a library area in the classroom so that children may reread their known selections. Copies of the children's rhymes bound in class-made books should also be available. Model silent reading and encourage children to try this as well as reading aloud.

Some whole language proponents seem to prefer using prepared literature to having children dictate. The material is exciting and the language is rich and predictable. We believe, however, that there is room for both literature and dictation in beginning reading programs. Using nursery rhymes as we have described here provides a wealth of learning opportunities. Language experience procedures allow the created text to relate directly to the experiences of the learner and give systematic attention to sight word acquisition, while nursery rhymes provide an easy introduction to children's literature and language structure. We recommend employing both as they are equally pleasurable and appropriate.

REFERENCES

Altwerger, B., Edelsky, C., & Flores, B. M. (1987). Whole language: What's new? *The Reading Teacher, 41,* 144–154.

Gillet, J., & Temple, C. (1986). *Understanding reading problems* (2nd ed.). Boston, MA: Little, Brown.

14 Linking Literacy and Lyrics through Song Picture Books

KATHY BARCLAY

Professor/Chairperson, Western Illinois University

Certain musical lyrics lure children into a web of imagination and enjoyment. Even very young children frequently memorize verse after verse of elaborate song lyrics, such as those from "I Know an Old Lady Who Swallowed a Fly," and, "Supercalifragilisticexpialidocious."

In *Joining the Literacy Club*, Frank Smith (1988) discusses the importance of introducing reading and writing to children in a variety of ways. He states, "the trick is to find something involving reading and writing that interests the learner and to engage the learner authentically in that area of interest, making the reading and writing incidental" (p. 125).

The language of song is a natural language for children. Through song children build language fluency that permeates every area of the school curriculum. Like the musician and the lyricist, writers and readers compose because they are all meaning-makers. Bill Harp (1988) suggests that "music and reading go together because singing is a celebration of language. Using songs to teach reading is consistent with the nature and purposes of language and puts readers in touch with satisfying meanings" (p. 454). Karnowski (1986) encourages the integration of writing with music and art. He advises teachers to place writing tools in the music area because "writing flourishes in a social environment where young children are free to use oral language, art, music, and drama to explore and enhance their writing" (p. 60).

[From "Linking Literacy and Lyrics in the Early Childhood Classroom," by Kathy Barclay, 1992, *Journal of Language Experience, 11*(1), pp. 26–33. Copyright 1992 by the Language Experience Special Interest Group. Reprinted and revised with permission.]

Using Song Picture Books

While children have always loved song picture books, these books have not usually found their way into school reading programs. Timeless tunes such as "Old Mac-Donald Had a Farm," and "There Was an Old Lady" have enjoyed a popular place in our classrooms for many generations, yet a widely growing genre of song picture books has not, as yet, gained any kind of consistent use or application.

Song picture books are appropriate for both library collections and instructional reading programs because they easily meet the criteria for both situations. First of all, they have wide appeal. Children of varied ages and abilities enjoy seeing favorite songs illustrated. Peter Spier's *London Bridge Is Falling Down* (1967) and Nadine Westcott's *The Lady with the Alligator Purse* (1989b) are two such examples. Secondly, they meet the current demand for books that follow a predictable pattern. Lydia Child's *Over the River and Through the Wood* (1987), Nadine Westcott's *Skip to My Lou* (1989c), Mary Maki Rae's *The Farmer in the Dell: A Singing Game* (1989), and Edward Bangs' *Yankee Doodle* (1976) are but a few of the many popular song picture books that contain well-known refrains repeated throughout. Finally, many song picture books provide an excellent source for vocabulary development and expansion. Books such as Pete Seeger's *Abiyoyo* (1989), Jimmy and Savannah Buffet's *The Jolly Mon* (1988), and Peter Spier's *The Erie Canal* (1970) possess a richness of language, as well as content, to be explored.

Lyrical Lesson Plans

The following procedures may be used to lead the children from the initial music experience with the song to reading experiences, and, finally, to writing tasks.

Stage One: Teaching the Song
1. Play the music, sing the song, and invite the children to sing along with you as you engage in several repetitions of the song.
2. Talk about the meaning of the song and discuss any special words that may be unfamiliar to the children.
3. Solicit the children's help in creating motions or drama to add to the song.
4. Enjoy singing the song with the added motions or dramatic activities.

Stage Two: Linking the Song to Print
1. Show the children the song picture book and ask the children to tell you about the cover and the pictures.
2. Read the book, allowing plenty of time for the children to savor the illustrations.
3. Reread the book, inviting the children to join in.
4. Show the children the lyrics written on a large piece of chart paper. Invite the children to read along with you as you point to each word in the song.

Stage Three: Developing Reading Skill

1. Build sight vocabulary by asking the children to locate words on the song chart that appear more than once. These words can be divided into function words, such as *in, an, the,* or content words, such as *lady, fly, spider*
2. Make a list of the high-frequency words contained in the song and use these words in various related reading and writing activities. These words can be added to the students' individual word banks, or to a class dictionary or word wall.
3. Select one or two phonic or word structure elements to work with as the children learn to read each set of lyrics. For example, the various ways that a "long i" sound can be spelled might be discussed as the children learn to read Bonne's *I Know an Old Lady* (1961). Words from the song with the "long i" sound would include *fly, my, spider, inside,* and *die.* The different sounds of *y* might also be stressed, using as examples the words *lady, fly,* and *my.*
4. Other phonic and/or structural activities could include asking the children to locate all the words on the song chart with a particular beginning/middle/ending sound, or with a particular prefix/suffix/common ending, and so on.
5. Phrase cards and word cards can be used for matching and sequencing activities. Ask the children to arrange the phrases in order as they appear in the song. Cover up particular words or phrases, and ask the children to supply the missing card(s).
6. Involve the children in extended comprehension activities. They might create, for example, a picture book graph depicting the events in the song picture book. Books that would be especially suitable for this purpose include Maryann Kovalski's *The Wheels on the Bus* (1987) and Nina Barbaresi's *Frog Went-A-Courtin'* (1985).
7. Other extended comprehension activities might include plotting relationships, such as problems and solutions, sequence of events, and causes and effects detailed in the songs. Song picture books such as Tracy Campbell Pearson's *Sing a Song of Sixpence* (1985) and Robert Quackenbush's *She'll Be Comin' 'Round the Mountain* (1973) lend themselves particularly well to these types of discussions and activities.

Stage Four: Developing Writing Skill

1. Create innovations based on the song Iyrics. For example, two preschool children changed the lyrics of "The Farmer in the Dell" to "The Bear in the Barn." The meaning pattern existing in the original is reflected in the children's new story. The lyrics now read:

   > The bear in the barn, the bear in the barn, heigh-ho the derry-o, the bear in the barn.
   > The bear takes a lion, the bear takes a lion, heigh-ho the derry-o, the bear takes a lion.
   > The lion takes a mouse, the lion takes a mouse, heigh-ho the derry-o, the lion takes a mouse . . . [and so on until] "the cheese stands alone."

2. The innovations can be enlarged on chart or poster paper, illustrated by the children, displayed on the wall, and later bound into a big book.

3. The children may wish to try writing new stanzas of the song, or creating their own song picture books based on the lyrics of their own favorite tunes.

Conclusion

The language of song is natural, joyful language. When combined with literacy development, using the approach recommended here with song picture books, the process of beginning reading and writing is as natural and joyful as a song. The following is a list of song picture books that can be used in the manner described.

A RESOURCE LIST OF SONG PICTURE BOOKS BY TITLE

A You're Adorable (1994). Buddy Kaye, Fred Wise, & Sidney Lippman. Martha Alexander [illus]. Cambridge: Candlewick Press.

Abiyoyo: South African Lullaby & Folk Song (1989). Pete Seeger. Michael Hays [illus]. New York: Scholastic.

Casey Jones: The Story of a Brave Engineer (1968). Glen Rounds. San Carlos, CA: Golden Gate Junior Books.

Clementine (1974). Robert Quackenbush [illus]. Philadelphia: Lippincott.

Do Your Ears Hang Low? (1980). Tom Glazer. Mila Lazarevich [illus]. Garden City, NY: Doubleday.

The Eensy Weensy Spider (1990). Alan Daniel [illus]. Bothell, WA: The Wright Group.

The Erie Canal (1970). Peter Spier [illus]. Garden City, NY: Doubleday.

Everything Grows (1989). Raffi. Bruce McMillan [illus]. New York: Crown.

The Farmer in the Dell: A Singing Game (1989). Mary Maki Rae [illus]. New York: Scholastic.

Frère Jacques (1973). Barbara Hazen. Lilian Obligado [illus]. Philadelphia: Lippincott.

Frog Went-A-Courtin' (1985). Nina Barbaresi [illus]. New York: Scholastic.

Go Tell Aunt Rhody (1986). Aliki [illus]. New York: Macmillan.

Hilary Knight's The Twelve Days of Christmas (1981). Hilary Knight [illus]. New York: Macmillan.

Hush Little Baby (1987). Margot Zemach [illus]. New York: Dutton.

Hush Little Baby: A Folk Lullaby (1989). Aliki [illus]. New York: Simon and Schuster.

I Know an Old Lady (1972). Rose Bonne [illus]. Music by Alan Mills. New York: Scholastic.

I Know an Old Lady Who Swallowed a Fly (1989). Nadine Westcott [illus]. Boston: Little, Brown.

I'm a Little Teapot (1966). Iza Trapani [illus]. Boston: Whispering Coyote Press.

In a Cabin in the Wood (1991). Darcie McNally. Rovin Michael Koontz [illus]. New York: Cobblehill Books/Dutton.

It's Raining, It's Pouring (1994). Kin Eagle. Robert Gilbert [illus] Boston: Whispering Coyote Press.

The Itsy Bitsy Spider (1993). Iza Trapani [illus]. Boston: Whispering Coyote Press.

The Jolly Mon (1988). Jimmy and Savannah Buffet. Lambert Davis [illus]. San Diego: Harcourt Brace and Jovanovich.

The Lady with the Alligator Purse (1989). Nadine Westcott [illus]. Boston: Little, Brown.

The Little Drummer Boy (1968). Ezra Jack Keats [illus]. New York: Scholastic.

London Bridge Is Falling Down (1967). Peter Spier [illus]. New York: Doubleday.

The Man on the Flying Trapeze (1975). Robert Quackenbush [illus]. Philadelphia: Lippincott.

Miss Mary Mack (1994). Alan and Lea Daniel [illus]. Bothell, WA: The Wright Group.

My Favorite Things (1994). Richard Rodgers and Oscar Hammerstein. James Warhola [illus]. New York: Simon & Schuster Books for Young Readers.

Oh, A-Hunting We Will Go (1989). John Langstaff. Nancy W. Parker [illus]. Boston: Houghton Mifflin.

Old MacDonald Had a Farm (1989). Glen Rounds [illus]. New York: Holiday House.

On Top of Spaghetti (1966). Tom Glazer. Art Seiden [illus]. New York: Grosset & Dunlap.

One Wide River to Cross (1971). Barbara Emberley. Ed Emberley [illus]. New York: Scholastic.

Over in the Meadow (1973). Olive A. Wadsworth. Ezra Jack Keats [illus]. London: Hamilton.

Over the River and Through the Wood (1987). Lydia Child. Brinton Turkle [illus]. New York: Scholastic.

Pop Goes the Weasel and Yankee Doodle: New York in 1776 and Today (1976). Robert Quackenbush [illus]. Philadelphia: Lippincott.

Shake My Sillies Out (1987). Raffi songs to read. David Allender [illus]. New York: Crown.

She'll Be Comin' 'Round the Mountain (1973). Robert Quackenbush [illus]. Philadelphia: Lippincott.

Sing a Song of Sixpence (198S). Tracy Campbell Pearson [illus]. New York: Dial.

Skip to My Lou (1989). Nadine Westcott [illus]. Boston: Little, Brown.

The Star Spangled Banner (1973). Peter Spier [illus]. New York Doubleday.

Sweet Betsy From Pike (1970). Roz Abisch [illus]. New York: McCall.

Teddy Bear's Picnic (1992). Jimmy Kennedy. Michael Hague [illus]. New York: Holt.

There Was an Old Lady (1975). Pam Adams [illus]. England: Child's Play.

There Was an Old Woman (1974). Steven Kellogg [illus]. New York: Scholastic.

This Old Man (1974). Pam Adams [illus]. New York: Grosset & Dunlap.

The Twelve Days of Christmas (1990). Jan Brett [illus]. New York: Putnam.

We Wish You a Merry Christmas (1983). Tracy Campbell Pearson [illus]. New York: Dial.

The Wheels on the Bus (1987). Maryann Kovalski [illus]. Boston: Little, Brown.

Yankee Doodle (1976). Edward Bangs. Steven Kellogg [illus]. New York: Parent's Magazine Press.

Yankee Doodle (1992). Alan Daniel [illus]. Bothell, WA: The Wright Group.

What a Wonderful World (1995). George Weiss and Bob Thiele. Ashley Bryan [illus]. New York: Atheneum Books for Young Readers.

REFERENCES

Bangs, E. (1976). *Yankee doodle*. New York: Parent's Magazine Press.
Barbaresi, N. (1985). *Frog went-a-courtin'*. New York: Scholastic.
Bonne, R. (1961). *I know an old lady*. New York: Rand McNally.
Buffet, J., & S. (1988). *The jolly mon*. San Diego: Harcourt Brace and Jovanovich.
Child, L. (1987). *Over the river and through the wood*. New York: Scholastic.
Harp, B. (1988). Why are your kids singing during reading time? *The Reading Teacher, 41*, 454–456.
Karnowski, L. (1986). How young writers communicate. *Educational Leadership, 46*(3), 58–60.
Kellogg, S. (1974). *There was an old woman*. New York: Scholastic.
Kovalski, M. (1987). *The wheels on the bus*. Boston: Little, Brown.
Pearson, T. C. (1985). *Sing a song of sixpence*. New York: Dial.
Quackenbush, R. (1973). *She'll be comin' 'round the mountain*. Philadelphia: Lippincott.
Rae, M. M. (1989). *The farmer in the dell: A singing game*. New York Scholastic.
Rounds, G. (1989). *Old MacDonald had a farm*. New York: Holiday House.
Seeger, P. (1989). *Abiyoyo*. New York: Scholastic.
Smith, F. (1988). *Joining the literacy club*. Portsmouth, NH: Heinemann.
Spier, P. (1967). *London Bridge is falling down*. New York: Doubleday.
Spier, P. (1970). *The Erie Canal*. New York: Doubleday.
Westcott, N. (1989a). *I know an old lady who swallowed a fly*. Boston: Little, Brown.
Westcott, N. (1989b). *The lady with the alligator purse*. Boston: Little, Brown.
Westcott, N. (1989c). *Skip to my Lou*. Boston: Little, Brown.

15 Beginning Writing

Where Does It Really Begin?

KATHY BARCLAY

Professor/Chairperson, Western Illinois University

A four-year-old handed her mother this piece of paper (see Figure 15.1) announcing, "Here's all the words I know!" She then proceeded to "read" the words as follows: *Pepsi, park, mom, dad, coconut, orange,* and *hot dog.*

In past years, adults have frequently failed to attach any real significance to these early attempts at writing words, yet this short writing sample is an illustrative

FIGURE 15.1   A Four-year-old Child's Attempt at Writing

[From "Beginning Writing: Where Does It Really Begin?" by Kathy Barclay, 1992, *Journal of Language Experience, 11*(1), pp. 34–42. Copyright 1992 by the Language Experience Special Interest Group. Reprinted with permission.]

example of what Marie Clay meant when she stated, "The child in thinking, in oral language, in reading for meaning, and in early writing is motivated to make the world make sense" (Clay, 1979). Actually, the child was telling her mother that she understood quite a bit about written language. She understood, for example, the concept of a word as a cluster of letters. In fact, she was using acceptable English letters in her writing. She also understood that words could be written in list form, and that each word that is written has a spoken equivalent.

Like many other children who are approximately this age, this child is in the emergent literacy stage of development. Children in this stage frequently engage in play with written language as they attempt to solve the written language puzzle (Dyson, 1982). It is as if they are asking "How do these puzzles called reading and writing really work?" When early childhood teachers use a language experience approach in combination with an abundance of free, or independent, writing, young children have a greater opportunity to discover for themselves how these puzzles work.

Through careful and systematic observation and reflection about what young children already know about literacy, researchers have identified stages through which most young children progress as they emerge into beginning writers and readers (Allen, et al., 1989; Barclay, 1990; Clay, 1979; Genishi & Dyson, 1984; Sulzby, 1985). While researchers often apply somewhat different terminology when labeling each stage, the sequence, or progression of stages noted, and the characteristics ascribed to each stage, are quite similar. The purpose of this chapter is to discuss each stage of early writing development, and to provide examples of each, using writing samples created by preschool, kindergarten, and first-grade children.

The Emergence of Written Letter Forms

A child's first exploration with writing, as opposed to drawing, can occur before the age of two. The onset of this first stage of writing development, scribbling, is often signaled by the young child scribbling a few random marks on a slip of paper, and then announcing "This says Terry!" (child's name). Quite often, young children make random scribbles on the same page with an accompanying drawing; however, the scribbles represent an abstract form of meaning-making, as opposed to their more concrete pictorial representations. Again, as adults, we frequently neglect to notice these scribbles—or to assign any special meaning or significance to them. Yet, this first stage of writing development is an important one, for it shows us that the child has learned a critical concept about print—that written language has meaning.

The child enters the next stage of writing development when he or she becomes more aware of the adult style of cursive writing. In the mock-handwriting stage (see Figure 15.2), the child produces lines of wavy scribbles. Note the way this child is writing on what are relatively small lines and spaces. It is important that we provide the child with many types of writing papers and utensils. Old

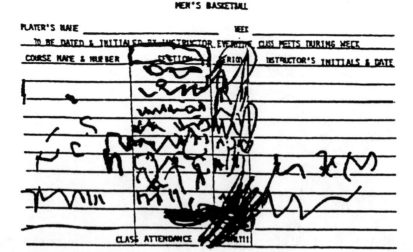

FIGURE 15.2   Example of Mock-Handwriting Stage

forms, such as the one depicted in Figure 15.2, can be recycled for use. They provide young children with a sense of real writing. Much of what we consider "junk" mail makes perfect writing paper for young children. Old catalog order blanks, magazine subscription forms, and other such printed materials have a great deal of appeal to young children. We do not need to worry about providing nice, clean, blank paper at these early stages of writing development, for as one child told her mom, "I can't write on the back because there's no writing! Writing goes with writing. See?"

As children begin to notice more and more print in the environment, they also begin to notice that writing doesn't always consist of continuous lines of print, but rather individual letters, or squiggles, that are separated by spaces. As young writers begin to experiment with forming these letters, or squiggles, they typically make letter forms that resemble acceptable letters. These mock letters (see Figure 15.3) are usually spaced in a random order on the page.

Through numerous experiences with print in books and in the environment, the young child's mock letters become more and more like acceptable letters. Finally we see the child emerging into the next stage of writing development (see Figure 15.4), combining real letters plus inventions.

Early Attempts to Form Words

When young children are fairly comfortable with their attempts at writing acceptable letters, we usually see them begin to cluster letters together, making wordlike forms. The child's first written words typically consist of several letters spaced closely together. These first words, however, seldom bear any resemblance whatso-

FIGURE 15.3   Example of Experimentation with Mock Letters in Random Order

ever to any phonetically or conventionally spelled words. That is, the words are purely invented and neither sound, nor look like, any words in the English language system. The example depicted earlier in Figure 15.1 is an example of this stage of writing development. The words that the child has written, while resembling words written in the English language system, do not resemble any conventionally or phonetically spelled words.

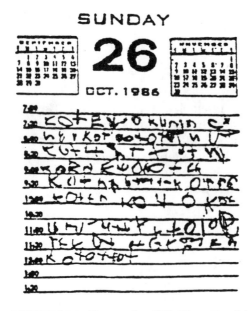

FIGURE 15.4   Example of Writing Combining Real Letters Plus Inventions

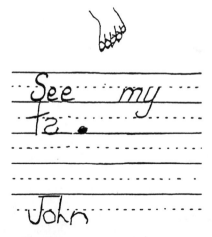

FIGURE 15.5 Example of John's Writing Combining Real Letters Plus Inventions

As children begin to develop an awareness of the relationship between certain letters and sounds, they will begin to form words that more closely resemble real words. After a discussion of body parts, one kindergarten teacher gave each child a piece of paper on which to draw a body part, and fill in the blank with the name of the body part. In Figure 15.5, we see John's attempt at drawing and at filling in the blank with the word *toes*.

John's writing sample provides us with the knowledge that he is beginning to function in the phonetic, or approximated spelling, stage. We know this because he is using his knowledge of letter–sound relationships to attempt the spelling of a new word. He is able to recognize the correct initial consonant *t* and the ending sound *s*, and thus uses these letters to form his spelling of the word *toes*.

A young child might also approximate spellings of words by using primarily visual clues. Such is the case when a child first tries to write his or her name. Usually the first letter and one or two other letters are written from memory, and then the child fills in with other letters to make the name appear to be the "right" length.

Beginning Phrases and Sentences

Once children begin to approximate the spellings of some words, they usually begin to hook words together to form simple phrases and sentences. These beginning sentences frequently appear in connection with a drawing (see Figure 15.6).

Four-and-a-half-year-old Katherine reads this sentence as "The cat and dog is in a house." Notice the beginning of conventional spelling with the words *cat*, *dog*, *a*, and *by*, as well as evidence of the approximated or phonetic spellings of *es*

FIGURE 15.6   Example of Katherine's Writing Using a Combination of Conventional and Approximated Spelling

for *is*, and *hs* for *house*. Function words *the, and, in,* are provided in oral rather than written form, thus indicating an awareness of correct syntax.

A young child's knowledge of conventional spelling will grow with time. We do not see an overnight move from one stage of writing development to another, but rather a gradual building of stage upon stage. It is certainly not uncommon to see what we, as adults, may believe to be a regression in writing development. In a more recent writing episode, Katherine, who is now five-and-a-half, explained her list of written clues gathered to solve a make-believe mystery (see Figure 15.7). The impetus for this particular dramatic play interlude came from the popular children's television show "Inspector Gadget."

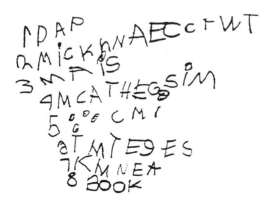

FIGURE 15.7   Example of Katherine's Writing Using Pure Invented Spelling

FIGURE 15.8　Example of Child's Writing Employing Several Stages of Writing

The only conventionally spelled word included on the list is the word *book*. The other words bear no resemblance to the way the actual words sound or look. Thus they are further examples of pure invented spellings of words, as opposed to approximated or conventional spellings.

As children progress in their writing we would like to see evidence of several stages of writing development as they more confidently exercise their word-making and meaning-making strategies. Gradually, we see the shift to more and more conventional spellings, approximated spellings, and even the use of pictures and symbols, yet the meaning is quite clear as this child records his favorite part of the story "The Three Little Pigs" (see Figure 15.8).

The Developing Sense of Story

As children hear many stories read aloud, they begin to develop a sense of story. That is, they understand that stories contain characters, and have a beginning, middle, and an end. Young children also have many personal stories and experiences to talk and write about. Aaron, a first grader, writes a touching story about his dog's death (see Figure 15.9).

> My dog died yesterday. My dad took her to the vet. [By] the time he got there she died. He brought her back and buried her in the backyard. Me and my brother tries [to] help. She's in my backyard. I don't know if we're going to get another dog. We feel sad for her. We'll never see her again.

Aaron's story, rich in content and personal experience, reveals many important understandings about written language. He has used many approximated, as well

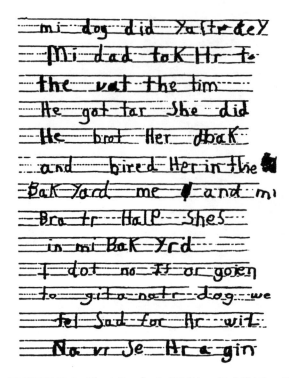

mi dog did YaftrdeY
Mi dad toK Hr to
the vat the tim
He got tar She did
He brot Her dbaK
and bired Her in the
BaK Yard me and mi
Bro tr HalP Shes
in mi BaK Yrd
I dot no If or gojen
to git a notr dog we
fel Sad for Hr wil
Now Je Hr a gin

FIGURE 15.9   First Grader's Writing Exhibiting Developing Sense of Story

as some conventional, spellings. His story clearly conveys a sequential order of events, and he has certainly managed to invoke in the reader a feeling of presence, of being there. Aaron is definitely on his way to becoming a writer!

As adults, we must support our young children by encouraging their early attempts at writing. A combination of language experience and personal writing allows the emergent writer to see good writing and reading modeled and allows ample opportunity for the young child to naturally and independently progress through the stages of writing development.

As Crystal, a first-grade pupil, wrote in an April journal entry: "I like reading. I learn so much without Mrs. T, and Mrs. T can take a break. I like reading so much." In our work with emergent readers and writers like Crystal, Katherine, Aaron, and the other children whose writings are included in this article, we would do well to remember that young children need the time to explore writing and reading independently as they develop a personal understanding of and appreciation for the power of the printed word.

REFERENCES

Allen, J., Clark, W., Cook, M., Crane, P., Fallon, I., Hoffman, L., Jennings, K., & Sours, M. (1989). Reading and writing development in whole language kindergartens. In J. M. Mason (Ed.), *Reading and Writing Connections*, pp. 121–146. Boston: Allyn & Bacon.

Barclay, K. (1990). From scribbling to "real" writing: What parents and teachers of young children should know about literacy development. In Nancy B. Cecil (Ed.), *Literacy in the 90's: Readings in the language arts*, pp. 4–13. Dubuque, IA: Kendall-Hunt.

Clay, M. (1979). *Reading: The patterning of complex behavior*. Portsmouth, NH: Heinemann.

Dyson, A. H. (1982). Reading, writing, and language: Young children solving the written language puzzle. *Language Arts, 59*, 829–839.

Genishi, C., & Dyson, A. H. (1984). *Language assessment in the early years*. Norwood, NJ: Ablex.

Sulzby, E. (1985). Kindergartners as writers and readers. In M. Farr (Ed.), *Advances in written research: Vol. 1. Children's early writing development*, pp. 127–199. Norwood, NJ: Ablex.

16 Using LEA to Assess Literacy in the Primary Grades

ELIZABETH GIBBONS PRYOR

Reading and Language Arts Curriculum Specialist, K–12, Columbus (OH) Public Schools

Daily, ongoing assessment of literacy in the context of instruction is particularly critical in the primary grades as children learn to read and write. Johnston (1984) asserts that a particularly critical time for literacy assessment is in grades one through three because reading and writing are such cumulative processes. Such assessment, according to Johnston, should focus on students' strengths, strategies, knowledge, and reasoning behind their responses so that their reading and writing processes can be examined and the learning context, materials, and instruction adjusted accordingly.

Emergent literacy research during the last twenty-five years has considerably altered perceptions of how children learn to read, write, speak, and listen (Bissex, 1980; Clay, 1972; Harste, Woodward, & Burke, 1984; Read, 1975; Sulzby, 1985; Teale & Sulzby, 1986). Today, these language processes are understood to be interrelated, dynamic, interactive processes of meaning construction. As a consequence of revised perceptions of how children learn these processes, literacy instruction has changed. Since 1986 there has been a national trend away from relying solely on standardized tests to accepting multiple assessments of literacy. These assessments occur within the context of instruction so that children's language processes can be examined and instruction adjusted in process.

Why Not Focus on the Curriculum and Tests?

Imagine you are a five-year-old who has already learned to read, but you have to spend nine months in a kindergarten class where the literacy instruction is focused on learning the alphabet letters and their sounds—BORING AND INSULTING! Now imagine you are a kindergartner who has had very limited experiences in reading and writing at home, and you are in the same classroom, receiving the same instruction—NONSENSE AND CONFUSION!

Such insults to children often happen when teachers focus on instruction that is covering the curriculum and preparing students for the next grade rather than basing literacy instruction on assessments of what children already know! Regardless of the subject, age, or grade level of students, the most effective teachers begin by finding out what their students know and can do.

Effective teachers, for example, might begin assessing students' literacy by asking questions such as: "What do my students already know about reading, writing, speaking, listening?" "What experiences have they already had?" "What can they already do in reading, writing, speaking, listening?" "What do they need to know in order to become better readers, writers, speakers, and listeners?" Teachers who follow this type of reasoning use information about their students to teach more complex processes and procedures by structuring a wide variety of meaningful opportunities that provide choices and engage students in active learning.

Linking Instruction and Assessment

The Language Experience Approach (LEA) is the ideal way to assess what students know and can do because it is real, in context, authentic, easy to do, flexible, integrates all of the language processes, and can be used for both instruction and assessment. Language experiences that are especially useful for both instruction and assessment in the primary grades are individual or group experience stories, interactive writing, book talks, retellings, reading response logs, dialogue journals, and learning logs.

An experience shared in common may become the source for a group experience story, or the individual's experience can be the topic of an individual experience story. The following explanation illustrates how one primary teacher uses a group language experience for both instruction and assessment in her classroom:

> During the study of change we shared a popcorn experience. First, we examined unpopped corn using our five senses and discussed our discoveries. Next we popped the corn and reexamined it using our senses. As we devoured our popped corn, we discussed and wrote a group language experience story about the changes in the popcorn, with the children telling me what they wanted to have written on chart paper about their experience and what they had learned from it. If this experience was early in the school year, I wrote their dictation on chart paper, using an instructional think-aloud (e.g., saying out loud my thoughts regarding where I began writing, how I figured out how to spell the words, why I skipped spaces between words, why I wrote capital letters in certain places, etc.). Then I had the children reread each sentence as well as the whole piece.

For the next several days, we used the chart story for shared reading, for instruction, and for assessment opportunities (e.g., "Who can find a letter or word or sentence they know and can show us and tell us what it says?" "What kind of letter is this—capital or lowercase? Why do we use that kind of letter here?" "Where did I begin writing this word?" "Why did I begin there?" "What word comes next?" "Can you find the same word in our story that is on this card?"). If this experience was later in the year, instead of writing their dictation, I involved the children in interactive writing (Button, Johnson, & Furgerson, 1996). After the children decided what they wanted to say, they each actively participated in constructing the experience story by actually writing a letter or a word on the story chart. I provided the scaffolding needed by writing and explaining aspects or elements of language that the children did not yet know. For example, when writing the word *oil*, most young children could not provide the standard spelling of the vowels, so that became an opportunity to introduce the *oi* vowel pattern and explain how it is used in other familiar words such as *foil, boil*, and *soil*.

Interactive writing lessons like this one provide a wealth of opportunities for both instruction and assessment of language elements (e.g., spacing, capitalization, directionality, phonemic awareness, syllabication, punctuation, pronunciation, phonics, sentence structure, and spelling). Such lessons, in fact, are so loaded with opportunities for children to learn and for the teacher to teach and assess, that little text actually gets generated in one lesson. Sometimes it is only one sentence! The point to remember is that generation of text is not the goal; the goal is students' learning via the language experiences of reading, writing, speaking, and listening during text construction.

A variety of information about children's literacy development can be assessed using LEA in the classroom. Although the categories of information differ from more traditional skills-based assessment, the information is similar and more user friendly when planning future instruction. The assessment information that can be easily collected in an LEA classroom can be categorized under three specific headings: (1) Meaning-Making Processes, (2) Knowledge about Language, and (3) Personal Attributes.

Assessing Meaning-Making Processes

Teachers can observe how children make sense of language by observing how they use language as well as how they interpret what they hear, read, or write. Here are some questions that may be used to assess particular aspects of their students' processes:

- Can the child already read or write?
- Does the child understand what she or he is reading, writing, hearing, and saying?
- Does the child understand that print conveys meaning and that reading and writing are supposed to make sense?

- Can/does the child elaborate in writing and/or when speaking?
- What language arts strategies does the child use to figure out an unknown word, to spell a word, to revise her or his writing, to listen?
- What are the speech patterns in the child's oral language?
- Does the child speak a dialect? If so, does it enhance or interfere with meaning-making?
- When reading, does the child self-correct and reread for sense?
- Can the child self-select a topic for writing?

Assessing Knowledge about Language

Another major area of literacy assessment is knowledge about language. The following questions can be used to identify what the child knows about conventions, rules, patterns, and sequence of oral and written language during language experience activities:

- Does the child know directionality?
- Does the child understand basic concepts about language (e.g., letter, word, phrase, sentence, paragraph, the function of space)?
- Does the child know language mechanics such as capitalization and punctuation?
- Can the child match letters, words, sentences, and so on?
- Can the child identify the capital and lowercase letters and their sounds?
- Does the child have phonemic awareness? For example, can the child hear the individual sounds in words? Can the child segment words into sounds?
- What is the child's developmental spelling stage?
- What writing conventions does the child know? For example, when writing a story can the child create a title, beginning, middle, and end?
- Does the child understand prefixes, suffixes, contractions, and compound words?
- Can the child identify rhyming words?
- When editing, how accurately and extensively can the child identify what needs to be corrected?

Assessing Personal Attributes

Finally, by using language experiences, teachers can learn much about children's personal traits and their prior experiences with literacy. Here are a few key questions teachers may use to guide their inquiry:

- What prior literacy experiences has the child had at home? Elsewhere?
- How willing is the child to take risks in learning?
- How interested is the child in learning to read and write?
- What are the child's interests?

- What is the child currently reading and writing at home?
- Does the child have physical, social, or emotional problems that might be obstacles to learning? Does the child have any vision or speech problems that need specific attention?
- Is the child self-confident as a communicator? As a learner?

Documentation of Assessment Is Essential

Keeping written documentation of the assessment data collected during language experience activities is essential for several reasons. First, teachers probably know their children as learners better than anyone since they are with them five days a week for nine months. If teachers do not document their children's learning, who else can or will? Second, written documentation is essential for reporting progress to families. Traditional report cards alone are too superficial in giving an accurate picture of the progress of a learner. Third, assessment is like research—one has to be able to see and analyze assessment data gathered over a period of time in order to discover the patterns. This cannot be done when the bulk of the data is stored and carried around in memory. It must be documented in writing or recorded in another form, such as an audiotape, so that it can be analyzed and reflected on at a later time. Trying to remember and balance so much assessment information in one's head is too stressful. Furthermore, such data is too likely to be remembered inaccurately, if at all.

Keeping anecdotal notes, also known as observational notes, is the most beneficial way to document assessment data, yet it is also the most difficult. Maintaining anecdotal notes is difficult because teachers need to write them either as they are teaching or as soon after the incident as possible. The richness of the data from these notes makes the effort well worth it.

Keeping Anecdotal Records: A Scenario

As a classroom teacher, I tried a number of ways to keep anecdotal notes until I finally found one that worked for me. All day, every day, I carried pages of self-stick mailing labels on a small clipboard that had a pencil attached. I explained to the students that part of my job as their teacher was to keep records about their learning. I told them that I cared deeply about how each of them learned, so they should expect to see me writing on my clipboard often. Each day I targeted my observations on five students. The date and each of their names was written on the top of a sticky label. I also carried extra labels for unexpected, incidental observations of other students.

At the end of each day, I transferred the anecdotal notes I had taken on the sticky labels into a loose-leaf notebook that contained pages for each student. I arranged the labels in chronological order down the left side of the student's page, keeping the right side clear for additional comments and notes about the patterns and instructional needs that I observed while reflecting on the anecdotal notes. Each week, prior to writing the following week's lesson plans, I reviewed and analyzed the anecdotal notes, seeking data about individual and whole-class instructional needs. This helped me to determine what I should teach next and to whom. For example, if I found that a group of students was having difficulty using the context to figure out new words, I would plan a series of mini-lessons with that particular group focused on ways to use context to figure out new words.

In addition to [recording] anecdotal notes, I also used a wide variety of other documentation methods over time. Some of the more effective methods are [collecting and analyzing]: samples of students' work, audio- and videotapes of students engaged in language experience activities, students' learning logs or journals, teacher-made checklists, notes from conversations/interviews/conferences with students and parents, surveys of students and parents, and student self-assessments.

How Do You Report Children's Growth in Learning?

For most teachers, the traditional report card is required. However, some schools now are revising their report cards to be more congruent with current literacy research and instruction. For example, teachers at Dunbar Elementary School in Tallmadge, Ohio, have revised their report card so that learning is defined by various performance continuums. The marks children get on their progress report cards indicate the range within which that child falls on each of the continuums so that learning is seen as a never-ending process. Families can see what their children have accomplished in their learning and what accomplishments they can expect to see next.

Although traditional report cards inhibit and reduce the amount of assessment information that can be shared with a child's family, teachers can balance the lack of rich information by having children develop learning portfolios to share with their families at the end of each grading period. Many teachers use these portfolios for family–teacher conferences where the child is present and participates in the conference. Others have a "Portfolio Night" several times a year when children can bring their families to school to see their portfolios and discuss and demonstrate their learning.

Another way to augment traditional report cards is to add a teacher's report on a separate sheet of paper that is inserted in the report card. This additional report can be anything from a checklist to a narrative profile of the child as a learner. The idea is to share as much information as is reasonable with families so they can get a more accurate picture of their child as a learner.

Summary

Language experience activities provide the ideal way for teachers to assess children's knowledge and use of language. Effective teachers design effective literacy instruction based on children's learning needs and literacy development, rather than artificially imposed curriculums. These teachers are focused on their students—not on getting through the prescribed curriculum by the end of the year. Language experience activities put children at the center of the learning while providing opportunities to assess their meaning-making processes, knowledge of language, and personal attributes. Thus, child-centered classrooms and language experience activities are key components for primary-grade teachers who want to assess literacy growth and development in the context of instruction.

REFERENCES

Bissex, G. (1980). *GYNS AT WRK*. Cambridge, MA: Harvard University Press.

Button, K. Johnson, M., & Ferguson, P. (1996). Interactive writing in a primary classroom. *The Reading Teacher, 49*, 446–454.

Clay, M. (1972). *Reading: The patterning of complex behavior*. Auckland, New Zealand: Heinemann.

Harste, J., Woodward, V., & Burke, C. (1984). *Language stories and literacy lessons*. Portsmouth, NH: Heinemann.

Johnston, P. H. (1984). Assessment in reading. In P. D. Pearson (Ed.), *Handbook of reading research*, pp. 147–182. New York: Longman.

Read, W. C. (1975). *Children's categorization of speech sounds in English*. Technical Report No. 197. Urbana, IL: National Council of Teachers of English.

Sulzby, E. (1985). Children's emergent reading of favorite storybooks: A developmental study. *Reading Research Quarterly, 20*, 458–481.

Teale, W., & Sulzby, E. (Eds.) (1986). *Emergent literacy: Writing and reading*. Norwood, NJ: Ablex.

17 Tying Assessment to Instruction

Adam Learns to Read the LEA Way

OLGA G. NELSON

Associate Professor, Eastern Michigan University

PATRICIA A. CHARLES KALMES

Director, St. Paul (Ann Arbor, MI) Early Childhood Center

ELIZABETH HATFIELD-WALSH

Elementary Teacher, Farmington (MI) Public Schools

The profile of at-risk youngsters learning to read is a rather complex one. Children not only face the anxiety of having to figure out how to read and write, they also usually experience a myriad of stressful situations at school and at home that may impede learning and interfere with establishing positive self-esteem (Hutinger, 1988; Wood, 1988). Therefore, establishing positive social learning environments for children who are at various developmental stages of literacy learning is a key element to success (Teale & Sulzby, 1986). Children need to feel comfortable in order to take risks. It is equally important to provide lots of encouragement for these youngsters so they receive feedback that affirms each success they experience.

The Language Experience Approach (LEA) provides children with opportunities to affirm what they know, what they can do, as well as what they can express orally and in writing. Social environments and interactive situations that support and recognize children's strengths as language users and literacy learners establish the foundations for growth (Hall, 1981; Nelson, 1989; Taylor and Nelson, 1990). LEA capitalizes on children's own vocabulary, experience, and natural desire to express themselves through listening, speaking, reading, and writing (Davidson, 1986; Stauffer, 1980).

This chapter presents a descriptive profile of one at-risk student's literacy assessment and growth as a reader and writer over the period of one year in the Reading Clinic at Eastern Michigan University. Students are referred to the university's Reading Clinic by their teachers and/or parents for initial assessment. Clinicians who conduct the initial assessment are graduate students enrolled in the Diagnosis and Remediation course. Parents and caregivers bring the children to the university one evening per week for the Reading Clinic.

Adam was referred to the Reading Clinic during the second semester of his second grade for a preliminary literacy assessment. Initial assessment indicated that Adam needed experiences to promote the connections between reading, writing, listening, and speaking. Although preliminary results indicated he had some knowledge of letter–sound relationships and his comprehension was fair, he did not have many strategies or incentives to read and did not want to read or write. Thus, language experience activities were used for assessment and instructional intervention purposes to motivate Adam and to help him gain success as a reader and writer.

Adam's Initial Reading Assessment

Results of the *Qualitative Reading Inventory* (QRI) (Leslie & Caldwell, 1990) indicated that Adam was at the frustration level at the primary reading level. When he looked at the isolated words on the primer list, he said, "I am not used to such big words. I don't know any of these in this line [list]." He attempted to read the words but was unsuccessful. To assess Adam's knowledge of words in context, the clinician had Adam read the first primer passage in the QRI entitled "A Trip" (p. 91). When the clinician talked with Adam about the title and what he thought it might be about, he appeared to have some background knowledge about field trips and farms. When he began to read, he was able to read the title and the following words in the passage: "It was a," "to a farm," "going to," and "a book." Thus, although he could not read any of the words in isolation, he did appear to have some word recognition in the passage. However, he made several miscues, appeared frustrated, and stopped reading.

Several other alternative assessment activities were conducted with Adam to assess his knowledge of story grammar, comprehension, and word recognition. The clinician read the book *Polar Bear, Polar Bear, What Do You Hear?* (Martin, 1991), and then they made their own pattern book together. Adam seemed to enjoy this activity and was successful at reading his own pattern book. A check of his prior knowledge with the QRI story "The Pig Who Learned to Read" (p. 92) indicated that he had quite a few predictions about what might happen. The clinician employed a web as a prereading activity to activate his prior knowledge. After this, he made four predictions about the story. He was able to read eight words in the story: *the, he, on, a, to, learn, read,* and *I.* However, at no time did Adam appear to use any strategies to help him decode or encode a word. If he did not know the word by sight, he made no attempt to decode the word. Although his comprehension was good, it appeared to be based on his prior knowledge of the topic and guessing.

An assessment of his interests indicated that Adam liked watching TV, playing baseball, and whales. Therefore, the clinician chose a book about whales to motivate him and to assess his prior knowledge, comprehension, and letter–sound recognition. She employed a K-W-L as a prereading activity (Ogle, 1986). Adam volunteered several facts about whales and then generated some questions. During the reading, he and the clinician were able to answer his questions and add to what he already knew. Adam enjoyed this activity, but he relied on the clinician to do the reading of the story. However, he was able to read his own dictation on the K-W-L chart with some help from the clinician. This activity indicated that reading had more meaning for Adam when it was related to his own interests, he had some prior knowledge about the topic, and he read his own writing.

Adam seemed most interested in reading and writing when he was composing his own story with the clinician. He displayed confidence and enthusiasm for reading that he did not exhibit when he was reading the QRI. Therefore, the clinician recommended that Adam read in meaningful situations every day, employ prereading activities, compose his own stories, and use context and picture clues to help him encode words. Based on Adam's initial assessment, it was determined that Adam was a suitable candidate to participate in the Reading Clinic.

Adam's First Semester in the Reading Clinic

Adam worked with two different clinicians during the fall and winter semesters of third grade. Both clinicians had experience teaching children in the primary grades and were graduate students enrolled in the Practicum in Reading course at the university, completing course work for their M.S. in reading. Liz Walsh, a kindergarten teacher, worked with Adam and another boy, Kevin, each week for an hour and a half. The boys were paired because their initial assessment indicated that they needed similar instruction and were at or close to the same reading level.

Tying Instruction to Assessment

The first thing Liz did after she received the initial assessment report, which was completed the preceding spring and before she met both boys, was to complete a K-W-L for each boy. In writing what she knew about Adam, she noted that he (1) had interests in baseball, TV, and whales; (2) viewed himself as an OK reader; (3) liked pattern books; (4) did not like to write; (5) had a good attitude about working with another person and complied with tasks; (6) had minimal knowledge of letter–sound relationships; and (7) appeared to be at an emergent reading level.

The questions she did have were (1) What was Adam's attitude toward reading at home and at school? (2) Did he visit the school or public library? (3) What was the extent of his knowledge of letter–sound relationships? (4) How well did Adam comprehend narrative and expository text? (5) What types of books did he like? and (6) Why didn't Adam like to write? In order to answer her questions, Liz made a plan for herself employing a variety of strategies that she could use to give her more information (see Table 17.1). These strategies were used to assess

TABLE 17.1   Liz's Initial Literacy Assessment of Adam

K Know	W Want to Know	L How to Find or Learn
• Interested in baseball, TV, and whales • Viewed himself as an OK reader • Liked pattern books • Did not like to write • Had a good attitude about working with another person and complied with tasks • Had minimal knowledge of letter–sound relationships • Appeared to be at an emergent reading level	• What was Adam's attitude toward reading at home and at school? • Did he visit the school or public library? • What was the extent of his knowledge of letter–sound relationships? • How well did Adam comprehend narrative and expository text? • What types of books did he like? • Why didn't Adam like to write?	**Affective Diagnosis** Conduct affective/interest surveys **Knowledge of Letter–Sound Relationships** Conduct spelling features analysis **Comprehension** • Use DR-TAs to assess comprehension • Use webbing for prereading and prewriting activities and to generate vocabulary **Word Recognition Activities** • Use pattern books to generate stories and motivate him to write • Use word banks and concentration games employing words that Adam learns from his own reading and writing activities **Fluency** Employ echo reading, reading aloud activities to model and build his fluency, rhythm for reading, chunking, and interest **Writing** • Summary writing as postreading activities with both narrative and expository text to help his comprehension • Journal writing for enjoyment and to motivate the use of invented spelling

Adam's and Kevin's knowledge about various things as well as guide her instruction during the fall semester.

Adam's Affective Assessment

Through the use of the Attitudes/Interest Survey (Strang, 1967), Liz discovered that Adam thought "reading is nice"; he enjoyed picture books; he would rather ask his teacher to help him, but sometimes he skipped a word when he did not know it. Adam also said he felt scared when he had to read aloud in front of others. He stated that he "gets bored" when he writes a paper and that he usually does not go to the library at school or when at home.

Assessment of Adam's Knowledge of Letter-Sound Relationships

Results of the Print Awareness Evaluation (Clay, 1972)) indicated he did well identifying words, word boundaries, sentences, parts of a book, and all the letters of the alphabet, and matching unfamiliar words with text. To assess his knowledge of letter–sound relationships with whole words, Liz administered a Spelling Features Analysis (Gillet & Temple, 1986). Results indicated that Adam was able to represent some initial, middle, and final sounds with appropriate letters. He spelled one word out of sixteen in a conventional way. Some of his letters and numbers were reversed or upside down, and he used the letter *h* to represent the *ch* and *sh* sound. After analyzing Adam's spelling, Liz determined that Adam was a Letter-Name speller, which means that "half or more of the sounds in words are represented by letters, the relation between the letters and sounds rests on the similarity between the sound of the name of the letter and the sound to be represented" (Gillet & Temple, 1986, p. 300). For example, Adam spelled *late* as *lat*, *learned* as *lrd* and *shove* as *huv*.

Based on this information, Liz decided to engage Adam in language experience activities that would encourage him to dictate, write, and reread his own stories. These activities built success, motivation, and interest as they increased his vocabulary, word recognition, and reading comprehension. As Adam engaged in these activities, he learned to apply strategies to build on what he already knew. He employed picture and context clues to gain meaning and encode unknown words. He engaged in repeated readings and word games to build fluency, sight words, vocabulary, and confidence.

Strategies Aimed to Increase Fluency, Vocabulary, Word Recognition, and Confidence

Liz employed word banks as a basis to play word concentration games. Word banks are groups of words on cards that are used to help an individual remember and review new words, in addition to other sight words. The words came from

Adam's and Kevin's own writing, and therefore the words had some familiarity and meaning for them. The concentration game is played using two identical sets of word cards with no more than fifteen words in each set. The words are chosen from students' word banks. All the cards are turned over blank side up and put in random order on the table. The student who is first turns over one word card, reads the word, and then must choose another card and read that word. If the student turns over a card with the same word on it, then the student may continue turning cards over and reading the word each time until a match is not found. The next student then takes his or her turn and does the same thing until all the cards are turned over and matched. The student with the most pairs of word cards wins. As students read these words week to week, it reinforces their automaticity, improves fluency, boosts self-confidence, and expands vocabulary. Adam enjoyed playing the concentration game with Kevin. The more they played, the more they enjoyed the game, and the more competitive they became. The desire to win as well as the need to know the words set the purpose for playing. Through this process, it was determined that retention and comprehension was increasing. As words became automatic, they were replaced with new words chosen from the boys' reading and writing activities.

Liz employed reading and buddy reading techniques to build Adam's confidence level in oral reading. In echo reading, Adam and/or Kevin would repeat phrases already read by the clinician. Buddy reading promoted positive social interaction as Kevin scaffolded for Adam. As it became evident that Kevin was a more competent reader, he often served to scaffold for Adam by reading or attempting something first, thereby allowing Adam to learn from him and gain a sense of confidence before he attempted something new.

By the end of the semester, Liz determined that Adam was at the learning-to-read stage. At this stage Adam was reading with assistance from a more knowledgeable and proficient reader. He was gaining reading fluency, and expanding and developing his sight vocabulary so that it more closely matched his spoken vocabulary. In addition, he was increasing his knowledge of decoding and encoding strategies, and improving his comprehension of text. At the completion of this semester, Liz completed a summary of the results of her ongoing assessment and made recommendations for the next clinician (see Table 17.2).

Adam's Second Semester in the Reading Clinic

Pat Kalmes, Director of an Early Childhood Center in a nearby community, was selected to work with Adam during the winter semester. The decision was made at this point to team Adam with Heidi, a new student admitted to the Reading Clinic who was the same age, grade, and reading level. Kevin, Adam's former partner, was assigned his own clinician at this time because his abilities had increased, thus, the focus of his instruction centered on comprehension with narrative and

TABLE 17.2 Liz's Final Literacy Assessment of Adam

Key Summary Statement	What Does This Mean?	Goals	Strategies	Results
Attitude/ Interest Survey • likes baseball, whales, dinosaurs, and TV • likes pattern books • thinks he is an OK reader • willing to try but not a risk taker • does not like to read at home • reading is not a first choice • prefers dictating over writing himself	**Attitude/ Interest Survey** • try to capitalize on his interests and do writing with pattern books • not confident in his reading ability and does not read for pleasure • communicates ideas orally but not in writing	**Attitude/ Interest Survey** • get books from the library based on his interests to motivate him to read • build his confidence by extending what he can do successfully, thereby increasing his willingness to read and write	**Attitude/ Interest Survey** • encourage parents to take him to the library to find books of interest to him and to purchase books as gifts • do choral, echo, and buddy reading • use webbing, journal writing, and word banks • employ story-starter activities	**Attitude/ Interest Survey** • increased comprehension • demonstrated eagerness to read • increased confidence and sense of success • all strategies should be continued in clinic
Word Recognition • some knowledge of letter–sound relationships • limited sight vocabulary	**Word Recognition** • at times has trouble with blends and two- or more-syllable words • does not have many words committed to memory	**Word Recognition** • build his knowledge of letter–sound relationships • increase sight vocabulary	**Word Recognition** employ LEA activities such as: • predictable books • stories that use blends that give him trouble (*ch, sk,* and reading *b* for *d*) • word banks • word cards • concentration • echo reading • choral reading • pattern books	**Word Recognition** • all strategies were successful and should be continued in the reading clinic

continues

TABLE 17.2 (*Continued*)

Key Summary Statement	What Does This Mean?	Goals	Strategies	Results
Comprehension • is beginning to read for meaning • limited sight vocabulary hinders fluency • difficulty with letter–sound relations limits comprehension • understands texts when read in groups	**Comprehension** • does not always self-correct • looks to the teacher to help with unfamiliar words • can retell story events and facts from expository texts	**Comprehension** • continue success in gaining meaning • take more risks when reading • build vocabulary	**Comprehension** • picture clues • employ questions when reading, for example: • Does that make sense? • Does that word fit there? • Does that look like a real word? • choral reading • buddy reading • repeated readings • K-W-Ls • DR-TA	**Comprehension** • strategies used were successful • continued use recommended • K-W-Ls were not used but could be successful
Writing • uncomfortable with writing at first • writes in complete sentences but words are not recognizable at times	**Writing** • beginning to take more risks • limited vocabulary	**Writing** • provide meaningful writing situations for Adam • improve risk-taking • build vocabulary	**Writing** • word banks • story mapping • summary writing • response writing • story tellings • concentration	**Writing** • strategies were successful and motivated Adam to write • recommend continued use in clinic

expository texts. Subsequently, he was teamed with another boy and clinician for activities.

Examining Liz's assessment of Adam, Pat determined that Adam still had a limited amount of sight vocabulary, remained hesitant to write, and still needed to make the connection between spoken and written language. Therefore, she concurred with Liz's recommendation that language experience activities be continued. Pat felt strongly that Adam needed to be successful every time he sat down to read and write so that he would want to engage in these activities. In order to accomplish this, she chose materials that both Adam and Heidi were interested in, and selected activities that built on their strengths and could be completed successfully in an evening.

Language Experience in Action

Relying on her past experiences working with young children, Pat decided to employ activities that had Adam and Heidi use all of their senses and knowledge of the world and stories. For example, one evening Pat chose to use Laura Numeroff's book *If You Give a Moose a Muffin* (1991), because the book had predictable language patterns and both children were familiar with the book. Pat initially employed a Directed Listening-Thinking Activity (DL-TA) (Stauffer, 1975) with the book, and then the students read the book with her and tasted some muffins. Finally they talked about the flavors, texture, taste, and what they did and did not like about the muffins. She followed this activity by having Adam and Heidi talk about Numeroff's book and ways they could use similar language patterns to make their own book. Subsequently, Adam and Heidi made their own stories following the same pattern, for example, "If you give _____ a _____, he/she will _____ . . ."

Building Motivation and Competency

Pat decided to continue developing Adam's word bank and to use the words with other activities. She discovered that riddles and riddle books (Cerf, 1966; Rosenbloom, 1979) had many of the basic sight words she knew he was learning. She also knew that Adam and Heidi both needed practice with similar words, word patterns, and sight words that were in the riddle books. At the same time Pat was working with the riddle books, she also themed her sessions around students' interests, holidays, and seasonal events such as Valentine's Day. Both children were excited about the word concentration games, so these were continued and found to be successful with both of them. Capitalizing on their interests and growing sight words, Pat incorporated the riddles on the valentine cards to play the word concentration game. She brought in two identical sets of valentine cards and used these to play the concentration game. Adam and Heidi took turns reading a valentine card they had turned over and then looking for its match. They were both extremely successful at the game and never tired of playing. Playing the game reinforced their sight recognition, improved their fluency, and provided lots of practice reading whole words and sentences.

Reasons for Writing

Pat decided to employ a dialogue journal with both Adam and Heidi. She began this the first night of class, writing in their journal, "What did you like about Clinic tonight?" Adam responded: "I libefofeth [I liked everything]." In responding to Adam, using conventional spelling, Pat wrote this back: "Hi, Adam! I'm glad you liked everything! I enjoyed spending time with you. We will read and write more tonight. Happy Birthday! Pat." Adam read this message in his journal when he came back to class the next time. By not correcting Adam's spelling but modeling writing and conventional spelling, she hoped that he would see the correct spelling and, more important, that he would be inspired to write back to her and create ongoing, meaningful communication with her. This was important to Pat because she believed Adam needed to make connections between reading and writing, but that he also needed to see and use language for meaningful purposes and for a variety of functions. Thus, journal writing became an integral part of each week's session. Adam's final entry (see Figure 17.1), about monsters, exemplified his growing willingness to take risks by writing longer messages and using invented spelling.

Pat chose specific children's literature books to use with the children because she wanted to introduce good literature to them, but she also felt the books lent themselves well to extended listening, speaking, reading, and writing activities. On one occasion, she chose *The Jolly Postman or Other People's Letters* by Janet and Allan Ahlberg (1986). Pat introduced the book, then the children looked at each picture to determine which fairy tale was on each page, and then she had Adam and Heidi read the correspondence in each pocket. As they read these, Adam and Heidi helped each other as Pat did an informal miscue analysis on their oral reading. Pat followed the reading with a Closed Word Sort Activity (Gillet & Temple, 1986). She made two sets of word cards; on one set she wrote the names of the characters in the book, and on the other she wrote descriptive words or phrases from the story. Adam and Heidi had to read and match the characters with the description or phrase that best described them. Talking, sorting, and categorizing together, Adam and Heidi were able to complete this activity successfully and seemed to enjoy it. Finally, the children wrote and addressed postcards to each other, which Pat mailed

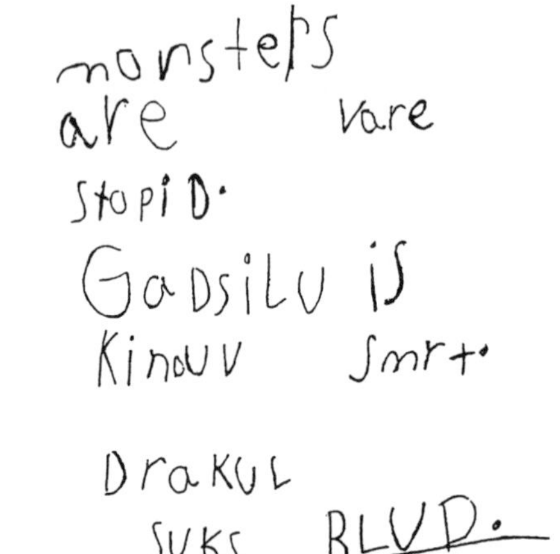

FIGURE 17.1   Adam's Writing Sample Using Invented Spelling

the next morning. Adam wrote: "Der Heidi, I think your funny and I lik basbolle [baseball]. Adam." The children were delighted to receive mail during the week and wanted to do more of this again. In evaluating this activity, Pat felt Adam was (1) gaining confidence in his writing, (2) taking risks with his spelling, (3) improving his knowledge of letter–sound relationships, and (4) gaining a sense of purpose for writing as well as enjoying the writing experience.

Building Expository Comprehension Strategies

Knowing that both Adam and Heidi loved anything to do with oceans, whales, and other sea animals, Pat felt she had the perfect content for reading and writing with expository texts. She brought in a variety of items from the ocean, such as sea horses, conch shells, shark teeth, sand dollars, starfish, coral, and sponges. First, Pat had both children explore the items by holding them, talking about them, and comparing what they knew and had learned about them. Next, she had them lay the items out on the paper; then they labeled and described them in whole sentences. After this, the children did buddy reading using books about the ocean (Buxton, 1987; Rinard, 1990), followed by a discussion about what they learned. On a large piece of paper in the shape of a fish, the children wrote sentences about the ocean, employing some of the words they had used on the chart they had created earlier in the session. Finally, Pat brought in a flannel board that had an ocean background with a variety of flannel ocean plants and animals pieces that could be placed in specific habitats. The children were so involved in matching the plants and animals with the appropriate habitats that they stayed after Reading Clinic to place all the flannel pieces in just the right habitats.

Ongoing Informal Assessment

Following each session with Adam and Heidi, Pat wrote evaluations of how she perceived the sessions had gone, noting strengths and weaknesses and suggesting goals and strategies for the following week's session based on what she had learned. During the nine sessions that were conducted, Pat evaluated, monitored, and guided both children in gaining success as learners, readers, and writers. As she employed intervention strategies to help Adam and Heidi achieve success, Pat continually assessed them. Thus her lessons were based on the information she was constantly collecting and interpreting about both children's strengths, weaknesses, and needs.

In her final assessment report on Adam, Pat stated this overall instructional goal: "Adam needs to be engaged in literacy activities that will produce success, maintain his interest in reading and writing, and promote his sense of self-esteem in order to be successful in his attempts to read and write." To meet these needs, she suggested the following kinds of language experience activities: (1) Adam needs to read and write pattern stories to acquire a rhythm and pattern of language, sense of story structure, and appreciation for good children's literature. (2) In order to develop his sight vocabulary, automaticity, and fluency, Adam should continue to build and use his word banks, play the concentration game, read and write his own stories and journal entries, and correspond with a friend by writing postcards. (3) In order to help improve his comprehension, Adam should be encouraged to retell stories in his own words and to construct webs to help organize his thoughts before writing. In addition, she suggested the use of K-W-L to organize his thoughts, to read for a purpose, and to summarize what he had learned. She recommended the DR-TA to get him to focus on meaning and to encourage him to make predictions as he reads. She also recommended that Open and Closed Word Sorts be used for both pre- and/or postreading activities to set a purpose for reading, to activate and integrate prior knowledge, to introduce new vocabulary terms, and to evaluate what Adam learned after reading.

Reviewing how the social aspect of learning supported Adam's growth and success as a learner, Pat further recommended that Adam be paired with another student or a small group of students at or above his reading level as often as possible. These social inter- and intra-actions (Bloome & Green, 1984) would serve as scaffolds for him to learn, take risks, achieve success, and feel good about himself as a reader and writer.

Departing Words

During one of the last sessions, Adam was able to read the book *Zoodles* by Bernard Most (1992). In order to be able to read this book, he had to access his prior knowledge about animals, employ picture and context clues, use some sight words he knew, and employ newly acquired knowledge about letter–sound relationships. To predict what the next fantasy animal would be on each succeeding page, Adam had to obtain meaning from the text, take existing words such as *kangaroo*, and combine them with a part of another word based on picture clues on the page to construct a totally new fantasy animal. For example, the printed text might read: "What do you call a kangaroo who wakes you up in the morning?" The answer on the next page would be: "kangarooster." Adam was tickled when he discovered that he surpassed Heidi, the Clinic Director, and Pat in his ability to accomplish this task. It seemed like everything clicked all at once for Adam.

At the final session, as Pat was talking with Adam and Heidi about their accomplishments over the past semester, she asked them how they felt about what they had learned. Adam turned to Pat and said, "I kept it a secret for a very long time that I did not know how to read. I am happy that you [Pat], the Clinic, and the school helped me learn how to read." His own statement clearly indicates that by the end of Reading Clinic, Adam recognized his own growth and perceived himself to be a reader.

Finally, the language experience activities worked for Adam and matched his needs most appropriately. The activities Adam engaged in provided rich social environments that invited him to build on his interests, past experiences, and knowledge about language and other topics. These activities supported his risk taking because they accepted his approximations and built on his growing knowledge and use of language, its functions, and patterns. His confidence grew as he experienced success so that he felt more comfortable and motivated to engage in future literacy experiences.

Tying Assessment to Instruction in the Classroom

Although the context for planning instructional activities to meet Adam's needs was conducted in a clinical experience, the basic principles, philosophy, documentation methods, and instructional approaches may be applied in the classroom. That is, similar kinds of affective instruments may be used to assess interests, attitudes, and perceptions of reading in the classroom. Any informal reading inventory can provide baseline information about many facets of a reader's strengths and weaknesses. Ongoing assessment of a reader's reading and writing may be observed, collected, and documented with anecdotal notes and writing samples. These assessment documents may be kept in individual student portfolios for reference in order to develop specific instructional activities to meet students' literacy needs. Although clinicians had to keep these kinds of ongoing records during the entire semester as part of their assignments, they all agreed that examining weekly anecdotal notes and establishing goals made them much more cognizant of students' needs and much more thoughtful about selecting strategies they could use to meet those needs. The format used to document summary information was provided for the clinicians, but classroom teachers may adapt this form to their own needs or generate their own form or framework for maintaining records.

Both teachers who worked with Adam were able to employ and monitor the language experience activities they used with Adam. Each week Liz and Pat engaged Adam in a variety of language experience activities and used these activities as opportunities to observe and document his progress. Classroom teachers can employ similar activities to monitor growth and success, recommend specific activities, and have documentation to share with parents about their child's progress. All of this can be part of the normal, daily classroom routine. Although these assessment activities take thought and time, they are not additions—they are replacements for some of the current classroom assessment practices. Teachers may want, therefore, to change their assessment activities slowly and work with them until they feel comfortable using them effectively and efficiently. As teachers become more comfortable employing assessment to direct their instruction, the teaching/learning process should become much more dynamic.

REFERENCES

Ahlberg, J., & Ahlberg, A. (1986). *The jolly postman or other people's letters.* Boston, MA: Little, Brown.

Ashton-Warner, S. (1963). *Teacher.* New York: Simon and Schuster.

Bloome, D. & Green, J. (1984). *Directions in the sociolinguistic study of reading.* In P. D. Pearson (Ed.), *Handbook of reading research* (pp. 395–421). New York: Longman.

Buxton, J. H. (1987). *Strange animals of the sea*. Los Angeles: F. A. Carbajal for Intervisual Communication.

Cerf, B. (1966). *Bennet Cerf's book of riddles*. New York: Random House.

Clay, M. (1972). *The early detection of reading difficulties: A diagnostic survey*. Auckland, New Zealand: Heinemann.

Davidson, J. (1986). *The language experience approach to teaching reading*. Illinois Office of Education.

Gillet, J. W., & Kita, M. J. (1979). Words, kids, and categories. *The Reading Teacher, 32,* 538–542.

Gillet, J. W., & Temple, C. (1986). *Understanding reading problems* (2nd ed.). Boston, MA: Little, Brown.

Hall, M. A. (1981). *Teaching reading as a language experience* (3rd ed.). Columbus, OH: Merrill.

Hutinger, P. (1988). Stress: Is it an inevitable condition for families of children at risk? *Teaching Exceptional Children, 20*(4), 36–39.

Leslie, L, & Caldwell, J. (1990). *Qualitative reading inventory*. Glenview, IL: Scott, Foresman.

Martin, B., Jr. (1991). *Polar bear, polar bear, what do you hear?* New York: Henry Holt.

McKie, R. (1978). *The riddle book*. New York: Random House.

Most, B. (1992). *Zoodles*. San Diego, CA: Harcourt, Brace & Jovanovich.

Nelson, O. G. (1989). Storytelling: Language experience for meaning making. *The Reading Teacher, 42,* 386–390.

Numeroff, L. J. (1991). *If you give a moose a muffin*. New York: HarperCollins.

Ogle, D. (1986). K-W-L: A teaching model that develops active reading of expository text. *The Reading Teacher, 39,* 564–570.

Rinard, J. E. (1990). *Whales, mighty giants of the sea*. Singapore: Tien Wah Press for National Geographic Society.

Rosenbloom, J. (1979). *Biggest riddle book in the world*. New York: Sterling.

Stauffer, R. G. (1975). *Directing the reading-thinking process*. New York: Harper & Row.

Stauffer, R. G. (1980). *The Language-Experience approach to the teaching of reading* (2nd ed.). New York: Harper & Row.

Strang, A. T (1982). Using children's dictated stories to assess code consciousness. *The Reading Teacher, 35,* 450–454.

Strang, R., McCullough, C. M., & Traxler, A. E. (1967). *Improvement of Reading* (4th ed.). New York: McGraw-Hill, Inc.

Taylor, N., & Nelson, O. G. (1990). Collecting, writing, and telling family folklore stories. *Journal of Language Experience, 10*(2), 16–20.

Teale, W. H., & Sulzby, E. (Eds.). (1986). *Emergent literacy: Writing and reading*. Norwood, NJ: Ablex.

Wood, F. H. (1988). Learners at risk. *Teaching Exceptional Children, 20*(4), 4–9.

18 My Experience with Language Experience

MARILYN L. FLETCHER

Title I Reading Teacher, Ozark (MO) R–6 School District

When I first began teaching first grade, I was leery of the students and unsure of the curriculum, especially the critical area of reading. Within a few days, however, I was charmed by and felt comfortable with those ever-active six-year-olds. To make sure I covered all the subject matter, I carefully followed the instructions in the teacher's manuals. For reading, my class was properly divided into the traditional three reading groups, and with each group I conducted a directed reading lesson. Motivation was set, difficult words were introduced, and silent reading was used so students would answer the questions I posed or that were at the end of the reading passage. Silent reading was followed by oral reading, and then the students returned to their desks for enrichment in the form of workbook pages and ditto sheets (Harris & Sipay, 1978). We did relatively well that year, the children and I, but somehow I sensed that we, or at least I, could have done better.

That summer I decided to enroll in some university courses to improve my teaching of reading skills. It was in one of those introductory classes that I first heard about the use of language experience as an alternate approach to the teaching of reading. To me it sounded as though it might be fun for the students, but hardly a viable or realistic total reading program. However, I decided to include it in my teaching plans for the upcoming year, but only as a filler, a reward, or a follow-up exercise after field trips and special events.

During the next year our language experience stories were always whole-class projects based on a discussion that school occasions prompted. As different students told of their impressions or remembrances l would transcribe their words on the chalkboard exactly as spoken, prefaced with their name (Stauffer, 1970). Our stories were generally quite long since each child was eager to participate. It was pleasing to see that everyone could recognize their own name as well as some basic sight words. The students seemed to really enjoy this activity, and I enjoyed watching them discover the relationship between the oral and written word. I took time to copy each story on paper from the chalkboard, and at the end of the year we were able to put together a memory booklet from the collection of stories.

By my third year of teaching first graders, I had taken several more graduate courses in reading and continued to hear and read more about language experience instruction. Nevertheless, I still could not convince myself to implement the teaching techniques as an integral part of my curriculum because I didn't feel I had enough time, patience, and additional hands to help me. I could not envision how only one teacher could take separate dictation from twenty-five pupils in any reasonable period of time. I could foresee no way to keep the other twenty-four children purposefully busy while only one student was helped. Therefore, I continued to use language experience activities for group enrichment, but the better students were encouraged to write individual stories during their free time and at home and to turn them in for extra credit. I was surprised and impressed by the quality and quantity of the stories written by these pupils and also by their enthusiasm, creativity, and independence in developing them. By the end of that year almost all the children were writing individually composed stories and booklets, even those students who were not quite on level in the basal reader.

By my fourth year of teaching first grade, I had completed my M.S. in Reading degree and decided to give the language experience approach an honest chance in the reading curriculum. I decided to set aside one day of the week, Friday, for story writing. During the first quarter, when my students were truly beginning readers, our stories were written primarily as whole-class or large-group activities. These stories were based on a common class experience, perhaps a film, a trip, or simply a picture shown to the students. After the students' impressions were recorded, the story was read to the class, and then pupils read aloud the particular sentence or idea they had contributed (Hall, 1970).

By mid-October the children were ready to begin writing their own individual stories but through my hand and pencil. There was still concern with keeping the remaining students interested and occupied while attention was given to one pupil. However, I soon discovered that many children did stay busy drawing and coloring their illustrations while I circulated and wrote other dictations.

Some pupils dictated a word or two per page, others dictated a phrase, but many dictated complete sentences. In just a short period of time the more advanced students began to print their own words, which was greatly encouraged. My pencil, however, always remained available for students who needed it. The pupils were encouraged to attempt spelling most of their words, but assistance was available for the more troublesome words. Picture dictionaries were introduced to foster independence, and while stories were never graded for spelling, writing form, or handwriting, neatness was encouraged and students' application of these skills was noted.

One of the most personally rewarding aspects of the use of language experience was the insight l gained about each student's mastery of language, phonics skills, spelling and writing form. Throughout the year, as the booklets became longer and the compositions more advanced, it was possible to ascertain each child's understanding and use of language in both its oral and written form. I observed which students understood the use of capital letters, commas, periods, and question marks. This greatly enhanced my ability to individualize instruction (Cramer, 1978). The children gradually came to understand the importance of proper story sequencing, attending to a main topic, and for varying sentence structure to enliven their written ideas. It was exciting and rewarding also to watch them discover their abilities to write fantasy and nonfiction, mysteries and biographies, poems, and even plays.

Throughout the year, Friday was the pupil's favorite day and not too surprising, I looked forward to Fridays also. I thoroughly enjoyed the children's imaginative ideas, refreshing use of the English language, and delightfully creative illustrations. I rejoiced as reading, phonics, spelling, and handwriting abilities grew and were applied to other content area subjects. The classwork and papers submitted for science and social studies reflected these growing abilities.

As the children shared their books with fellow students, and subsequently saw their edited and bound versions on display in hallways and in the school library, their pride and self-esteem were clearly evident. Other students, other teachers, the first-grade students themselves, and I were continually impressed by the amount they had learned and the progress they had made in just a few short months.

Today, I still employ the language experience approach in my classroom, only I do not delegate it to one day a week. Instead, language experience is incorporated daily in many activities we engage in across the curriculum. Over time, I have also come to believe how valuable the activities and approaches taught in education courses really are. As I grew comfortable and more confident with my own abilities to employ language experience activities in my classroom, I was motivated to continue my reading and study and to keep up with the current literature on teaching and learning. I have found that in teaching, as in all professions, when innovations are presented, each person has the choice to experiment and adapt, apply and/or reject different aspects of the innovation. Eventually, each person chooses a teaching style and approach based on his or her own philosophy and experiences.

REFERENCES

Cramer, R. L. (1978). *Children's writing and language growth*. Columbus, OH: Merrill.

Hall, M. (1970). *Teaching reading as a language experience*. New York: David McKay.

Harris, A. J., & Sipay, E. R. (1978). *How to increase reading ability* (2nd ed.). New York: David McKay.

Humphrey, J. W., & Redden, S. R. (1972). Encouraging young authors. *The Reading Teacher*, *25*(7), 643–651.

Stauffer, R. G. (1970). *The Language Experience approach to the teaching of reading*. New York: Harper & Row.

CHAPTER

19

A First-Grade Whole Language Teacher Talks about the Principles That Guide Her Practice and Decision Making

JANICE V. KRISTO

Professor, University of Maine

MARY H. GIARD

Teacher, Turner (ME) Primary School

We live in an exciting era, one that is charged with an explosion of information on literacy learning. Teachers all over the country are reading, writing, talking, and sharing what they know about whole language learning and thinking. It is important to explore ways of planning and organizing the classroom to parallel philosophical and methodological shifts in the ways teachers approach literacy teaching and learning.

I was involved in a case study research that focused on one first-grade teacher, Mary Giard, and how she goes about planning and organizing a whole language literacy program. There are many guiding principles that have shaped her philosophy about teaching and learning. For instance, Mary strongly believes in the following: (1) that she present herself as both a reader and writer; (2) that the children see her engaged in reading and writing for different purposes

[From "A First Grade Whole Language Teacher Talks About the Principles That Guide Her Practice and Decision-Making," by Janice Kristo and Mary Giard, 1992, *Journal of Language Experience, 11*(1), pp. 6–9. Copyright 1992 by the Language Experience Special Interest Group. Reprinted with permission. This chapter is included because whole language teachers have similar philosophical beliefs as language experience teachers.]

throughout the day; and (3) that she discuss issues pertaining to becoming skilled readers and writers, such as goal setting, making good choices about what to read or write next, and strategies for becoming better readers and writers. She does not function as a separate entity in the classroom but as one who is also immersed in wanting to know more about her own reading and writing. Probably the best way to describe the environment is that of a learning community—collaborative and cooperative in all of its tasks.

There are strong contributing factors to Mary's success as a whole language teacher. One factor is her consistent demonstrations of ways to become a skilled reader and writer; another is her ongoing planning and organization of a classroom environment that is consistent with her beliefs about literacy learning. This classroom devotes a substantial amount of sustained time to actually reading, writing, listening to stories, responding to literature, discussing books, and talking about reading and writing as processes. It requires a high degree of orchestration and organization, of constantly thinking about the ways her students are growing as readers and writers.

What follows is an interview I conducted with Mary in which she discusses important considerations in planning and organizing for whole language teaching. We had several goals in mind in writing this chapter together. It is our belief that the principles and practices we discuss describe good whole language teaching at many grade levels. For instance, the beliefs previously described pertain to many whole language teachers from kindergarten through college level. We believe it is the teacher who sets the tone and atmosphere that is conducive to growth in reading and writing, not the text or materials used. We also believe that it is vital for teachers to understand what literacy is all about and how to help children uncover and discover a variety of aspects of reading and writing. It is important that teachers think about themselves as readers and writers so that they can begin to add ways to their repertoire of helping young readers and writers. Lastly, we wanted to leave Mary's unrehearsed statements untouched so that a genuine enthusiasm for her teaching would shine through as well as providing our audience with specific ways Mary's beliefs are implemented in the classroom.

Teacher as Decision Maker: Setting Goals

JANICE: What is the role of decision making in the whole language classroom?

MARY: Prior to the opening of school and constantly during the year, I do lots of thinking about myself, my students, and our program. I think about developing general long-term goals. Most decisions are based on a philosophy to be part of an interactive, integrated program where all of us collaborate to help each person stretch and grow. Decisions are based on high expectations of all the learners in the classroom. I consider the environment as I prepare for new students. I also think about how I can facilitate a program using a strong discovery-process model. Curriculum issues emerge as I make decisions about integrating the school system's goals with my philosophy. Perhaps the biggest decision is not to make too many decisions before school begins. I choose to have a master plan with alternatives in reserve, yet maintain flexibility to weave the children's talents and interests into our days.

I also make decisions about my roles. On any given day I may demonstrate a lesson, coach another person, offer a personal response to some writing, share a story, ask a question, solve a problem, conference over a piece, or observe another learner. I choose to foster alternative options for students as well. They might model reading and writing strategies with their peers, read to a friend, or conference with a peer over writing, to name a few possibilities.

I believe a whole language teacher makes more decisions when working in this kind of classroom environment. Some of those decisions tend to be of a different nature than in a traditional classroom. For instance, one of my most crucial decisions is planning how I can help the children become good decision makers. I don't want to make all the decisions about our classroom without involving the students in the decision-making process. My decision making goes beyond deciding where someone is going to sit, who is going to work with whom, who is going to be in what group, and so on. It is a much more collaborative decision-making plan. I do have goals and purposes in mind for lessons and units, but I use a guided discovery approach so that children can offer their suggestions for activities. [For example,] perhaps after a read-aloud we'll web a variety of ways to respond to the literature. Children are much more interactive with me and the other students in this model of teaching. I look at children closely—their ways of learning, what they need, what they seem to know, and what I need to do as the teacher.

Teacher as Reflective Practitioner

JANICE: Your role seems to be one of decision maker within a community of decision makers. Not long ago I visited a classroom and the teacher had a sign on his desk that read, "This is the way it is here because I'm the boss." This is obviously very different from your philosophy. It seems to be a more realistic picture of life because you live with these students all day long. Your decisions seem to be guided more by a philosophy of teaching and learning than materials. However, you still need to attend to the district's needs, which might not always be consistent with your way of thinking or your beliefs about literacy learning.

MARY: I have to meet the needs of the school system. I am accountable and responsible for attending to the district's curriculum, but I am like other teachers in that curriculum only represents part of what goes into my decision making about what we will do throughout the year. I've made a decision not to fragment my day. Instead, reading and writing are integrated throughout the entire day. I constantly think about what I do as I do it—self-debriefing. For instance, when demonstrating what to do when a reader comes to a word he or she doesn't know, I may do it one way one day but then try it another way another day to see what works best. I work from the standpoint that children are learners—not passively acquiring skills from the curriculum. I study how they learn.

JANICE: You just said that you don't do things the same way every day, and I know we've talked about the answer to this in other contexts, but I am wondering, what remains constant for you?

MARY: Probably what remains most constant for me is reflecting on what children teach me about what they know. I look more at the philosophical aspects of what I believe about teaching and learning. I also examine my questioning strategies. How am I able to get information the children do or do not know? How well have I sharpened my observational skills? These are important to me rather than looking only at curricular issues. I feel that these will come easily compared to how I am able to present and help children learn. These things remain more constant than the actual material we use.

Teacher as Learner

JANICE: To what extent do you think this kind of decision making could be used by teachers?

MARY: I think demonstrating strategies or ways to do things is incredibly important for learners of all ages. Therefore, I would demonstrate decision-making strategies for teachers and ask questions such as What do you notice? What did you discover? Why did you do that? I would do it much the same way I do it with children.

I think many teachers don't trust their own decision making or their own judgment. They have a hard time seeing themselves as learners. We're constantly growing as teachers; the process never stops. It's difficult to invite children to be a part of the process when, as a teacher, you remain detached from the process yourself.

Teacher as Community Planner

JANICE: Discuss how you go about organizing a whole language classroom. What decisions do you make?

MARY: As I prepare for incoming students, I think about whether or not the classroom environment will say what I want it to say. I know I need to consider interests and strengths so I provide a wide variety of materials on day one. Accessibility is a key issue and organization is a must. I think about what the children will need and what they may be interested in when they come to school at the beginning of the year. I try to have classroom materials accessible to the children, displayed and organized in a manner that make the room inviting and interesting to them. I have classroom areas very clearly delineated so that they can find, for example, the math center, the writing area, and the classroom library. I display the books but do not categorize or label them. I leave that for the children to do. I try to have things very well organized and structured. Plenty of room is left for children to make their decisions. It is our room, not mine. It is my hope that they see it as an inviting, collaborative environment with plenty of room left to add their personal touches. Very little wall display space is in use at the beginning as an invitation for the children's input. Journals, learning logs, lab sheets, and other materials are strategically placed at appropriate spots. A variety of writing tools are available as are content-related materials. Easels and chart stands can be found around the room. Students gather on the floor at such spots for group lessons at storytime. I use tables, so that they can sit next to each other rather than at desks. Because of the room arrangement, the children can really begin to get into a collaborative mode the minute they enter the classroom. My desk is out of the way of classroom flow.

I think about what I want to share about myself. I consider what I want to have available to model my investment in the classroom as part of the community. I strive to model lifelong learning beyond academics. I often share ideas from a new form of cooking or perhaps a new sport I'm learning. I enjoy sharing what I read and write with my children. I want students to see that literacy is a life issue, that everything I experience contributes to my own growth as a learner.

Students and Teachers as Decision Makers

JANICE: What do you want students to, specifically, notice about the classroom?

MARY: I want them to notice that the room is set up for them. I give them a tour of the room so that they know where things are, and I ask them what they notice about that area. They may even work in that area for a while. Then we'll come back together as a group to discuss the logistics of working in that space. We'll talk about how sensible it is to have twenty children working there at the same time. It takes time to help them understand what makes good sense, how to use the materials, and how to work well as a group. I also ask them why they think I might have set up an area as I have, such as the writing center.

Should we consider reorganizing or using the area in a different way? Do they see things are stacked in a certain way or do they notice that certain materials are there? In terms of organizing the books, they come up with their own labeling procedure. I try to set it up so that they see some sort of sense to the whole thing or some sort of organization. Hopefully they'll begin to internalize how to put things back, what is there, why it is there, and how to use it.

Teachers and Students as Learning-Community Builders

JANICE: What factors seem to be the most important for you as you plan and organize for whole language teaching?

MARY: Establishing a learning community is extremely important. In fact, I think it is probably the most important aspect. For me a learning community is collaborative in nature. It is a situation where everybody learns from everybody else. I try to get all the children involved in decision making and to accept everybody's opinion. It is important for us to talk about what we are going to do before we do it, actually go through with our plan, and then debrief or talk about it. This is an integral part of planning in our learning community.

Before school starts, I send letters to my incoming students asking them to come on the first day prepared to share their interests and plans for learning during the year. I feel it begins to set the stage for a collaborative year together. I join in sharing my ideas and opinions as well. It is important to begin to build support and gain knowledge from all the learners in the room. I want them to become more conscious about the decisions they make and to talk about what makes for good decisions. I ask them how they can get the most out of working in this classroom and how to get the support and help of others in the room, as well as in the school. I also point out from the beginning that there is no one way to do anything, that there is not usually one right answer, and that the most important thing is to think about a lot of different ways to figure out something. I spend time each day debriefing with them. We talk about what's going on for us as readers, writers, and mathematicians, and about how our room is being run in general, etc. Their expectations of themselves and their peers rise as the year progresses. My decisions to trust the children and foster collaboration reap great benefits. Independent, collaborative learners emerge making powerful decisions about their needs as learners both individually and collectively.

Another extremely important aspect of my classroom is the invitation to parents to play an active role in our classroom. This demonstrates to the children that our learning community extends beyond our group.

Parents become aware of what we are doing and, hopefully, better invest themselves in their children's education. Within the first couple of weeks, the parents are invited to come for an evening when I explain the program, my long-term goals, and what I'm hoping the children are able to do and are going to be involved in. I explain updated research on reading, writing, spelling, math, and science, so that they get an overview of what I am trying to achieve. I also have books and articles that parents are most welcome to borrow. Also available are our district's curriculum guides so that they can look at what would be expected from first graders. I encourage parents to get involved, providing them with options of ways they may want to consider.

Parents as Partners

JANICE: How do parents work within your literacy program?

MARY: I find most parents were taught to read using phonics exclusively. What I try to do right from the start is some instructional work with them so they realize phonics is only a part that contributes to reading and that there are many other options available. Not all children learn the same way, and the children need to develop a strong battery of strategies that they can use to help them in their reading and writing. Parents also help with our writing time. Most parents feel very comfortable with publishing. Others conference with students, again using the same strategies I develop with the children.

Another home/school reading link is in the book-bag program coordinated by one of the parents. I have enough canvas bags for each child in my class. Each bag is filled with a selection of books such as old favorites, books by Ezra Jack Keats, fairy tales, etc. Each child may check out a bag for a week to share the books at home. Children also have the opportunity to choose the bag containing a bear (students name it each year) and a journal. They record their experiences with the bear in the journal and share this with the class the next morning.

This classroom involvement invites parents to become much more invested in our program. It is really helpful to me once we get going because it frees me up to work with students on a more individualized basis. I have to be organized in order to prepare parents. It takes a lot of time just like it does with children the first month or two of school to get everybody in gear and to teach parents strategies for helping with our reading and writing program. However, once this is accomplished, it really flows very nicely. I try to schedule activities not only during the school day but in the evening so that parents who work still feel involved in our program. I keep them informed through a parent letter every week and sometimes more than one. The letters are very informal and conversational in tone. My aim is to keep parents informed of general classroom activities and important events. I also ask them to keep in touch if they have something they want to talk about or invite them to come in; I try to keep the lines of communication open.

Students as Decision Makers

JANICE: Let's return to your role in the learning community. I notice that you talk with your students a lot; you seem to want to understand how they are thinking, and you'll admit that they may have thought of something you hadn't thought of before. I don't think we hear teachers say that enough at any level. We give the message that we have all the answers, or we're waiting for the right answer and nothing that anybody says could really be that intriguing. Teachers don't seem to ask enough questions that puzzle themselves as well. I think some of the questions that you ask in every area of curriculum authentically change you as well. Doesn't this take an incredible amount of time? Do you ever feel a sense of frustration over the time this kind of processing takes?

MARY: It takes a very long time, and usually the first six weeks of school I'd like to rip my hair out, but I feel that the benefits in the long run are definitely worth it. Suddenly the children start to tune in and are able to articulate some incredible things. I have found that the same thing happens with parents. It takes us quite a while to build a community of learners because of a variety of personalities and learning styles. It can be frustrating but I think the long-term benefits of what [children] can do emerge in January or even May or June. It's worth it. They could literally run the room on their own and that is the ultimate goal as far as I'm concerned. They become seekers of knowledge on their own. They go ahead and work with someone else rather than expecting the teacher to have every answer for them.

    Children become really involved with each other as far as the time it takes. It is so exciting as the year progresses when one child realizes another's accomplishment. They can applaud a person and support him or her.

JANICE: Because of the constant decision making, you are not afraid to revise on an ongoing basis and say to yourself, I need to change this question or I need to revise the strategy or approach I'm using in this kind of way. How do you help the children make decisions? Do they make decisions all the time in your classroom? How do you help them do that?

MARY: What I try to do is be a risk taker myself. That in itself provides children with a model because I do what I think is right. The key is starting right at the beginning, asking questions and making the children commit to decisions. If children don't commit verbally, on paper, or don't somehow let there be public awareness of it, then are they really sure that is what they think? There are always children in the group who are going to be more verbal and aren't going to be afraid to say what they think. Others observe that it's risk free, but an answer is expected. I always try to rotate so everyone gets a turn and may gently nudge some so that they all share.

JANICE: Talk about the trust you have in children that they will make good decisions.

MARY: I believe if there's trust that children can accomplish a great deal, then they can. Teachers need to take time to talk to children about what they are learning. I always take time to help children discover why some decisions are more appropriate. With time, practice, and experience they are all very capable of valuing themselves and others as learners. They respect their materials and make good decisions.

Teacher as Kid Watcher

JANICE: What kinds of observations do you make of children? How do these observations give you direction?

MARY: I find out a lot by carefully watching children. I observe body language. I observe how they approach a reading and writing task, how they interact with peers, and how they interact with me. How honest are they in a group discussion? Who is a risk taker? Who is not a risk taker? How am I going to nudge that child into becoming more of a risk taker? Who is conscious of other people in their space? Who is not? How much more time do I have to spend on the environment or how we interact with each other? My observations are constant. I don't assume much unless everybody is given equal time to share. When the year starts, many children aren't comfortable yet to be able to do that. One of my jobs is to get them more comfortable with sharing and being a risk taker with their learning. I don't want them to be afraid to try new things. It is easy to be on the fringes of something and be on the outside and that is not what I want children to do. I want them to be part of the community, and the only way they are going to do that, in some cases, is if I give them a nudge. Sometimes I find myself, even with children whom I think I know well, assuming something even as late as May, and they'll shock me with something that is not at all what I thought they would say. Or a child might make an incredibly profound statement that I would not have assumed he or she would be able to make. It is a constant reminder to me.

JANICE: You've asked the children to think about things; you've spent an incredible amount of time processing with them. In what ways do children grow in this classroom? What do you see happening in May that you didn't see happening in September?

MARY: Children often come to our room unsure of what they know and what they should know. They may expect their lives to be planned for the year and their interests to be unimportant to people outside their families. They often expect little of themselves as they may not realize their potential and importance in our classroom community. Some children may have strengths in traditional academic areas—others may not, or assume that they have no strengths. That small facet in itself may set the stage for the initial social structure of the room. September brings a melting pot and with it disequilibrium.

As the year unfolds, children's personalities, real interests, and talents emerge. The melting pot transforms itself into a room of experts and consultants who can assist one another with learning, sharing, and risk taking. Children bring materials and ideas from their homes to aid in their learning and the learning of their colleagues. The environment becomes more flexible depending on needs. Learners freely move and choose what they need to continue their inquiry. In May, an observer might describe the learners as independent, helpful, and collaborative. Children mature a great deal in nine months of working together.

Teacher as Model

JANICE: Their growth is really a tribute to all the things that you have demonstrated throughout the course of the school year: the way you talk about books, the value you place on them, the way that you want children to treat each other, and so on. Children witness this on a daily basis with you so it is not something you tried once but things you work on throughout the year.

MARY: I realize that everything I say and do is really demonstrating some aspect of my attitude toward learning, working, and getting along with others, and so on. I just try to be myself, and I try to really talk with, not at, them. I live what I believe and try to help the children learn that, as well.

Teachers and Students: Setting Goals for the Future

JANICE: These ideas that you have put into practice seem very generic. They could cross age and grade-level barriers, couldn't they? These principles could, indeed, be put into practice at any grade level. Your students leave with certain ideas about literacy and ways to get along with each other, how to be responsible decision makers, and so on. What are your concerns about the years that follow? I would think you, as well as many parents, would want to see their children continue with similar classroom practices during the next year of school. What if it doesn't? What are your concerns about your students as they leave to go to another grade?

MARY: I think my main goal is to help children get along with others and become strategic learners. No matter what happens, I feel most children leave this room knowing how much I trust and respect them. I think the children gain a lot of self-confidence in here because there is a lot of community support for them. I've talked with the children very candidly in May or June; what if your room next year is different? What can you take from here that you can use there that will help you? We talk about teachers not doing things the same way and how their classrooms might be different. We discuss strategies we've learned in first grade that will help them in many years to follow.

One thing the children really like is all the strategies they've developed for reading and writing. They know that if they forget any, they can stop by and we'll talk about them or even write to me for a copy! The children feel so involved in what we've done that they want to take a copy of our strategies to share with their next year's teacher. We also set goals for what else they need to learn, what goals they want to work on through the summer and next fall in reading, writing, math, science, and social studies. We talk about how to set new goals for themselves. I feel that even if they are going into a situation that is very different from this, my hope is that there has been enough of a spark as a beginning learner that they will continue on with some of those strategies.

JANICE: In conclusion, what stories do you tell yourself about teaching? What do you want to try? What do you want to learn next?

MARY: I am constantly reminding myself that I need and want to be a learner and risk taker. Perhaps a key issue is self-monitoring. I attempt to foster that concept in children so I certainly expect to refine my understandings of myself as well. Metacognitive work with young children also intrigues me. I have found that they are very capable of understanding themselves as learners. I plan to research the issue more thoroughly and draw some more concise conclusions. I know I'll continue to investigate learners—how they learn and how best to meet their needs and interests. There will always be new challenges.

20 Language, Experience, and Learning

A Natural Connection for the Middle Grades

ELIZABETH G. STURTEVANT
Coordinator, Middle Education, George Mason University

In a middle school near Washington, D.C., two hundred seventh graders recently studied the Industrial Revolution. Textbooks and a wide variety of other print and nonprint materials served as sources of background knowledge on the time period, with writing, discussion, and hands-on activities interwoven into the curriculum. The unit culminated with an interdisciplinary project in which students built and decorated wooden toys on an assembly line in the industrial arts and art rooms. Designs for the toys were selected through a voting process including all students, while records of each student's contribution were recorded on "work cards" and charts by student "managers." After toy production, written reflection and discussion occurred in social studies classes. The toys were then donated to a local charity. A variety of teachers, including technology, art, social studies, English as a Second Language (ESL), and special education, participated in the planning, teaching, and assessment of learning (Sturtevant & Linek, 1996).

In the first chapter of this book, Nancy Padak and Timothy Rasinski explain that language experience is well suited for students of any age: "LEA practices work effectively in all instructional settings, with all learners, in all content areas." While teachers familiar with "language experience charts" may think of language experience as a method only for the primary grades, many language experience instructional practices are especially valuable for middle-grade students. Simply stated, a language experience curriculum provides well-coordinated opportunities for students to use both language and experiences for learning. On a daily basis, teachers encourage students to draw on previous experiences and apply them to new concepts. Learning opportunities include both hands-on experiences (experiments, trips, interviews, real-life mathematical problems, and so forth) and relevant, interesting uses of reading, writing, and discussion. Throughout, students are encouraged to become inquirers and are given frequent choices of topics, materials, and forms of expression. The earlier scenario illustrates the LEA concept at work in a middle school. The chapters that follow in this section of the book present in-depth portrayals of middle-grade LEA instruction in various disciplines. But first it seems useful to explore the rationale for LEA in the middle grades, beginning with a look at the middle-grade learner.

Who are Middle-Grade Learners?

Middle-grade teachers know one thing above all else—their students are in a time of change—physically, emotionally, socially, and intellectually. Roughly defined as between ages ten and fourteen (National Middle School Association, 1992), any class of middle-grade students will be an interesting mix: tall and short, mature and childlike, accomplished in literacy and just developing. Indeed, each young person may be at different levels of maturity in different areas, and likely will appear to change daily! Cognitively, students in the middle grades become more ready for abstract thinking and problem solving, while socially they thrive on positive interpersonal relationships and seek to feel both special and part of a group (Preisser, Anders, & Glider, 1990).

Certainly, teaching middle-grade students demands enormous flexibility and creativity. As students go through this transition in their growth from childhood to adolescence, they need a school curriculum that values their diversity, challenges their intellect, and creates numerous opportunities for purposeful social interaction. A program anchored by a language experience philosophy can provide this environment.

Why Use Language Experience?

A language experience philosophy has both ancient and modern roots. As Russell Stauffer succinctly noted, "Across the centuries scholars have ridiculed rote memory and its alleged role in the learning-thinking process" (1969, p. 293). Nonetheless, studies of instruction in the United States have found that over at least the last century, curriculum in the middle and upper grades has primarily emphasized factual learning (Cuban, 1986; Goodlad, 1984).

Early proponents of building conceptual learning through experiences included Aristotle and Socrates (Lavine, 1984), Dewey (1916), and Piaget (1926). Later in the twentieth century, scientists, historians, and educators working on educational reform at the prestigious 1959 Woods Hole Conference insisted that school curricula should be designed to help students learn the structure of a discipline, rather than isolated bits of information (Bruner, 1963). Jerome Bruner, who chaired the meeting, believed one way to accomplish this was through experiences at school that resemble work done by professionals in a given field: "The schoolboy learning physics is a physicist, and it is easier for him to learn physics

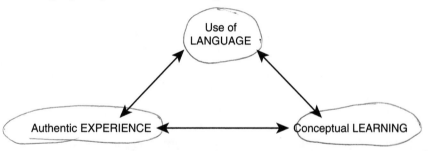

FIGURE 20.1   Interconnections between Language, Experience, and Learning in a Language Experience Curriculum

behaving like a physicist than doing something else" (p. 14). In planning curriculum, Bruner's example is still very useful as we consider ways we can immerse our students in activities that require them to "think like" and "act like" scientists, historians, artists, or mathematicians. Similar to their adult counterparts, our "schoolboy" (and girl) physicists can make predictions, conduct experiments, take notes, make charts and diagrams, write summaries, read background information, and have discussions with colleagues.

Research on the role of language and social interaction in learning, including Vygotsky's (1962) influential work, also supports the rationale for a language experience curriculum. Numerous studies have found that reading, writing, and discussion are active thinking processes and that conceptual learning is enhanced through use of these processes (e.g., Langer & Applebee, 1987). In addition, we know that as students use various language forms for learning, their proficiency as language users also improves (Vacca & Vacca, 1996). This reciprocal process (illustrated by the triangle in Figure 20.1) means, for example, that as the sixth-grade students in Vicki Duling's class (see Duling, Chapter 36) learned about themselves and others through their writing, they also became better writers. While this concept seems simple on the surface, it can provide a powerful framework for designing learning experiences.

Other Advantages of a Language Experience Curriculum

Two additional, compelling reasons for developing a language experience curriculum are that it is both motivating and appropriate for all learners. First, student motivation has been found to be an "overriding concern" of teachers and may be central to learning (Gambrell, 1995, p. 3). In numerous studies, middle-grade students have been motivated by experiential activities and language activities that allow choice, discovery, and interaction between students (e.g., Gambrell, 1995; see Standerford, Chapter 31). This type of instruction is the hallmark of the LEA classroom. Second, the language experience curricular emphasis on valuing students' past experiences while providing new, common experiences is especially appropriate for diverse populations. Long-term studies of bilingual students in North America, for example, have found that the most effective instruction helps these students develop concepts through a combination of experiential learning and extensive use of both their first and second languages (Collier, 1995). The seventh-grade participants in the team activity described in the beginning of this chapter were very diverse in cultural and language background, prior academic achievement, and learning needs. All were able to benefit from the project because of the support provided by both the content area and the special needs teachers.

National Standards Support Language Experience

Finally, a language experience curricular framework is supported by National Standards across a wide range of subject areas (e.g., National Council of Teachers of Mathematics, 1989). While the Standards documents do not use the term "language experience philosophy," they specifically suggest hands-on, inquiry-based, experiential forms of learning combined with group discussion, reading of relevant, interesting materials, and written reflection and synthesis. Zemelman, Daniels, and Hyde (1993), in their recent book *Best Practice*, call this emerging consensus among fields of study that have been traditionally separated a "coherent philosophy and spirit . . . [that is] . . . reaching across the curriculum and up through the grades" (p. 7). While, as mentioned earlier, recommendations for this type of curriculum are not new, during that past thirty years an expanded research base in cognition and human learning has provided a depth of support that was not previously available (Zemelman et al., 1993).

In sum, language experience has been called an elegant concept because it allows for both unity and diversity. The major premise, that learning takes place through both language and experience, can be applied across disciplines, age groups, and learner characteristics. Teachers can easily look at individual lessons, units, or an entire curriculum to analyze whether students are provided opportunities of both kinds. Diversity also is expected, however, because the balance in the way language and experiences are used will differ according to the concepts studied, local conditions, and needs of particular learners. Thus, a distinguishing feature of language experience for the middle grades is not so much its difference from other related philosophies, but rather its potential to help educators conceptualize and implement a powerful framework for instruction. The chapters that follow give further insight into the multiple ways such a framework looks in action.

REFERENCES

Bruner, J. S. (1963). *The process of education*. New York: Vintage.
Collier, V. P. (1995). *Promoting academic success for ESL students: Understanding second language acquisition for school*. Elizabeth, NJ: Teachers of English to Speakers of Other Languages-Bilingual Educators (NJTESOL-BE).

Cuban, L. (1986). Persistent instruction: Another look at constancy in the classroom. *Phi Delta Kappan, 68*(1), 7–11.

Dewey, J. (1916). *Democracy and education*. [On-line]. xx. Available http://www.ilt.columbia.edu/academic/texts/dewey/d_e/contents.html

Gambrell, L. B. (1995). Motivation matters. In W. M. Linek & E. G. Sturtevant (Eds.), *Generations of Literacy* (Seventeenth Yearbook of the College Reading Association), pp. 2–24, Harrisonburg, VA: The College Reading Association.

Goodlad, J. I. (1984). *A place called school: Prospects for the future*. New York: McGraw-Hill.

Langer, J., & Applebee, A. N. (1987). *How writing shapes thinking: A study of teaching and learning*. Urbana, IL: National Council of Teachers of English.

Lavine, T. Z. (1984). *From Socrates to Sartre : The philosophic quest*. New York: Bantam.

National Council of Teachers of Mathematics (1989). *Curriculum and evaluation standards for school mathematics*. Reston, VA: NCTM.

National Middle School Association (1992). *This we believe*. Columbus, OH: NMSA.

Piaget, J. (1926). *The language and thought of the child*. Trans. by M. Worden. New York: Harcourt Brace Jovanovich.

Preisser, G., Anders, P. L., & Glider, P. (1990). Understanding middle school students. In G. Duffy (Ed.), *Reading in the middle school* (2nd ed.), pp. 16–31. Newark, DE: International Reading Association.

Stauffer, R. G. (1969). *Directing reading maturity as a cognitive process*. New York: Harper & Row.

Sturtevant, E. G., & Linek, W. M. (1996). Unpublished data.

Vacca, R. T., & Vacca, J. L. (1996). *Content area reading* (5th ed.). New York: HarperCollins.

Vygotsky, L. (1962). *Thought and language*. Cambridge, MA: MIT Press.

Zemelman, S., Daniels, H., & Hyde, A. (1993). *Best practice: New standards for teaching and learning in America's schools*. Portsmouth, NH: Heinemann.

21 The Group Mapping Activity for Instruction in Reading and Thinking

JANE L. DAVIDSON
Professor Emerita, Northern Illinois University

To develop students' reading and thinking skills, the Group Mapping Activity (Davidson, 1978; Davidson & Bayliss, 1978) is an instructional strategy that provides dynamic interaction through discussion. After reading, students produce a map or diagram of relationships or ideas, a graphic representation of their interpretations of information in the text, or their personal responses to the text based on their knowledge of the world.

After students have finished reading a passage, the teacher gives them the following instructions. "Map your perceptions of the passage on a sheet of paper. There is no 'right' way to map. Elements, ideas, or concepts are simply put in diagram form. You might choose to use boxes or circles. You may also wish to draw lines to show relationships. Your map will represent your interpretation or perceptions of information from the passage. Do not look back at the passage at this time."

Following is an example of how the strategy works. In this transcription of a discussion, students were sharing maps they drew after reading a short passage entitled "All the Years of Her Life" by Morley Callaghan (1935). This story, described by Squires (1964) as containing ambiguity, involves a boy who was caught stealing. His mother convinces the owner of the store to release the boy to her instead of turning him over to the police. Later, the boy realizes that his mother is tired, alone, and frightened; he feels he understands her for the first time in his life.

One student had produced the map shown in Figure 21.1. The discussion started as this student explained the map.

"The curving wavy line shows how Alfred's life has gone—not a 'straight' life, because he gets into trouble constantly. His mother's life line has waves in it— she's had her share of troubles as she has grown older. The lines intersect when she helps Alfred out of his most serious trouble and he begins to understand her, but the lines move away from each other, because I don't think they'll ever touch again. Alfred's line is now straight, because I don't think he'll get in trouble again, however."

"I don't see why you think they'll never get together again. What are you basing that on?"

"It says in the story that although he wants to talk to his mother, he doesn't say a word. He may think he understands her for the first time in his life, but he doesn't go and talk to her even though he realized she's feeling so alone. If he were ever going to talk to her, now would be the time to do it. And, he doesn't."

"Alfred's mother has had so many unpleasant things in her life. My map shows her life line. Now that she's reached old age, she has nothing good to look forward to" (see Figure 21.2).

"Why do you say that when it looks like Alfred is finally going to appreciate her?"

"It says her face looks broken—I think it's too late."

"But it says that at that moment, his youth was over—that means he's finally grown up and I think he'll be able to talk to her."

"I kind of felt like that, too. My map shows the relationship between the mother and son, that's what I think it's all about. All the years of her life, she's been trying to get through to him, and she's finally done it. This new awareness

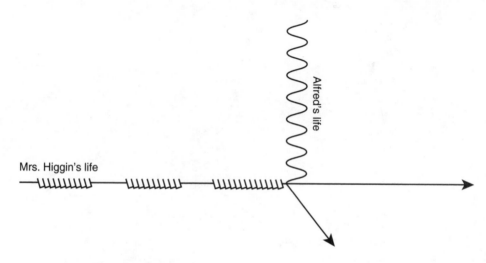

FIGURE 21.1   First Student's Map

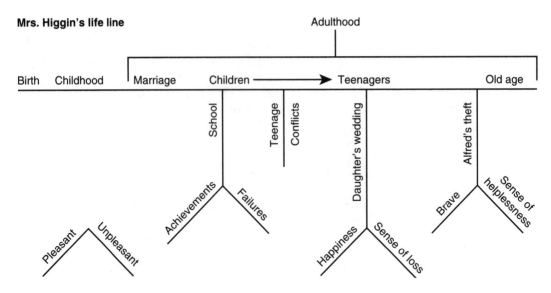

FIGURE 21.2   Second Student's Map

of his that she's really been trying to help him is what causes him to grow up" (see Figure 21.3).

"She may be handling him differently, too. It says that he expected her to come in the drugstore and yell at him or cry. He wasn't expecting her to be calm. So she must have done those things in the past. Now he's surprised at her. He can't figure her out. He felt proud of the way she acted, which made him more aware of her. That's why I put those arrows in leading to his growing up."

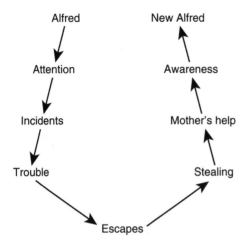

FIGURE 21.3   Third Student's Map

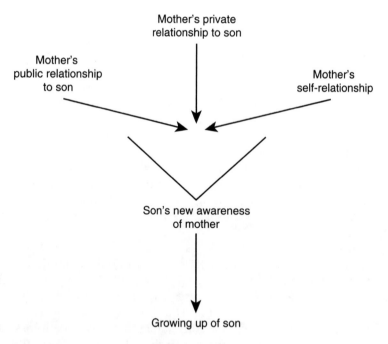

FIGURE 21.4   Fourth Student's Map

"My map shows what happens to Alfred. First he needs attention when he's growing up and he doesn't get it from his mother. I put in incidents, because he does little things to get attention, but nothing that's really serious. Then he gets into more trouble, but he always escapes before he's caught. Finally, the stealing incident occurs and he's caught. She has to come and help him. He sees what he's missed all these years—that she really does care about him. This new awareness—that she's always cared for him—causes him to be a new Alfred" (see Figure 21.4).

Encouragement Is Helpful

When students first begin to draw maps they may experience some frustration. The teacher may encourage students by showing them the maps accompanying this chapter to help them get started. However, the teacher should provide very little additional information about maps because it is important to let students generate their own individual structures. Some students become frustrated because they're used to being told exactly how something is to be done. The teacher should simply remind them that each map will be different and that there is no "right" way.

Students' initial frustration at their first Group Mapping Activity is rarely repeated in subsequent experiences with the strategy. After they have been involved in discussions following mapping and have had an opportunity to see and analyze others' maps, their frustrations subside. In subsequent Group Mapping Activities, students feel free to create their own structure for maps, convinced that there truly is no one right way to map. The process of mapping is learned by trying out and then experiencing the maps of others.

After most of the students have completed their maps, the teacher begins the discussion by inviting all students to hold up their maps so that they can see what others have drawn. The teacher then provides the following guidelines for discussion. "I will ask for a volunteer who will share her or his map with the rest of the group by explaining the map and sharing their reasons and interpretation or perceptions of the passage. When the person is finished, anyone in the group may question the person about anything in the map or any information that was shared. Anyone may refer to the passage for specific information to support a point. When there are no more questions, I will ask for another volunteer and the questioning time will be repeated."

During the first few discussions, if students don't raise questions, the teacher may ask a question or two to demonstrate the procedure. Students may freely question one another; they don't need to be called on by the teacher. The teacher's basic role is to moderate the discussion, facilitate the group's interaction, and occasionally provide questions that will serve as models for students.

The discussion period can be sensitive and intense as students ask each other about various elements in maps, agree with shared interpretations of the passage, or disagree with various interpretations. Students challenge one another, and their questions and responses represent high levels of critical thinking (Greenslade, 1981). The teacher must keep in mind that students' interests and experiences are different and their interpretations of the same passage may also differ. The discussion encourages different kinds of thinking, and as students interact with one another by sharing maps and asking questions, they gain insights about the various reasoning processes used by others. They are able to analyze their own purposes for reading.

Results of an investigation of comprehension instruction (Durkin 1978–1979) in reading and social studies in grades three through six caused Durkin to conclude that little comprehension instruction is provided in most classrooms. She felt that whatever attention was given to comprehension focused on assessment through teacher questioning, a process she described as interrogation. She reported that written assignments, particularly duplicated sheets, constituted most of the instructional program in the classrooms she observed. The Group Mapping Activity actively involves students in the reading–thinking process and has long been urged by reading authorities who believe that active involvement maximizes students' comprehension of text (Henderson, 1977; Huey, 1908; Russell, 1964; Smith, 1979; Stauffer, 1980).

The Group Mapping Activity helps readers recall and retain text information. The strategy also provides a means for students to generate personal responses in their interpretations of passages. The act of mapping requires students to make intellectual commitments about their perceptions of the meaning of a passage as they draw relationships, details, or ideas from information in the text. "When discussions vary in the story dimensions considered, when different kinds of thinking processes are encouraged, and when they become true occasions for dialogue, then students have a stimulating thinking experience" (Hall, Ribovich, & Ramig, 1979, p. 151).

REFERENCES

Callaghan, M. (1935). All the years of her life. *The New Yorker, 11,* 17–19.

Davidson, J. L. (1978, April). *Mapping: A dynamic extension of the DR-TA.* Paper presented at the IRA Language Experience Special Interest Group meeting, San Antonio, TX.

Davidson, J. L., & Bayliss, V. A. (1978). Mapping. *The Journal of Language Experience, 1*(1), 6–9.

Durkin, D. (1978–1979). What classroom observations reveal about reading comprehension instruction. *Reading Research Quarterly, 14,* 481–533.

Greenslade, B. C. (1981). *The quality, quantity and variety of teachers' and pupils' questions and pupils' responses in discussions following Group Mapping Activities.* Thirtieth Yearbook of the National Reading Conference (pp. 240–244). Clemson, SC: National Reading Conference.

Hall, M. A., Ribovich, J. K., & Ramig, C. J. (1979). *Reading and the elementary school child* (2nd ed.). New York: D. Van Nostrand.

Henderson, E. H. (1977). The role of skills in teaching reading. *Theory into Practice, 16,* 348–356.

Huey, E. B. (1908). *The psychology and pedagogy of reading.* Cambridge, MA: MIT Press.

Russell, D. (1964). The prerequisite: Knowing how to read critically. *Elementary English, 40,* 579–582.

Smith, F. (1979). *Understanding reading.* New York: Teachers College Press.

Stauffer, R. G. (1980). *The language-experience approach to teaching reading* (2nd ed.). New York: Harper & Row.

22 Awareness and Anticipation

Utilizing LEA and DR-TA in the Content Classroom

BONNIE C. WILKERSON

Director of Research, Evaluation and Assessment, Elgin, IL

"Based on what you already know about the subject, what information do you expect to find in the passage?" Thus, a lesson is begun, based on a teaching strategy designed to facilitate comprehension through critical reading–thinking. The purpose of this question is to focus on the students' prior knowledge and experience as a basis for interaction with the text.

Learning occurs as learners are able to relate new information and concepts to their existing understandings of the world. In a teaching/learning situation the teaching task includes helping students become aware of what they do indeed already know and helping them find a basis for relating new information to existing understandings. Included also in the teaching task is facilitating the reader's interaction of existing knowledge with new information and concepts. The interaction of the learner's prior knowledge with the textual information is essential for learning.

An ongoing concern of content area teachers is that many of their students seem unable to understand their textbooks. Though students demonstrate the ability to read the words, the concepts seem beyond their grasp. Many suggestions have been made for teaching practices and strategies to help solve this dilemma. Questioning has been a major approach. Study questions—pre-, post-, and within-text have been and are used as a means of having students look critically

[From "Awareness and Anticipation: Utilizing LEA and DR-TA in the Content Classroom," by Bonnie C. Greenslade, 1980, *Journal of Language Experience, 2*(2), pp. 21–29. Copyright 1980 by the Language Experience Special Interest Group. Reprinted with permission.]

at what they are reading. These questions are meant to present purposes for reading, since it is through purposeful reading that interaction with the text occurs. The problem that develops, however, is that students do not comprehend the questions or use them to interact with the text.

Frank Smith (1978) discusses comprehension as relative: "It depends on the questions that an individual happens to ask" (p. 67). This seems reasonable. Why then the difficulty of students in interacting with questions included in the textbook or supplied by the teacher? The answer lies in the word *individual*. Smith is referring to having "one's own" questions answered. Questions included in the text or supplied for the reader are developed by teachers or author, not the learner. As such, they are not necessarily meaningful to the reader and do not help in comprehending the text.

Manzo (1975) states that students do not learn to ask appropriate questions of themselves. This would suggest a need for teaching practices that encourage the development of appropriate questions. Smith (1978), in his definition of comprehension, states that "prediction means asking questions—and comprehension means getting these questions answered" (p. 66). The asking and answering of appropriate questions by the process of prediction is inherent in the Directed Reading-Thinking Activity (DR-TA) suggested by Stauffer (1969). In the DR-TA, questions, or purposes for reading, are developed through anticipating what is to be found in the reading based on an awareness of prior knowledge.

In the DR-TA *awareness* is facilitated by brainstorming prior knowledge, causing the student to focus on what he or she already knows about the subject in order to make predictions. Thus, reading of the text is approached with some *anticipation* of its content. In the DR-TA, critical reading, including reading to confirm or refine hypotheses and evaluate responses of others, is facilitated by group interaction. The group interaction provides the learner with the opportunity and purpose to use information from the text for justifying and modifying his or her own understanding, questioning and evaluating the views of others, and organizing and clarifying his or her thinking.

Stauffer (1969) has identified the steps in the DR-TA as:

1. identifying purpose for reading;
2. adjustment of rate to purposes and material;
3. observing the reading;
4. developing comprehension;
5. fundamental skill training activities.

The DR-TA is introduced as a group activity. The discussion that occurs as an integral part of the activity occurs openly and spontaneously with students encouraged to react directly to other students. In a DR-TA the teacher is not the center of communication. The teacher's role is that of facilitator, providing impetus for further discussion and encouraging higher-level discussion by asking students to explain and/or justify their responses.

1. Identifying Purposes for Reading

Students are given the opportunity to read the title or appropriate subheading and are asked, "Based on what you know, what do your expect to find in this passage?" Students, in predicting what they expect to read in the passage, become aware of prior knowledge and begin to organize what they already know about the subject at hand. By making predictions they are anticipating what they will find in the text, developing a purpose for reading—to find out if their predictions are correct.

Responses elicited from the students (as purposes are identified throughout the lesson) may be informally recorded on the chalkboard for later reference and comparison. The chalkboard notations are useful for student reference during the discussion and serve an important function later for extending type activities.

2. Adjustment of Rate to Purposes and Material

In this step students read the text to confirm and refine their predictions. Students are directed to read a portion of the text (the amount having been predetermined by the teacher). The description of this step refers to rate because flexibility of rate is an essential component of effective reading. Flexibility of rate is particularly important in content area reading where overall concepts must be grasped as facts and details are gleaned for study purposes and for proof of hypotheses. The rate of reading will depend on the individual purposes of students as they seek to confirm their expectations, and on the complexity of the material.

3. Observing the Reading

The teacher observes the reading and has the opportunity to observe student involvement with the text, effectiveness of each individual's purpose setting, ability to adjust rate and skim, scan, or read carefully for different purposes. The teacher also has the opportunity to offer assistance to those having difficulty with word recognition or in understanding particular concepts.

4. Developing Comprehension

After students have read, the teacher encourages response and critical reaction to the text by asking, "Now what do you think? Why?" These questions provide opportunity for students to confirm or refine earlier expectations, using evidence from the text to support, extend, refine, or reject hypotheses. Students can verify predictions they or others have made by pointing out evidence in the text. They can question the validity of predictions based on new information and formulate new predictions or hypotheses based on new information, thus setting further purposes for reading.

The amount of material read at any one time is directed by the teacher as the cycle of identifying purposes, adjustment of rate, observing the reading, and developing comprehension is repeated while learners read and react. It is the teacher's role to motivate the discussion when necessary by asking questions that require students to explain, justify, or extend their responses. Research has shown that teachers providing instruction by means of a DR-TA ask chiefly interpreting, inferring questions and that students make responses that are chiefly critical and represent higher levels of thinking, going beyond the literal level (Davidson, 1970).

The example in Table 22.1 is from a transcription of a DR-TA. The lesson was an introduction to the Great Depression using a fifth-grade social studies text, *Many Americans, One Nation* (Noble & Noble, 1974):

TABLE 22.1 DR-TA Transcript

Questions	Responses
Looking at the title and thinking about what you might already know about the subject, what do you think this unit will be about?	Something that happened back in the twenties.
What kinds of things about the twenties?	Troubles in the twenties. Prosperity means troubles.
(Students read silently.)	
Now what do you think?	People were paid during the war and they could buy more goods. They could buy now and pay later.
Have you changed your mind about the meaning of the word *prosperity*?	Yes, it means good things.
Why have you changed your mind?	Well, I read the book and it means a different thing. The people are having good things happen.
What kinds of good things?	Food was cheaper. Gas was cheaper.
Why do you think things were cheaper?	Well, they really weren't, because the people didn't have as much money to buy them. You could buy now and pay later.
Why do you think the buy now, pay later is important here?	Well, you wouldn't have to pay for the food or goods all at once. You could pay a little each month.
Do you think that is a good thing or a bad thing?	Good. (All)

TABLE 22.1 (*Continued*)

Questions	Responses
Why?	If you need something now but don't have the money you could get it anyway and pay for it by the month.
Do you think the prosperity will continue?	Probably. No.
Why?	I don't know. Well, they way things are today, it couldn't have continued. Prices went way up.
Are we prosperous today?	No. Things started going down when prices started going up.
What do you expect to read next?	That prices start to go up. And keep going up. Rising prices will ruin the prosperity.
(Students read silently.)	
Now what do you think?	We were right because it says that wages went from $13.00 in 1925 to about $25.00. The prices are rising.
What makes you think prices are rising?	It's the wages that are rising not prices. Well, when pay goes up, prices go up too.
What do you expect to find next?	There will be more things to buy.
Why?	Because if factories hire more workers then they're able to make more of the products they're manufacturing.
Where will this lead?	To more inflation.
Why?	Prices will rise higher and higher. That's what happens today. It's been going up since then.
(Students read silently.)	
Based on new information, what do you think now?	I was wrong. Everybody needs jobs now. Everybody is bankrupt. The banks tried to get their money from the investors and they didn't have it. They couldn't get their money back.
What happened?	They started closing. They were losing all their money. By 1932 the banks were closing. People had borrowed money and couldn't pay it back so they had to close up.

Questions	Responses
What is going to happen next?	Inflation is going to go higher.
Why?	Because the production went down and they need more money. They'll have to raise the prices. Stores need more money to stay open.
Where will the money come from?	Not from the banks. They're all closed. They can fire workers and save money. But the factories are already bankrupt. You can't save money you don't have.
What else will happen?	The people will be in trouble. They won't have the products the factories make. They won't have money to buy the goods because they won't have jobs. They won't have money to buy food.
(Students read silently.)	
Have any of your predictions been confirmed?	It says children had torn clothes at school. Children were asking for food from the schools. Stores offered to give away food and so many people wanted some that there was a riot. The government should have given everybody enough to live on.
Why do you think that?	Nobody should have to starve. It was the government's fault that the problem started.
Why do you say that?	Because they were involved in a war and the depression started because of changes after the war.
Did you find that information in the text?	No, but I thought it implied it. It said people had lots of money to spend after the war and began to overbuy. It says that American factories produced huge amounts of supplies for our troops and our allies during World War I. Everybody had jobs. Everybody saved their money during the war because there really wasn't much to buy. It was all going to the war. After the war, they were so happy they began to buy just for the heck of it. They started to buy on credit and then they got in trouble. When the bills came they couldn't pay. Then the banks went bankrupt. They lost all their money because nobody could pay them.

5. Fundamental Skill Training Activities

Throughout the strategy, as purposes are set by making predictions, the teacher has made note (informally, on the chalkboard) of students' expectations, representing their expressed prior knowledge. As the text is read and reacted to, a modified outline of the text may be developed. This outline can serve two important functions.

First, it serves as a study guide. It is a record of literal information and fundamental concepts presented in the text, and a reminder of the discussion with its critical response and reaction.

Second, it can be used to compare students' prior knowledge with information presented in the text. A comparison can be made of the informal notations made prior to reading portions of the text, and of the modified outline. Information and concepts introduced by students but not covered by the text may be used as topics for individual research and inquiry. The notations made prior to reading portions of the text may in general be used to define individual interests and areas for further study. An example of notations as they could appear at the completion of the group activity is provided in Table 22.1.

Additionally, the DR-TA is in itself a "fundamental skill training activity." Students, through involvement in a group DR-TA, experience the developing of individual purposes for reading, experience reading for those purposes, and experience critically reacting to text. Students who have experience with a group DR-TA can be encouraged to use those same skills of developing purposes, reading for purposes, and reacting critically to text in their individual reading. Thus, use of the DR-TA, in addition to improving comprehension, can also facilitate students' improvement of study skills, individual inquiry and research, and critical reading–thinking on an individual basis.

Conclusion

If we hope to encourage critical reading and understanding of content area text, we must facilitate students' interaction of prior knowledge with the information and concepts presented in the text. This can be accomplished by means of a questioning strategy if the questions are meaningful to the learners and if the strategy encourages higher-level response and critical thinking.

The DR-TA is a questioning strategy that utilizes higher-level questions and evokes higher-level responses even when students have no prior experience with the strategy (Davidson, 1970). It requires involvement of the learner in meaningful interaction and encourages students to read and think critically. It provides purpose and motivation for individual research and study as well as facilitating the improvement of study skills. The DR-TA is a viable and valuable teaching strategy for use with content area text.

REFERENCES

Davidson, J. L. (1970). *The quantity, quality, and variety of teachers' questions and pupils' responses during an open communication structured group Directed Reading-Thinking Activity and a closed communication structured group directed reading activity.* Unpublished doctoral dissertation, University of Michigan, Ann Arbor.

Manzo, A. V. (1975). Guided reading procedure. *Journal of Reading, 18,* 287–291.

Noble and Noble Basal Social Studies Series. (1974). *Man and his world.* New York: Noble & Noble.

Smith, F. (1978). *Understanding reading.* New York: Holt, Rinehart, & Winston.

Stauffer, R. G. (1969). *Directing reading maturity as a cognitive process.* New York: Harper & Row.

23 Sorting

A Word Study Alternative

JEAN WALLACE GILLET

Reading Specialist, Charlottesville (VA) Public Schools

Author's Note

This chapter appeared in *The Journal of Language Experience* in 1980. At that time, basal readers and language arts systems dominated the instructional scene. Children were taught to recognize words using sight recognition of whole words and phonic decoding skills. Although language arts systems typically presented both methods, and each had its staunch supporters, phonic decoding skills were usually emphasized. Phonics advocates often compared whole-word recognition to the so-called "look-say method" of the 1950s, thereby inferring that it was hopelessly dated. They advocated letter–sound drills and materials in which almost all the words were easy to sound out, which often limited the story content of the text. With adherents of each method declaring theirs the most effective, relatively little attention was paid to helping children develop a variety of strategies that would be effective in many different reading contexts.

Today the face of literacy instruction has changed dramatically. Whole language and literature-based reading instruction approaches focus less on a particular "best" reading method and more on helping readers develop a range of strategies they can use independently in authentic reading tasks. Strategic readers use different strategies to identify words and get meaning from text depending on the difficulty and content of the text, their purposes as readers, and the prior knowledge they bring to the act of reading. As they gain facility in using effective strategies and acquire greater automaticity in word recognition, they develop what Clay (1985) has called "a self-improving system"; that is, they learn more about reading every time they read. Rapid, accurate recognition of words makes comprehension possible, which in turn makes reading meaningful. Skillful word recognition is enhanced when students are able to perceive similarities and differences among words sharing certain features, form concepts about how word patterns work, and use these patterns to help them recognize new words.

The word study activity described in the original article, which follows, is based on a concept formation approach to studying words. In it, children categorize written words based on their analysis of specified features. Words sharing the same feature or features are grouped together, and generalizations are developed about how such words go together. Features may be phonological, orthographic, syntactic, semantic, or a combination of these.

At the time the original article appeared, few commercial instructional programs utilized a concept formation approach to word study. Today, this approach is much more widely recognized. Sorting and categorizing, whether in word study, math, science, or other subject areas, are widely recognized as effective ways of teaching thinking skills. "Strategies for thinking about printed language," Clay (1985) wrote, "are an important part of a self-improving system" (p. 14). The word sorting activities detailed in this chapter are now cornerstones of a whole language word study program.

Text of the Original Chapter Published in the *Journal of Language Experience*, 1980

A review of the word analysis strands of today's front-running language arts reveals a perhaps startling finding: we're still arguing the Great Debate. In that milestone of reading education, whole-word and phonics methods squared off against each other. Some may view Chall's 1967 work as dated and believe that the issue has been argued to death. However Groff's article (1979) decrying what Hoskisson (1979) and others have called "assisted reading" is proof that the issue is still viable.

Many have felt for some time that neither word recognition method is altogether satisfactory. Certainly some youngsters can be taught to productively apply phonic generalizations, but for many children in the beginning stages of reading, phonics skills and rules are apt to be awkward at best, incomprehensible at worst. Before children have developed a stable concept of what words in print are, and have acquired a store of words recognized at sight, phonetic segmentation of words is a nearly impossible task (Henderson, 1976; Morris, 1979).

According to many programs, if a word can't be sounded out it must simply be committed to memory as a whole. Most children acquire their first sight words, often brand names and labels frequently encountered in context, in just this way; however, committing large numbers of individual words to memory, as children have attempted to do with basic sight vocabulary lists for years, is apt to be as frustrating and unproductive as the overuse of phonics.

In our desire to decide which of these two methods is best, we have over-looked the possibility that a way of helping children recognize words can be developed that uses phonics without distorting or overemphasizing the role of speech sounds in print, and that springs from the natural spontaneous way in which children learn to recognize whole words before they are taught. An alternative to teaching children to use pre-set letter–sound correspondence, or to rely on their brute memory of whole words, is to lead children to compare and contrast whole words and discern for themselves the features words have in common. There is nothing new about this, for it is the basis of concept formation and discovery learning. Children can frequently discriminate between several words in print far more quickly than we can come up with language to describe the differences to them. It is just this power and economy that a concept formation approach to word study offers.

Word Sorts: Discovery Concepts and Features of Words

A concept formation approach utilizes the "word sort," an activity in which children physically arrange words printed on cards into groups. Word banks are ideal for sorts. All words in a group share a common feature. All words have a number of features, for they all have letters, letter–sound combinations, spelling patterns, and possible meanings. All these features are important, allowing us to distinguish words from each other. In word sorting, children are led to discover for themselves the features words have in common, rather than being told how words are similar and being expected to remember and apply these generalizations. Word sorts are different from traditional word study activities in that sorting helps children discover and make sense of word features for themselves; traditional word study focuses upon *telling* children, or *showing* them, word features rather than guiding them to *discovering* them. Word sorting rests upon a discovery learning foundation, which makes the method a natural extension of the language experience approach.

Word Sorting Strategies: Closed and Open Word Sorts   There are two general types of word sorts, closed and open. In closed sorts, the category or common property of the words to be included in the group is stated before sorting. This forms the basis for including or excluding any word in forming groups of words. The common property might be the same initial letter or medial vowel sound, part of speech, or a shared meaning relationship. With the criterion stated, words are examined for presence of the stated feature. Thus, closed sorts help children develop convergent thinking and the ability to compare and contrast.

In open sorts, no criterion is stated in advance. Instead groups are formed as the word bank is examined and relationships among words are spontaneously noted by children. Because all words have a number of concurrent features, a word can properly belong to several groups simultaneously. As more words are examined new relationships appear and word groups can change in size and composition. In open sorting children consider several features at once and examine other words for shared features; this requires divergent thinking and induction.

Sorting Using Picture Cards   The technique of sorting can be introduced even before children have any word bank words, by sorting picture cards. Forming categories of pictures of things that go together can be done in the reading circle, with direct supervision so that all children become familiar with the sorting procedures. Independent activities, sorting picture cards or collecting pictures of things that belong together, can be easily devised for seatwork and centers. This practice provides a solid foundation in the process of classifying. As the children begin to collect sight words in their word banks, sorting can be extended to include pictures and printed words, and finally to sorting word cards alone.

Sorting Activities Using Word Bank Cards   Children's word banks provide the ideal source of words for word study. Using immediately recognized word bank words, collected from dictated stories as well as from other sources, frees children from having to figure out what a word is before they begin to compare it to others. Comparing a word to others, a high-level thinking task, can only be accomplished when the words to be manipulated are immediately recognized. Puzzling over the identity of a word precludes the possibility of placing it in a category; in other words, we must know something in order to do something with it. Also, sorting recognized words into patterns means that we are always working from the known, building upon what is already familiar. The foundation of all learning lies in moving from the known to the as-yet unknown, the familiar to the new. This is a basic tenet of the language experience approach, which can be extended to word study.

Sorting the word bank words is an excellent word study activity for the reading circle. Beginning with sorting picture cards, then moving to sorting word cards, is done by each child in the circle simultaneously. The teacher presents the examples of the word feature to be studied, for example an initial consonant sound. The teacher presents and the children identify picture cards, and the children sort their words for those that begin like the pictured words, examining their cards and laying down those they find that fit the pattern. The teacher immediately sees what each child produces and can provide immediate feedback while assessing diagnostically each child's progress. All children in the group are occupied with the task, rather than one working and the others waiting, and children work with their own word banks rather than someone else's. In this way, group instruction and feedback are provided while the activity is truly individualized. Finally, by sorting words with a pictured example, the children focus upon the sound similarity of the words, and the tendency to visually match letters to the example is minimized (Gillet & Kita, 1979).

The group activity just described, which can focus upon any other word feature as well as letter–sounds, is an example of a closed sort; the teacher directs what the children are to look for. Open sorts are just as easy to do in a circle. Children can be paired or put in smaller groups of three or four and an open sort done in a game format. Each child forms categories of word bank words, and the others must try to figure out the basis for the category by placing their own word cards correctly into another's sort. This mind reading game is one children love, for they try to stump each other while trying to break each other's categories. In doing so, they are engaged in induction as well as in examining words for many possible shared features. Also, this activity introduces reading each other's word cards as well as their own.

Conclusion

As a teaching technique, word sorts are highly individualized, yet they allow the teacher to bring children together in the classroom for group instruction that is focused and substantive. Word sorts can reflect any of the almost limitless ways English words can be related to each other. In their basic form, they require no materials other than word bank words, which students can easily make up themselves; additional game activities adapted from the sorts are quickly and easily made up with poster paper. As children's sight vocabularies grow, sorts continue to be useful, because what changes is not the activity but the features or common properties being examined. Sorting activities can be used with individual students, groups, or whole classes, conducted independently or during direct instruction.

Few other techniques for substantive word study are so flexible, retain students' long-term interest, or engage students in real reflection and high-level thinking. Probably most important, sorts put children to work discovering how words work, rather than remembering rules someone else has generated. Systematically incorporated into classroom instruction in word analysis, word sorts provide a sensible alternative to phonics or whole-word approaches.

REFERENCES

Chall, J. S. (1967). *Learning to read: The great debate*. New York: McGraw-Hill.

Clay, M. M. (1985). *The early detection of reading difficulties* (3rd ed.). Portsmouth, NH: Heinemann.

Gillet, J. W., & Kita, J. J. (1979). Words, kids, and categories. *The Reading Teacher, 32*(5), 538–546.

Groff, P. (1979). A critique of teaching reading as a whole-task venture. *The Reading Teacher, 32*(5), 647–652.

Henderson, E. H. (1976, May). *On learning to spell*. Paper presented at the meeting of the Language Experience Special Interest Group, International Reading Association Annual Convention, San Diego, CA.

Hoskisson, K. (1979). A response to "A critique of teaching reading as a whole-task venture." *The Reading Teacher, 32*(6), 653–659.

Morris, R. D. (1979). *The beginning reader's concept of word and its relationship to phonetic segmentation ability*. Unpublished doctoral dissertation, University of Virginia, Charlottesville.

24 The Directed Spelling Thinking Activity (DSTA)

Providing an Effective Balance in Word Study Instruction

JERRY ZUTELL

Professor, The Ohio State University

The current enthusiasm for whole language philosophy and language/literature-based approaches has had important, positive effects on literacy instruction in many classrooms and school districts: Children learn to read from meaningful, enjoyable texts that follow more predictable and familiar language patterns; they are encouraged to write early and often, with a focus on ideas they wish to express and on the writing process; teachers recognize the value of integrating reading, writing, and content area subjects into thematic units of instruction; more holistic and naturalistic approaches to evaluation (e.g., portfolio assessment) are gaining wider acceptance.

Underlying these changes is a belief that children best learn to read and write naturally, in meaningful contexts rather than from isolated skill-and-drill

[From "The Directed Spelling Thinking Activity (DSTA): Providing an Effective Balance in Word Study Instruction," by Jerry B. Zutell, 1996, *The Reading Teacher, 50*(2), 98–108. Reprinted with permission of Jerry B. Zutell and the International Reading Association. All rights reserved.]

Portions of this article have been adapted from J. Zutell (1994). Message from the guest editor. *Literacy Matters, 5*(4), Winter, 1–2, and from J. Zutell (1993). The Directed Spelling Thinking Activity (DSTA): A developmental, conceptual approach to advancing students' word knowledge. In *Literacy for the new millennium.* Conference papers from the 1st International Conference and 19th National Conference, Australian Reading Association, Melbourne, 184–191. They are used here with permission.

activities. But as teachers have moved in this direction many have begun to realize that, while such conditions provide necessary environment for literacy learning, such an environment may not be sufficient in itself. Most children also need more direct and explicit information about the forms and patterns of written words in order to acquire the full range of knowledge and strategies necessary for fluent reading and writing (Zutell, 1994).

As teachers move away from the use of traditional spelling books, materials, and activities, they must determine how to present information about words and their spellings in meaningful, appropriate, and effective ways. The Directed Spelling Thinking Activity (DSTA) is a technique that applies basic concepts from a language-based literacy learning approach to word study.

Overview

The name Directed Spelling Thinking Activity (DSTA) is directly borrowed from Russell Stauffer's Directed Reading-Thinking Activity (DR-TA) (Stauffer, 1969). Stauffer coined this term to distinguish his instructional activity from the traditional approach to organizing basal reading lessons at that time, called the Directed Reading Activity (DRA). In the traditional DRA format the teacher dominates the lesson, setting purposes for students' reading, asking specific detailed questions to check comprehension, and controlling the lesson in ways that allow for little student input.

In contrast, the DR-TA procedure encourages honest discussion, critical thinking, concept formation, and use of a problem-solving strategy (problem statement; hypothesis; data collection; acceptance, revision, or rejection of the initial hypothesis). The procedure involves students in predicting outcomes, reading to collect evidence about their predictions, revising predictions as more information becomes available through reading, and using evidence in the text and their own reasoning to defend their conclusions. The teacher guides and facilitates students' thinking, but the ultimate responsibility for making decisions and reaching conclusions lies with the group and its members. (Over the years, some of the innovative aspects of the DR-TA have been incorporated into many basal reader presentations of the DRA.)

The DSTA was so named because it shares with the DR-TA the spirit that students should be full participants in the lesson, actively engaged in discovering and thinking through the problem at hand. Although the content in the two activities is naturally quite different, the structure of the DSTA is similar to that of the DR-TA in several significant ways.

The teacher initiates student predictions by giving the group a brief spelling test on words that represent patterns related to a given contrast. Before the correct spelling of each word is presented, members share their attempts and discuss the strategies and reasoning they used in generating their spellings. As they listen to others' reasoning and compare their attempts to the correct forms, students gather evidence about patterns, which they often use to spontaneously revise their predictions of upcoming words.

Word sorting and follow-up activities actively engage students in refining their concepts and extending applications to their own personal examples. Thus the heart of both the DR-TA and the DSTA is a focus on active, thoughtful problem solving.

In the following sections a more extensive discussion of a conceptual framework supporting the DSTA is presented, followed by a detailed description of the specific steps involved in implementing the procedure.

Conceptual Framework

The DSTA activity is modeled on Stauffer's format, but its concepts are grounded in recent work on the developmental and conceptual nature of learning to spell. A developmental approach to spelling was inspired by the seminal studies of Read (1971), then advanced and extended by Henderson and his colleagues (see, for example, Henderson, 1990; Henderson & Beers, 1980; *Reading Psychology*, Vol. 10, Nos. 2 & 3, 1989; Templeton & Bear, 1992). Several important principles have emerged from that work and related scholarship:

- English orthography is not as arbitrary or irregular as is often assumed. It is a complex system involving relationships among sound, visual patterns, meaning elements, and word origins (e.g., Cummings, 1988).
- Learning to spell is more than a matter of rote memorization; it includes a strong conceptual component. Students not only learn individual words, but acquire progressively more complex ideas about "how words work."
- This development follows a broadly defined set of stages marked by advances in correct spellings and more sophisticated misspellings. (Henderson's 1990 labels for these stages are Preliterate, LetterName, Within-Word Pattern, Syllable Juncture, and Derivational Constancy. See Morris, 1981, and Gentry & Gillet, 1993, for slight variations.)
- Word familiarity and concept formation are mutually supportive in that relationships or patterns are first recognized in familiar words, then extended to less familiar ones, which become more memorable as they are fitted into an overall scheme. Expanded sight and spelling vocabularies provide more examples for making sense out of more complex patterns.

The findings from developmental spelling research support a conceptual approach to learning about words that focuses on the discovery of categories and relationships by building on previously acquired word knowledge. DSTA lessons provide opportunities to compare and contrast words in ways that clarify such relationships. Further, information about stages of development provides a rough guideline for the selection of lesson content in terms of order of difficulty and conceptual appropriateness.

Principles from Vygotsky's (1978) ideas about learning have also influenced the development of the DSTA. In contrast to more individualistic views, Vygotsky focused on the power of social engagement to transform children's thinking, the collaborative nature of learning, and the role of language in shaping mental functioning. He developed the construct of the Zone of Proximal Development (ZPD), defined as the region where mental abilities are transferred from the shared environment to individual control. Movement through the ZPD proceeds from performance assisted by teachers, peers, or other "experts" to self-assistance to internalized, automatic control (Berk & Winsler, 1995; Tharp & Gallimore, 1991).

The DSTA design reflects the application of these principles: The teacher aims for patterns and concepts within the students' ZPD (see the discussion of "using but confusing" that follows); students and teachers work collaboratively to discover patterns of relationships, both in a small group and in pairs; and word sorting activities, including, teacher and student verbalizations of strategies and decisions, provide the scaffolding for internalizing concepts and developing individual, automatic control.

Planning

Planning a DSTA involves deciding upon three things: (a) which students will participate, (b) which contrast and patterns will be discussed and examined, and (c) which words will serve as examples.

Because the primary aim of the activity is to generate interaction, discussion, and concept formation, the DSTA functions best with a small group of students (six to ten) at roughly the same level of spelling ability. The teacher applies her understanding of the spelling system and developmental patterns of student errors to samples of students' spellings (e.g., from developmentally based measures like the Qualitative Inventory of Word Knowledge [Schlagal, 1989], or from classroom writing activities) in order to determine which students need and are ready for help with a particular contrast and related patterns.

In choosing a contrast, the teacher looks for patterns for which students have some knowledge but lack full control or application, patterns that students are "using but confusing" (Invernizzi, Abouzeid, & Gill, 1994, p. 159). From these she or he chooses one from the earlier stages of word knowledge first. For example, a teacher may notice that some students are aware of long vowel markers (e.g., silent *e*), but are not always sure of when to use them in spelling single-syllable words. At the same time students are not yet doubling consonants when adding endings to appropriate single-syllable short vowel words (hop → hopping), a more sophisticated concept than the long vowel markers. The teacher would choose to work with the long vowel marker pattern first. Depending on students' familiarity with the concept, she or he might also choose to begin with a DSTA that features a simple, single contrast (e.g., long *a* represented by the silent *e* pattern vs. short *a*) to reduce the complexity of the task. Later, possibly as part of a sequence of DSTAs, other patterns (e.g., vowel digraphs, the other long vowels) might be introduced or incorporated.

Next the teacher thinks through the relevant patterns and selects a set of words (sixteen to twenty) to use in the activity. Some of the words will be direct examples of a pattern, others will provide contrast to see how patterns complement each other, and a few will be selected as exceptions. The words chosen should also be well within the students' speaking and reading vocabularies. (Teachers often find published word lists organized by patterns useful. See, for example, Appendix B in Henderson, 1990.)

As an illustration, suppose students are having difficulty with long vowel markers, and the teacher has chosen to work on the related contrast, limiting the activity to a single long vowel sound (long *a*) to reduce the complexity of the task. Next, she or he chooses some long *a* words with silent *e* markers (vowel digraphs as in *rain* might be presented in a later DSTA), some short *a* words, and a few that don't fit either sound-to-spelling pattern. The following two groups of words might be used: *brave, came, plane, bake, trade, page, tape, space; bag, plan, last, black, tap, mad, land, fast have, they, eight, far*.

The teacher makes a list for testing and also prepares individual index cards or strips of paper. Half the words from each category are jotted down in a randomly ordered list to be used as a pretest to begin the activity.

The Activity

Prediction and Discussion   The DSTA itself begins with a brief spelling test on the list words. While a general introduction to the task may be given, the teacher does not point out that the words are related to a specific pattern or contrast. Such cueing might well alter students' current sense of how the words should be spelled, and mislead the teacher's sense of what they really understand.

If the teacher has chosen the examples well, there will be a fairly even mix of correct and incorrect spellings. These attempts serve as student predictions about word form and pattern and as the basis for discussion and examination.

The teacher initiates discussion by asking individual students how they spelled specific words, what they were thinking about as they generated those spellings, and why they thought the words would be spelled in that way. Students listen to one another's explanations and decide which spelling is likely to be correct. Only then does the teacher present the correct spelling to the group, complimenting students on the reasonableness (and sometimes ingenuity) of their guesses and pointing out parts of the word that caused particular difficulty. (In my experience, the presentation of the correct spelling before discussion inhibits children's willingness to volunteer and explain their own attempts.)

After two or three of the words are discussed in this way, students begin to make connections across words and to use these connections to revise or confirm their guesses about other words. The teacher may stimulate comparison by asking directly whether a word is more like one or the other of two examples that have already been examined. The discussion continues in this way with all the words.

Assisted Word Sorting   Next, usually the following day, the teacher assists students through a group word sorting activity to further clarify the nature of the contrast and the differences in patterns. (A pocket chart is a very helpful aid in doing these sorts.) First, one word is chosen from each category to serve as a key for each column or pile. The cards for the remaining words are then mixed together. The teacher begins the sort by selecting the first card from the deck, pronouncing the word, and showing it to the group.

At this point the teacher can either solicit student ideas about the category in which to place the word and encourage students to explain their reasoning or place the word and verbalize her or his thinking as to why it belongs there. Teacher choices throughout this activity depend upon assessment of how much scaffolding is needed to assist students in discovering and understanding the relationships captured by the sort. As a general guideline, the aim is to maximize student input and control, so she or he continues through the deck, turning decisions over to the group or to individual students as appropriate.

A second deck of word cards, made up of the examples not used in the test, is presented as well (see Figure 24.1). Students are then encouraged to add their own examples to the sort, as the group (with teacher prompting only as necessary) provides feedback about the appropriateness of their choices.

In ending the activity, the teacher may decide to elicit from the group an explicit statement of the orthographic principle they have been examining. On succeeding days students engage in more individualized activities. These reinforce and extend the understandings presented in the first two parts of the activity.

Word Hunting   Scanning through familiar books, class lists, magazines, newspapers, and other regularly used sources of print is a way to build individual and group word banks. Students can also proofread or check their recent writings for examples of the patterns, noting their own control with words in context and adding found words to individual collections. Word hunting does more than simply provide additional words for the lesson. Hunting through their own writing and reading gives children a sense of connection between their everyday experiences with words and more focused contexts in which they are examined and studied. Furthermore, by observing the ease and accuracy with which an individual child locates and selects appropriate words, the teacher can get a clearer sense of how well that child understands the patterns being studied. Adjustments in instruction and activities can be made accordingly.

Personalized spelling lists can then be constructed from the two sources of teacher-selected and student-located words. The teacher might also choose one or two additional words that are not related to the patterns being studied but that deserve attention because of their high frequency, common misspellings, or special relevance to current classroom topics.

Cooperative and Individual Word Sorting   In order to extend and solidify their understandings of the patterns and contrasts under study, students work in pairs and then individually, sorting a combination of teacher-supplied words and their own examples.

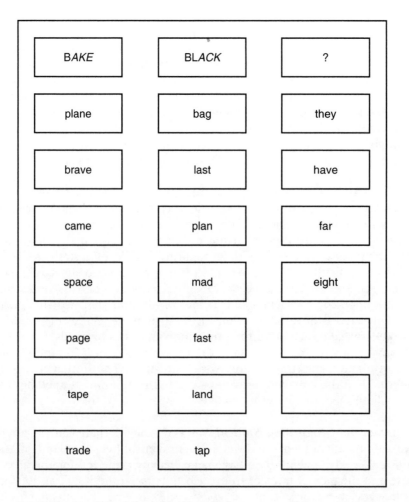

FIGURE 24.1   Word Sort for Simple Long *a* vs. Short *a* Contrast

In paired word sorting each student's set of words is collected into a deck placed face down on a desk or table. The key words from the group sort are put in a row to represent the various patterns. One student begins by picking the top word from his or her partner's deck and reading the word out loud. The partner indicates the key word under which the card should be placed. The student holding the card puts it there, and they both check to see if that choice makes sense. They continue in this manner, taking turns, until the words from both decks are sorted. Then they review their sort, making changes as they think appropriate. A final check is made either by the teacher or against a master list. On subsequent days students can sort with different partners to get a greater range of words and perspectives, or they might work together over several days before moving on to sorting their own words independently.

Word sorting is a particularly powerful form of learning as students working together discuss the reasons for their decisions and support or question each other's choices. Depending on their control of the contrasting patterns, some students do this easily, while others must initially work carefully and diligently. The teacher provides support by checking student attempts, demonstrating the sort as necessary, and providing intermediate feedback for managing corrections. ("Two words in the third column seem to be different from the others. Find them and consider where else they might go.") Only when students can sort quickly, as well as accurately, have they developed perceptual and conceptual fluency with the contrast and relevant patterns.

Practice Activities   Once individual students and the teacher have agreed upon specific sets of words for the lesson cycle, each student may choose from a variety of activities to practice and measure his or her control over those words. The best practice activities are those that not only give students many opportunities to write the words, but also help them to locate and develop strategies for remembering the difficult parts. These might include Have-A-Go sheets, the Look-Say-Cover, See-Write-Check procedure, games in which success or advancement depends upon correct spelling of personal words, and intermediate practice tests.

One successful variation of practice is structured peer testing. In this activity two students give each other their own individual sets of words. Key words head columns on a sheet of paper. Rather than write the words in random order, the student first matches the spelling word with the key word that shares the same pattern. Then the key word provides a cue to the appropriate spelling. The result is a spelling sheet that looks much like the earlier word sort.

Measuring and Recording Student Success   The ultimate aim of any spelling instruction is for students to develop fluent control over the words in their own writing. Weekly spelling tests have been heavily criticized for the anxiety they cause and the lack of transfer from such tests to writing. Still, an individualized spelling review at the end of the lesson cycle can help students determine what they have learned. Given the individualized character of student spelling lists, reviews are often done in a peer-checking format (see Figure 24.2).

Students then plot their own growth by keeping an ongoing list of new words learned. They might also assemble individual word study pattern books with key words (e.g., *bake*) or brief pattern descriptions (e.g., long *a* words) at the

1. Pretest for prediction and discussion
2. Assisted word sorting
3. Word hunting
4. Cooperative and individual word sorting
5. Practice activities
6. Measuring and recording student success

FIGURE 24.2   Steps in a Directed Spelling Thinking Activity

top of each page or column. Individual pages can be placed in a binder or folder, so that students can rearrange the pages to reflect the current contrast under consideration. For instance, the short *i* pattern might initially be contrasted with short *e* words, but later with long *i* words. A word might also be listed under two or three different patterns, depending on its features. For example, *trip* could be found under both beginning *tr* blends and short *i*. Lists can thus be reviewed and expanded at various times during the school year.

A Contrast for Older Students

The example just used, based on a single long vs. short vowel contrast, is simple, appropriate for students in an early phase of the Within-Word-Pattern stage of spelling development. For more advanced students, more complex or less familiar contrasts are appropriate. For example, DSTA lessons work well when students are using but confusing past tense markered with related homophones (e.g., *guessed* vs. *guest*), and patterns related to consonant doubling (e.g., *hoping* vs. *hopping*).

For an example of a lesson dealing with the spelling–meaning connection, consider the sets of words in Figure 24.3. For all words, the final syllable is pronounced /shun/. But in the first two sets, the spelling is *-ion*, while in the third it is *-ian*. This difference is predictable by meaning: words spelled with *-ion* are typically noun forms built from Latin roots or related verbs. In the second set this connection to a verb form is more apparent: *define-definition*. In the third set, *-ian* combines with words ending in *-ic* or *-ics* to form a specific kind of noun—one that labels a person engaged in a related activity or profession: *music-musician*. This lesson

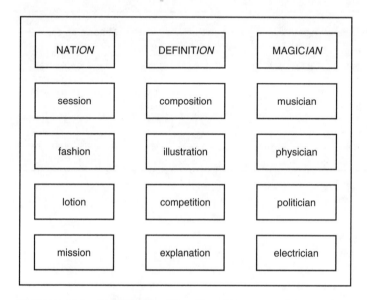

FIGURE 24.3 Spelling by Meaning Contrast: *-ion* vs. *-ian*

thus combines making sense of a spelling contrast with vocabulary and word formation concepts.

An Example from Student Writing

DSTA procedures and techniques can be modified to meet the needs of individuals and small groups; they work best when directly connected to patterns in a student's own reading and writing. In the following example a tutor applied the using-but-confusing principle to the journal writing of Steve, a third-grade student struggling with spelling.

An early selection from Steve's journal (see Figure 24.4) indicates confusion with long vowel marking and the use of silent *e* across several high-frequency words. The tutor tabulated a more complete list of Steve's attempts with such words, both correct and incorrect, across several journal entries (see Figure 24.5).

4-8-94

yesterday I went to the **mol** with my dad. he got me two **pars** of shorts and two **pars** of *jeans*. Then we went to a **Woch stor**. and behind it was a book **stor**. I got two **Goesbumps** books. then we went **two** a sports *store* and **bote** *some* **rollerblad laesis**.

FIGURE 24.4   An Early Sample from Steve's Journal Writing

Correct spellings	Misspellings	
sleep	pars	(pairs)
play	stor	(store)
stay	Goesbumps	(Goosebumps)
jeans	rollerblad	(rollerblade)
store	laesis	(laces)
some	ester	(Easter)
came	nams	(names)
liked	shar	(share)
base	gran	(drain)
glove	becaus	(because)
improve		
stone		
feel		
name		
read		
hide		
code		

FIGURE 24.5   A Tabulation of Steve's Relevant Spellings

Prediction, word hunting, and word sorting activities were used over several weeks (see Figure 24.6). Later samples from his journal (see Figure 24.7) provided some evidence that Steve had gained greater control over long vowel/silent *e*. Moreover, his tutor reported greater attention to visual detail and success with word forms across reading and writing activities.

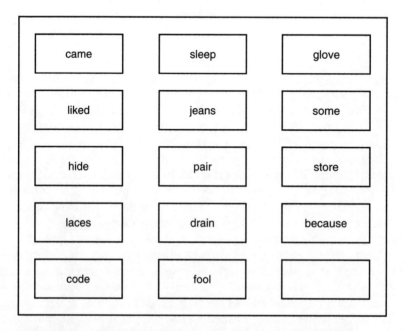

came	sleep	glove
liked	jeans	some
hide	pair	store
laces	drain	because
code	fool	

FIGURE 24.6 One of Steve's Word Sorts for Vowel Markers

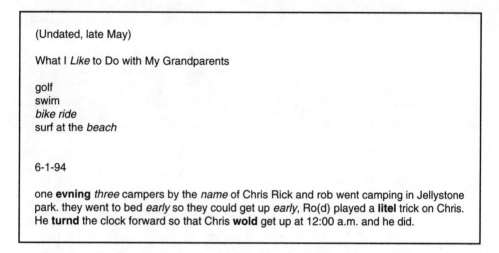

(Undated, late May)

What I *Like* to Do with My Grandparents

golf
swim
bike ride
surf at the *beach*

6-1-94

one **evning** *three* campers by the *name* of Chris Rick and rob went camping in Jellystone park. they went to bed *early* so they could get up *early*, Ro(d) played a **litel** trick on Chris. He **turnd** the clock forward so that Chris **wold** get up at 12:00 a.m. and he did.

FIGURE 24.7 Two Later Samples from Steve's Journal

Conclusion

An effective word study program provides students with many formal and informal opportunities to examine words carefully, explore their orthographic forms in relation to their meanings and uses, and develop reliable and efficient strategies for independent word learning. The regular use of Directed Spelling Thinking Activities should be an important component of such a program.

Although DSTA research is not yet extensive, initial feedback has been encouraging. Teachers using the technique have been very positive about the value of modeling, manipulation, and peer discussion for enhancing student learning (Compton, 1994; Wheaton, 1995). Students report that their spelling ability has improved, they have become more attentive to the details of print in their writing, and they have more strategies for generating spellings of unknown words (Compton, 1994). More systematic classroom studies of student interactions and long-range effectiveness are currently under way.

The DSTA procedure has many advantages over more traditional, drill-and-skill-based spelling lesson formats: It is based on findings from current research on word knowledge and spelling development; it treats learning about words as a conceptual process rather than as rote memorization; and students are actively engaged in problem solving, constructing knowledge as they discover complex relationships within and between words, and taking greater responsibility for their own learning. For these reasons the DSTA concept and format are compatible with child-centered, language-and-literature-oriented approaches to instruction. The DSTA can be used as one kind of mini-lesson in a whole language classroom. At the same time, the ideas and procedures involved in the DSTA can be incorporated into formal, sequenced plans for spelling instruction as presented in basal spelling series.

As with any instructional technique or procedural description, there is always the danger that the DSTA will be applied in a formulaic, rigid, step-by-step way. No worthwhile instructional innovation is meant to be "teacher proof," nor should it be our aim to make it so. As the extensive description in this chapter indicates, the successful use of the DSTA depends in large part upon the understanding, insight, and judgment of teachers knowledgeable about the nature of the spelling system and sensitive to the needs and abilities of their students. The format of the Directed Spelling Thinking Activity encourages teachers and students to work together in a spirit of genuine discovery in unraveling the complex relationships that govern English spelling.

REFERENCES

Berk, L. E., & Winsler, A. (1995). *Scaffolding children's learning: Vygotsky and early childhood education*. Washington, DC: National Association for the Education of Young Children.

Compton, C. (1994). What do we do for spelling? *Literacy Matters, 5*(4), 8–12.

Cummings, D. (1988). *American English spelling*. Baltimore, MD: Johns Hopkins University Press.

Gentry, J. R., & Gillet, J. W. (1993). *Teaching kids to spell*. Portsmouth, NH: Heinemann.

Henderson, E. (1990). *Teaching spelling*. Boston: Houghton Mifflin.

Henderson, E., & Beers, J. (Eds.). (1980). *Developmental and cognitive aspects of learning to spell: A reflection of word knowledge*. Newark, DE: International Reading Association.

Invernizzi, M., Abouzeid, M., & Gill, J. T. (1994). Using students' invented spellings as a guide for spelling instruction that emphasizes word study. *Elementary School Journal, 95*(2), 155–167.

Morris, D. (1981). Concept of word: A developmental phenomenon in the beginning reading and writing processes. *Language Arts, 58*, 659–668.

Read, C. (1971). Preschool children's knowledge of English phonology. *Harvard Educational Review, 4*(1), 1–34.

Reading Psychology. (1989). 10(2).

Reading Psychology. (1989). 10(3).

Schiagal, R. (1989). Constancy and change in spelling development. *Reading Psychology, 10*, 207–229.

Stauffer, R. (1969). *Directing reading maturity as a cognitive process*. New York: Harper & Row.

Templeton, S., & Bear, D. (Eds.). (1992). *Development of orthographic knowledge and the foundations of literacy: A memorial festschrift for Edmund H. Henderson*. New York: Erlbaum.

Tharp, R. G., & Gallimore, R. (1991). *Rousing minds to life: Teaching, learning and schooling in social context*. Cambridge, England: Cambridge University Press.

Vygotsky, L. (1978). *Mind in society*. Cambridge, MA: Harvard University Press.

Wheaton, A. (1995, November). *Exploring students' thinking during spelling word sorts: A longitudinal study*. Paper presented at the 45th meeting of the National Reading Conference, New Orleans, LA.

Zutell, J. (Ed.) (1994). Changing perspectives on spelling instruction. *Literacy Matters, 5*(4).

25 More than Just a Brownie

Language Experience and Edible Science for the Middle Grades

ELLEN LAWRENCE PESKO

Teaching Assistant, University of Michigan

Ask most elementary students "Where does milk come from?" and they will probably tell you, "the grocery store." Many children in the United States would name McDonald's, Arby's, Burger King, Wendy's, and Dairy Queen as the five basic food groups. It appears that some children know little about what they put into their bodies other than what they are told in commercials.

In 1997, approximately 40 percent of the calories in a typical American diet came from fat (*"American fat cat,"* 1997). Heart attacks, the number one killer in the United States, are directly linked to a diet high in fat (Bellerson, 1991). Clogged arteries do not begin a few months before a heart attack but are the result of a lifetime of choices. The Children's Nutrition Research Center (CNRC) has stated "that of the 10 top causes of death, five are attributable, in part, to dietary habits established in childhood" (1997, p. 1). A study of grade school children in Michigan showed that 98 percent had at least one major risk factor for heart disease. Twenty-eight percent had high blood pressure, 42 percent had abnormally high levels of cholesterol in the blood, and more than half had a combination of three or more risk factors (*"Fatty food's,"* 1997). The good news is that at least 90 percent of premature strokes and heart attacks are preventable (Piscatella, 1987). Thus, the questions facing educators are "How do we educate our students to make healthy diet choices?" and "Where do we add this to the curriculum?"

The Third International Math and Science Study (Checkley, 1997, p. 1) "reveals that U.S. students are introduced to a greater number of math and science topics than students in other countries, but they seldom explore these topics in much depth." At the same time, state and national testing programs are pushing for greater proficiency in reading and writing skills. President Clinton has proposed "using the National Assessment of Education Progress to test students in fourth grade reading . . . to make sure that students master key skills" ("Clinton pushes," 1997, p. A1). Given this scenario, integrating language arts skills and strategies with content area topics is essential.

Nutrition lends itself well to the Language Experience Approach (LEA). Choosing, tasting, and experiencing food is a daily experience whether it be for a fast lunch, snack, dinner, or celebrating a special event. It is easy to arrange a shared experience with food because it holds great interest for students who are becoming more and more aware of their bodies and how they are perceived by others. The whole concept of self-image is clearly evident in such books as *Are You There God? It's Me, Margaret* (Blume, 1970) and *Blubber* (Blume, 1974).

Integrating Language Arts and Science

Sampling food changes the classroom atmosphere because it invites social interactions such as the sharing of common experiences, and it sets the stage for learning activities built on conversation and discussion of a shared experience. The topic of food and nutrition encompasses a wide range of science explorations and activities that may be integrated with other topics, such as food preservation, analysis and testing, product development, marketing and advertising, additives, weighing and measuring, ecology, geography, and natural resources.

The Learning Cycle Framework

After reviewing statistics on young people's diets and eating habits, I developed a unit on nutrition using The Learning Cycle Framework (Biological Sciences Curriculum Study, 1993). The unit was designed to help students gain an awareness of the importance of nutrition, catch their attention, and make a lasting impression.

When students study content areas such as science, it is critical that they organize and connect what they have experienced and already know with new information (Santa, Havens, & Harrison, 1996). Therefore, it made sense to me to tie language arts activities with science, specifically nutrition-related topics, employing LEA. The philosophy and approach of the Learning Cycle Framework match those of LEA and provide clear, distinct procedures for planning and organizing lessons, involving students in active hands-on learning, and incorporating new information with existing knowledge. The Learning Cycle Framework consists of five stages:

1. *engage* the learner;
2. *explore* by witnessing an event or presentation, gathering data, examining pictures and text;
3. *explain* concepts and provide input;
4. *elaborate* by expanding and applying new concepts by making collections, identifying examples, using multiple sources to locate information;

5. *evaluate* students by what has been gathered in learning logs, displayed on posters, built as models, shared in oral presentations, and written on class wall charts.

The following is a description of one inquiry project (Zorfass & Copel, 1995) that uses the principles of LEA and The Learning Cycle Framework. Although a complete nutrition unit would include many other topics, this chapter describes one project that has students focus on the food they eat, the necessary ingredients and their origins, and the importance of maintaining healthy bodies.

Engaging Learners

To engage students' attention immediately, I bring in a large, clear plastic container filled with rich-smelling brownies and set it on the desk. Students all gather around and excitedly ask, "Is that for us? Do we get to eat?" I tell them, "Yes, we will sample some brownies today, but before we start, we want to really make this a memorable event by focusing on the scents, textures, and flavors." Recording observations is usually the first step in any scientific exploration. In order to prepare for that, I ask the students to think about some descriptive words that might describe the taste and flavors of the brownie we are about to eat. As the students brainstorm, I record their predictions on chart paper in the front of the room. This list is entitled *Brownie Sensations*.

Exploring Flavors and Ingredients

Next, I distribute the brownies. As they chew, I ask them to think about the actual flavors, aromas, taste, and textures. With a partner, they list all the words that come to mind that describe the actual brownie they are eating. Students write their list in their science learning logs. Next, I ask students to share new descriptive terms they have generated with their partner and add these to our chart.

With the same partner, students list the ingredients they think were used to make the brownies. As students brainstorm in pairs, they write their lists in their learning logs. This list usually includes the following: chocolate, nuts, sugar, applesauce, vanilla, butter and/or margarine. I find that students who have spent time in the kitchen with a parent, grandparent, or other family member will list additional ingredients: milk, flour, eggs, baking soda, and baking powder. After a few minutes, we group share these ingredients and I list them on another sheet of chart paper entitled *Brownie Ingredients*. This list prepares the students to think about the origins of the ingredients.

Next, I ask, "What plants were needed to make your brownie?" This question leads students to make connections between the tasting experience, the ingredients, and the larger concept that much of our diets comes from plants. Again in pairs, students now list the plants they think are used to provide the ingredients. Together, we group share and construct Chart 3, entitled *Plants Needed to Make a Brownie*. Together, the three charts look something like Table 25.1.

TABLE 25.1

Chart I Brownie Sensations	Chart II Brownie Ingredients	Chart III Plants Needed to Make a Brownie
Chocolate tasting	Chocolate	Bush or tree
Nutty	Nuts	Trees
Delicious	Sugar	Sugar cane plants
Yummy	Apple sauce	Fruit trees
Smooth	Vanilla	Wheat
Good	Flour	
Sticky	Eggs	
	Butter/margarine	
	Milk	
	Baking powder	
	Baking soda	

As we construct Chart 3, some questions arise: "Where do vanilla and chocolate come from?" "Do we need to list the plants that chickens and cows eat since we need the eggs and butter?" "What plants do these animals need to survive?" "What is baking powder?" "Do peanuts grow on a bush or a tree?" We list the questions on a large, separate piece of newsprint at the front of the room. These questions serve as the basis of our inquiry and prepare the students for researching the raw materials that are essential for producing the ingredients that go into making the brownie.

Explaining Concepts and Providing Input

In order to broaden the students' concept of what constitutes our daily diets, I ask them, "What did you eat for breakfast?" After listing their responses, I ask, "Which items on the list come from plants?" The list is usually varied but generally contains some of the following: cereal, fruit and fruit juice, muffins, toast, bagels, pancakes, waffles, pop-tarts, cold pizza—all of which are derived from plants in some way. I then ask, "What do you think would happen if all the plants disappeared? What would we eat?" Students might say "seaweed" or "fish." I ask, "Could we survive on a diet of only seaweed and fish?" It soon becomes evident to the students that if all the plants disappeared, we would have no vegetables, fruits, seeds, or grains. This realization then leads them to think of the immense impact this would have on their diets since there also would be no meat, eggs or dairy products as animals are dependent on plants for food. To impress students with the seriousness of this, I tell them that two-thirds of all plants growing on the earth are flowering plants with roots, stems, leaves, fruit, and seeds that we eat (Pearce, 1991). These reflections get students thinking about the importance of plants in their diets as well as why it is critical to maintain them and to insure that plants continue to thrive. At this point, I ask them if they can think of any other questions about plants they might have. These are added to the questions already listed on the newsprint.

Now is the time to introduce some of the many resource books I have collected for our plants and nutrition unit (see list of Science Resource Books for Inquiry Project p. 181). Some of these are *From Cacao Bean to Chocolate* (Mitgutsch, 1981) and *Plants We Live On* (Fenton & Kitchen, 1971). Two books that can lead to geographic and historical exploration are *People of Corn, A Mayan Story* (Gerson, 1995) and *Food and Feasts With the Vikings* (Martell, 1995). Before the books are distributed, I give a brief "Booktalk" (Tompkins, 1997) about each of them, pointing out unique information that may be found in each one. Since students have already thought about the importance of plants and have engaged in formulating questions, their curiosity is aroused about at least one question concerning plants, their diet, or food production. Students choose two or three of the questions that the class as a whole has generated, and gather information that either answers the questions or leads to further questions. Students enter the questions in their science learning logs and begin to search through the resource books for the answers. Sources as well as any additional facts about plants or diets they discover are also recorded. Illustrations, charts, and/or diagrams may also be included in their notes. I would recommend that if access to a CD-ROM or the Internet is available, students should also be encouraged to use the Internet and an encyclopedia on CD-ROM as additional resources for information.

The students continue their inquiries over two or three writing sessions. As they discover interesting pictures or information that answer their questions, much sharing goes on. During this time, students find pictures of cacao pods and/or vanilla beans and learn what countries grow these.

Some find information on how to feed and take care of cows and chickens in their own country as well as in other cultures. The mystery of "Where do peanuts come from?" is solved as a student discovers a picture that shows the developing peanuts as part of the peanuts' larger root system.

To display our findings, I select a few students to draw and paint a large brownie on chart paper. As a class, we display this on one of the bulletin boards in the hall. Next, students list the separate ingredients on cards, including the plant or plants needed to make each ingredient, and the country that grows the plant. These cards are placed on the brownie. Now it is time to also have the students share the findings of their investigations. Students state their questions and briefly provide the answers, sharing any illustrations or drawings they included that help explain or clarify. When the reports have all been shared, they are displayed on the bulletin board under specific questions the inquiry reports addressed.

Elaborate

This inquiry project provides a good transition for us to start talking about our daily nutrition and diets. During the same week the students conduct their inquiry projects, I have them keep a daily food diary of what they eat for every meal and snack for that week. Each morning we take some time to make sure that everyone is writing in their daily food diary and that they are all up to date. This information is used to categorize the food into the five food groups: fruits and vegetables, dairy, bread and grains, meat and fish, and fats and oils (see Table 25.2).

I display a wall chart with a food pyramid that indicates the number of choices we should eat from each area during a day. For example, five choices daily from the fruit and vegetable group and six servings of grain is recommended (*Health*, 1992). We take some time to define what belongs in each group. When we discuss grains, I bring in boxes from cereal and grain products, and we look to see what are the different types of grains—wheat, corn, oats, barley, and rice.

Finally, students fill in their individual food group charts using the information from their daily food diary. In comparing their charts to the daily recommended requirements, students are more acutely aware of what they eat as well as the ratio and proportional representation of some groups to another. This visual representation provides clear evidence of the nutritional composition of their diets as well as where they need to increase or decrease some things they eat. By comparing their food group charts with the U.S. Recommended Daily Allowance (USRDA) of meat, poultry, vegetables, fruit, cereal, bread, and milk (*Health*, 1992), students get a greater awareness of their diet and what they need to do to maintain a healthy body.

As a culminating activity, the class plans a nutritional lunch, basing their selections on the four food groups and the USRDA of nutrients. In planning the menu, students need to consider taste appeal, special dietary needs of individual students (e.g., vegetarians, diabetics), and nutritional demands.

Evaluating What Students Learn

This inquiry project, which focused on examining students' daily diets and their nutritional value, started with eating a brownie but expanded to include other topics: agriculture, botany, geography, mathematics, advertising, food shopping, and meal planning. As in the world of work, these subjects are blended in the application of their knowledge base to problem solving. The overall problem can

TABLE 25.2

Fruits and Vegetables	Dairy (milk, eggs, cheese, ice cream)	Bread and Grains (noodles, rice, pasta)	Meats and Fish	Fats and Oils

be stated as the following: If our present diets are inadequate and harmful to maintaining a healthy body, what do we need to know and do to change our food choices?

> Students need . . . to apply their knowledge and skills, with the result typically being a tangible product (written, visual, or three-dimensional) on a performance. These products and performances have an explicit purpose (for example, to explain, to entertain, or to solve a problem) . . . because real-world issues and problems are rarely limited to a single content area, authentic work often provides opportunities for making interdisciplinary connections. (McTighe, 1997, p. 9)

In planning this project, I wanted students to experience many of the activities that real scientists experience. I thought about the skills my students could take away from this experience:

1. Notetaking. Keeping detailed notes of the sources and information they located in seeking answers to the questions generated by the tasting experience.
2. Recording observations. Writing perceptions during the tasting experience, on trips to the grocery store, and while reviewing advertisements for food on television and in print media.
3. Research. Consulting multiple sources and becoming aware that there can be conflicting views on data, for example, the harm or benefits of caffeine or alcohol or the debate over whether high cholesterol is caused by diet or heredity.
4. Analysis. Thinking about what they eat and how it affects their body (cause and effect).
5. Application. Creating healthy meals and developing their own guidelines for snacks.

Effective language arts teachers plan units of study that will enable students to (1) expand their use of vocabulary, (2) write coherently, (3) use the conventions of writing, (4) use writing as a tool to learn, (5) use writing to inform others, (6) communicate their ideas orally, and (7) organize information for either verbal or written presentation. In addition to these language arts goals, this type of lesson tries to incorporate some of the goals of effective science teachers. Many science teachers are rethinking their goals in terms of:

> What does the 'doing' of mathematics, history, science, art, language use, and so forth, look and feel like in context? What are the projects and other kinds of synthesizing tasks performed all the time by professionals, consumers, or citizens that can be adapted to school use? (Wiggins, 1992, p. 29)

Much of the literature on assessment today focuses on student performance and problem-based learning. The language experience approach to teaching language arts parallels and enhances these science goals.

A Summary: Content and Process

The language experience approach has always involved engaging students in brainstorming and dialogue, in having students collaborate and interact on using their ideas and information they gather and on a question/problem solving-approach to communication of ideas (e.g., Why do you think the author has the character act this way or do this in the story? Would you have ended the story differently if you were the author?). Children are treated as authors and storytellers and researchers. To use this with science content means adding the role of scientist, that is, observer, former of hypotheses, information organizer, evaluator, and conclusion maker.

In planning lessons that combine the goals of both language arts and science, the model of engage, explore, explain, elaborate, and evaluate is an effective tool. It provides teachers with a model that supports what current research (Tompkins, 1997) and teacher-reported practices say must go on in the classroom for learning to take place ("Class acts," 1994, Willis, 1997).

In early 1994, the Department of Education invited two hundred outstanding teachers to Washington to get their views on education reform. The *New York Times* asked several of those voted Teacher of the Year in their respective states to write about what they do in the classroom. The following quote by Vicki Matthews Burwell, Teacher of the Year from Idaho, clearly supports the philosophy that students need to be investigators rather than passive learners and that teachers need to be facilitators rather than dispensers of information:

> We fell through our day like Alice in Wonderland, soaking up ideas, experimenting with and stretching our talents. We were civil engineers, archeologists, detectives, paleontologists, art critics, computer nerds, teachers and community planners. We used technology, bright construction paper, dog-eared books, parents. We used our imaginations, our background knowledge and our intuition. We went home exhausted and satisfied. Tomorrow we'll be back for print making and teamwork in long division. And Corey says he has a few card tricks to show us. Steven Spielberg never had it so good. ("Class acts," 1994, p. F19)

SCIENCE RESOURCE BOOKS FOR INQUIRY PROJECT

Aliki (1976). *Corn is maize: The gift of the Indians*. New York: HarperCollins.
Burns, M. (1978). *Good for me, all about food in 32 bites*. Boston: Little, Brown.
Carona, P. B. (1975). *Chemistry and cooking*. Englewood Cliffs, NJ: Prentice-Hall.
Christopher, J. (1956). *No blade of grass*. New York: Avon Books.
Dineen, J. (1991). *Chocolate*. Minneapolis: Carolrhoda Books.
Gerson, M. (1995). *People of corn, a Mayan story*. Boston: Little, Brown.
Gross, R. B. (1990). *What's on my plate*? New York: Macmillan.
Hausher, R. (1994). *What food is this*? New York: Scholastic.
Hays, W., and Hays, V. (1973). *Foods the Indians gave us*. New York: Ives Washburn.
Hyde, M., & Forsyth, E. H. (1975). *What have you been eating? Do you really know*? New York: McGraw-Hill.

Jones, H. (1976). *How to eat your ABC's, a book about vitamins.* New York: Four Winds Press.

Manushkin, F. (1990). *Latkes and applesauce.* New York: Scholastic.

Martell, H. M. (1995). *Food and feasts with the Vikings.* New York: New Discovery Books.

Meyer, C. (1974). *Milk, butter, and cheese: The story of dairy products.* New York: William Morrow.

Patent, D. H. (1991). *Where food comes from.* New York: Holiday House.

Rodanas, K. (1991). *Dragonfly's tale.* New York: Clarion Books.

Smith, D. (1993). *The food cycle.* New York: Thomson Learning.

Storms, L., (Ed.) (1985). *Cooking the Vietnamese way.* Minneapolis, MN: Lerner.

REFERENCES

"American fat cat" has new meaning. (1997). Reuters Limited, CNN Interactive. [On-line]. xx. Available: http://www.cnn.com/HEALTH/9703/06/health.fat.reu/index/html.

Bellerson, K. J. (1991). *The complete and up-to-date fat book.* Garden City Park, NY: Avery.

Biological Sciences Curriculum Study. (1993). *Developing biological literacy: A guide to developing secondary and post-secondary biology curricula.* Colorado Springs, CO: BSCS.

Blume, J. (1970). *Are you there God? It's me, Margaret.* New York: Bantam.

Blume, J. (1974). *Blubber.* Scarsdale, NY: Bradbury.

Checkley, K. (1997). International math and science study calls for depth, not breadth. *Education Update, 39*(1), 1, 3, 8.

Children's Nutrition Research Center—Research Overview. (1997). Available: http://www .bcm.tmc.edu/cnrc/cnrc-research.html

Class acts. (1994, February 12). *The New York Times,* F13, F19.

Clinton pushes standard testing. (1997, March 6). *The Ann Arbor News,* A1, A13.

Fatty food's damage begins in childhood. (1997, January 28). *The Ann Arbor News,* A1.

Fenton, C., & Kitchen, H. (1971). *Plants we live on.* New York: Harper Library.

Gerson, M. (1995). *People of corn, a Mayan story.* Boston: Little, Brown.

Health: Choosing wellness. (1992). Englewood Cliffs, NJ: Prentice Hall.

Martell, H. M. (1995). *Food and feasts with the Vikings.* New York: New York Discovery Books.

McTighe, J. (1997). What happens between assessments? *Educational Leadership, 54*(4), 6–12.

Mitgutsch, A. (1981). *From cacao bean to chocolate.* Minneapolis: Carolrhoda.

Pearce, M. (Ed.). (1991). *A big science teacher's guide: Plants we eat.* New York: Scholastic.

Piscatella, J. (1987). *Choices for a healthy heart.* New York: Workman.

Santa, C., Havens, L., & Harrison S. (1996). Teaching secondary science through reading, writing and problem solving. In Lapp, D., Flood, J., & Farnan, N. (Eds.), *Content Area Reading and Learning,* pp. 165–179. Boston: Allyn & Bacon.

Tompkins, G. (1997). *Literacy for the 21st century.* Upper Saddle River, NJ: Prentice-Hall.

Wiggins, G. (1992). Creating tests worth taking. *Educational Leadership, 49*(8), 26–33.

Willis, S. (1997). Field studies-learning thrives beyond the classroom. *Curriculum Update,* Winter 1997, 1–2, 4–8.

Zorfass, J., & Copel, H. (1995). The I-search: Guiding students toward relevant research. *Educational Leadership, 53*(1), 48–51.

26 Williamsville

An Integrated Language Experience Approach to Math

PATTY TARRANT

Math/Science Teacher, A. C. Williams Elementary School, Commerce, TX

When educators engage students in meaningful communication using the everyday language of words, mathematical symbols, and body language, this communication serves as a means to an end. Using language and expending effort is how we accomplish tasks, achieve goals, and develop relationships in the real world. With meaningful communication about math as my objective, I developed a simulation to use while teaching fifth-grade mathematics that I call Williamsville. I called our community Williamsville because the name of our school is A. C. Williams, and I felt this name would give the students a sense of ownership. I was right; they immediately adopted Williamsville as their own town and spoke of it as if it really existed.

Williamsville is composed of six centers that employ citizens. Each center in Williamsville has specific purposes, tasks, and employees. Although the teacher and citizens can adjust and modify the centers based on the curriculum, I found that a post office, city hall, newspaper, library, bank, and museum were good initial centers.

Getting Started

To begin the Williamsville simulation, two major components had to be in place. First, each student had to become a citizen that acquired and spent money. Second, the community needed an overall budget for the six centers.

Becoming Citizens

Students were initially identified by their social security numbers. Those who had not yet memorized this important row of digits did so and were required to use this number to log into computer classes. To establish themselves as citizens, they filled out an application for a bank account. This included their full names, actual addresses, telephone numbers, social security numbers, and other pertinent personal information. Next they had to fill out a credit history. We invented debts by giving each citizen balances for three credit cards. Again they were required to fill out a great deal of personal information to get the feel for paperwork firsthand. We also created collateral for each citizen, such as real estate, stocks, or other financial holdings that were not liquid so they could obtain loans for cars and houses.

After citizens were assigned jobs for the coming week and learned their monthly salary, they were required to buy a car and a house. They were advised as to the amount they could borrow based on what they earned per year and made their purchases accordingly. The papers they filled out for their bank accounts and loans were filed in the bank to be updated as needed.

The Community Budget

Our first project was making a budget for the community. Citizens were asked to create a community budget as a group within their centers, realizing that the maximum they could spend for all six centers was one million dollars. They had to decide how much each center needed for supplies, rent, utilities, salaries, and which centers needed the most money. At this point they began to realize just how quickly one million dollars can be spent. Each group presented their budgets, we discussed them, and we came to a consensus on the community budget.

The Centers of Williamsville

This section describes each center, its purpose, and its pertinent position.

The Post Office

Williamsville has a post office as its center of communication, with a postmaster and three mail carriers as employees. The post office is responsible for selling envelopes and postage, weighing and assessing postage for packages, and sorting and delivering the mail within and outside of the community. The employees start the year making posters that advertise the costs of various items. They routinely deliver mail that citizens generate, such as the bills and payments that are mailed in stamped envelopes each month, and they return graded papers from the teacher, which is a time-saving classroom management aid. Other activities of this center include creating stamps to commemorate holidays or special events within the classroom, developing lists and directories for original zip codes for different rooms within the school, calculating mileage between cities to determine special postage rates, and paying postal workers' salaries.

The City Hall

City hall has two purposes—to manage utilities and to administer justice. Jobs include a mayor, justice of the peace, city secretary, and utilities secretary. City hall calculates utility bills, mails them, and collects fees from each citizen on a monthly basis. Each citizen pays water, gas, and electricity bills, so a form for each type of bill is created and employees use calculators to figure a "units used" amount as well as a charge for each unit. Records are extremely important here because bills each month depend on present and previous readings to determine the units used. For example, on the utilities form there is a box for the previous readings of last month and the present readings of the current month. By subtracting these two amounts they find a units used amount. By multiplying this amount by a designated price per unit, the monthly bill is calculated. The employees must become organized and efficient record keepers, or the employees who are in that center next month are not able to accurately assess the billing amounts. Envelopes are addressed to each citizen, and stamps are purchased at the post office. Bills are mailed to and paid by each citizen the first week of each month for the previous month.

Another responsibility of city hall is related to the justice system and behavior management. The justice of the peace is responsible for fining students for irresponsible and/or reckless behavior during the Williamsville sessions. Fines are paid out of their bank accounts, which makes a more significant impression than missing recess or lowering a citizenship grade. The justice of the peace justifies his or her accusations in writing and the people involved have to appear before the mayor, who assesses the amount of the fine or other punishment. As the teacher, I function as the supreme court if any child feels his or her punishment is unjust. I have the final say, but I try to support the authority figure whenever possible.

The budget of the city hall is much larger than the other centers because of the demands made on the management of a community. For example, this center has amounts allotted for street repairs, the volunteer fire department, the emergency medical transport (EMT) service, and even gas for the police car. All citizens enjoy taking their turn working in city hall because of the feeling of being in charge.

The Newspaper

Our community has a weekly newspaper called the *Williamsville Warrior*. Employees use the computer to draft articles, format each issue, add clip art, edit, and refine the weekly paper. A typical issue includes a summary of what we are covering in all areas of study, a list of super citizens, special upcoming events, and information about extracurricular activities, such as the University Interscholastic League (UIL). A calendar is also included so parents are aware of when projects are due, imminent field trips, supplies needed for special assignments, and any other event that is tied to a specific date. It is printed on the class printer and copied on the school copy machine.

Newspaper employees use math concepts to measure the length of articles, resize and scale clip art, and calculate the use of paper for each edition. They also keep up with the volume and edition number, dates, time lapses, and budget requirements, which increase with advertising from businesses in the community. This center is another favorite of the students.

The Library

Items in the Williamsville Public Library are arranged according to the Dewey Decimal System, just like the school library, so that students have extra exposure to using a numerical organization system. Citizens borrow and return books on a regular basis, so librarians are responsible for checking out books, reshelving them, assessing fines for late books, keeping track of overdue books, and making recommendations for purchasing. The employees create their own system of check-in and check-out and make sure citizens are held accountable for the books they borrow. The librarians also give book reviews, so citizens are aware of popular and new books that are available.

The Bank

The First National Bank is the busiest center in Williamsville. Bank employees are responsible for depositing weekly payroll checks, canceling the checks received from each citizen, and balancing ledgers so that accounts are kept current and accurate. They account for house and car loans, loan payments, credit card purchases, credit card payments, and credit card balances. At the end of each month, bank statements are compiled and citizens receive copies of their checks as well as statements of current balances. This is a busy place that always has plenty of work for employees. Calculators are used so that accuracy is at its peak.

Bankers are also responsible for foreclosing on properties that are in arrears. Any citizen that goes two months without making a payment is foreclosed. Citizens must have collateral before they are allowed to borrow money for houses or cars. At the beginning of the year this collateral is established and can be used as needed until it is gone.

The Museum

The Science Place is a museum in which employees create research presentations in the format of an experiment to entertain and inform the community. They have materials for research related to the science curriculum, and the museum staff presents their research to the citizens each Friday. The content must be relevant to the course of study going on at the time, but the methods and delivery are left up to the ingenuity of the employees involved. Employees in the Science Place include a research leader, a presentation leader, a materials leader, and a design leader, who are responsible for these four facets of their production.

The Big Picture

Williamsville is an ongoing simulation that I flexibly schedule as it relates to billing and payment cycles. One week I may schedule Williamsville for ninety minutes every morning. Other weeks we may do it two to three times or not at all. To plan and schedule one must consider community projects, assessment, and the challenges that arise when implementing a new approach.

Community Projects

Throughout the year there are community projects, such as the initial budgeting, that all students are required to complete. For example, one project was related to budgeting for holiday gifts. Before Christmas each person made a wish list of gifts they wanted to buy for their families. We used catalogs to figure out the purchase price of items so everyone could create their own budget while keeping their account balances in mind. Then we revised our lists noting the item, who it was for, and the price. We figured sales tax, wrote checks, and mailed our orders. The checks were processed by the bank and accounts were charged. During this activity the cost of items was frequently discussed, and individuals often remarked about how they would not ask for so much at Christmas in the future.

Another community project is paying taxes and insurance. We study percentages and how to calculate them, and then we do these calculations on the values of our houses and cars. Each citizen pays their yearly taxes from their bank accounts. Next comes the car insurance payment. An insurance agent comes in and figures the amount of insurance for each car. Citizens fill out application forms and are required to pay their insurance. If they cannot afford to pay, they have to park their cars until the money is earned.

Assessment

The Williamsville project is assessed with a portfolio at the end of the year. Students keep files of their account balances, their bill receipts each month, and reflections on what they are learning from each experience. They often comment on the relevance and importance of learning how real life works and how this program is beneficial to them as math students.

Facing the Inevitable

No matter what kind of program an instructor implements, there are times when one realizes it should have been done differently. I have had problems with Williamsville and am trying to keep notes and records to avoid them in the future. I realize how carefully I must first consider the personality of the class when planning the timing and initial center assignments. Some students typically need more structure than I had initially prepared for in some of the centers. For example, children who constantly need redirection or detailed instructions may not find Williamsville an enjoyable way to learn. Frustration, boredom, and/or misbehavior result when they wait to be told what to do next. I realize I'll have to more thoroughly assess student maturity, more carefully plan center assignments, be ready with a variety of thought-provoking questions, and provide options to help students figure out what is possible so that they can be more creative. Although this program works well with gifted and talented students, in no way should it be limited to them. I have found that many average, slightly below average, and slightly above average students soar to heights of creativity and excellence that I didn't think were possible.

A problem with some centers is that there is not a constant flow of activity. Employees of the post office, library, and museum often find themselves searching for meaningful activities to fill the ninety-minute period devoted to their jobs. Task sheets are distributed at the beginning of each session listing what each center is expected to complete. Although task sheets are changed for each session and regularly have challenging and fun activities, it has been difficult to devise relevant activities for these centers. After employees in these centers get their basic jobs done, they find themselves doing things that don't relate to their center. Our plan is to visit with real-world employees and take field trips so that we can gain more insight into these jobs and create tasks that truly reflect the requirements of that job.

A Personal Perspective

Prior to implementing Williamsville, I found myself refereeing arguments, struggling to get late assignments in, dreading grading, and constantly asking myself why I was not enjoying my job. I came to the conclusion that maybe it was time for a change. I believe I am a good teacher, but just being a good teacher was not always helping my students have good learning experiences in the classroom. I was not the mentor, guide, or coach I wanted to be. I was the dictator, the person who made students do it my way instead of helping them find their own best way. Williamsville has been my wake-up call. My students ask for responsibilities, they want to work, and they want to be busy. For the most part, I don't have to find things for them to do—they create their own assignments. I look forward to seeing what they will come up with each session. I don't dread arguments or disagreements because most of them are related to the requirements of a job and, just as in real life, students want to discuss and have some control over decisions that affect them. I find myself giving them more and more control each session.

In the big educational picture we still learn how to do long division, common denominators, cross multiplication, and how to use the metric system. Now each aspect of the math curriculum has a purpose, and I can give students real reasons why we need to learn about abstract mathematical concepts instead of just telling them it is on the test. Williamsville not only develops students' appreciation for the financial struggles their families face, it also gives them a purpose for their day, improves their attitudes toward school, toward me, toward each other, and toward the language of mathematics.

27 Collecting, Writing, and Telling Family Folklore Stories

ANNETTE NANCY TAYLOR
Teacher, Saint Michael School (Columbus, OH)

OLGA G. NELSON
Associate Professor, Eastern Michigan University

Storytelling was the focus and framework for a family history project in a fourth-grade classroom. By exploring existing children's literature, personal experience stories, and already published family folklore scrapbooks, children became immersed in an extensive project that spanned seven weeks. They interviewed relatives, transcribed family stories, published family heirlooms, and told their stories to classmates and other classes in the school. Children were excited and eager to interview relatives and to share their experiences with classmates. As action researchers and authors of family reminiscences, they were alert to the value and importance of all the activities involved with the project. Fridays were devoted to working on the project that integrated social studies (family life and cultural heritage), reading, writing, and storytelling.

Storytelling as a Means to Lift Sense of Story

In order to activate the children's concepts about stories and story components, the class first reviewed parts of a story. Since the class had written original stories and presented puppet plays earlier in the school year, the students had no diffi-

[From "Collecting, Writing, and Telling Family Folklore Stories," by Nancy Taylor and Olga G. Nelson, 1990, *Journal of Language Experience, 10*(2), pp. 16–20. Copyright 1990 by the Language Experience Special Interest Group. Reprinted with permission.]

culty with this task. Then Mrs. Taylor, the teacher, told a story, she entitled "Robin for a Day." Students discussed that story in relation to the six story parts they had established: (1) setting, (2) mood, (3) character's physical and emotional trait, (4) character's problem, (5) sequence of events, and (6) closing. This activity prepared them for thinking and talking about the "Family Folklore Scrapbook" project that entailed interviewing relatives and writing their own family stories.

Children's Literature as a Way to Generate Story Ideas

Mrs. Taylor brought in her own illustrated family scrapbook and other trade books and journals (Brooke, 1986; Smithsonian Institute, 1982; Weitzman, 1975) to share with the class. As specific pictures were shown that illustrated some family occasion or event, such as a birthday, holiday, vacation, birth, or wedding, students volunteered similar recollections from their own families. Children were encouraged to talk freely about the pictures and to suggest similarities with their own families. Many picture books featured younger characters (Dembar, 1986; Flournoy, 1952; Hazer, 1979; Langner, 1979; Miles, 1971; Rylant, 1985; Williams, 1982; Yoder, 1979), and this prompted students to talk about their own childhood memories. Group discussions gave students opportunities to talk about and listen to ideas that could be incorporated into their own stories.

Storytelling as a Way to Generate Personal Incidents

On the second Friday, Mrs. Taylor told the story *When I Was Young in the Mountains* (Rylant, 1982). The class talked enthusiastically about how interesting it was to hear stories about their parents' childhoods. They also shared incidents that had happened in their own families. Students discussed the possibility that some of these incidents could become stories to include in their family albums. Talking about ways to save these family stories followed. Students became excited at the prospect of publishing and telling their own family stories. They decided that these family stories might make perfect gifts for a parent, grandparent, uncle, or aunt. However, the importance of preserving family history was emphasized. Everyone agreed that these literary heirlooms could be shared with others but would eventually be returned so students could save them for their own children.

Writing Activities to Generate Story Ideas

In order to generate ideas for students to explore, Mrs. Taylor handed out a list of topics to start the discussion. Topics included such things as a most embarrassing moment, funniest thing that ever happened, most unforgettable character, and so on. These ideas fostered more discussion among students and generated even more topics for students to investigate and talk about with their relatives. The brainstorming activities served to give students ideas to promote conversations among themselves first and then with adult family members. In addition, Mrs. Taylor shared personal stories from her own family to stimulate students' thinking about different topics that might be used for their own stories. After sharing some of the traditions in their own families, students compared the similarities and differences among their traditions. For example, most students said they received gifts for Christmas; however, some opened presents on Christmas Eve and others opened gifts on Christmas morning. From these activities and discussions, students learned how to start conversations, take notes, and finally how to put their notes together to write a story.

Collecting Personal Family Stories

At this point, the children were very excited to go out and get their stories and the class talked about relatives they might interview. Since Thanksgiving was approaching and children would have many opportunities to see and speak with relatives, the class discussed how they would conduct the interviews. The children talked about the importance of explaining the project to family members, how to take notes, and how to determine the sequence of events for their family stories.

The Writing Process

After conducting the interviews, the children worked on their rough drafts, conferenced with the teacher, and revised their final copies for three weeks. They put their books together and designed quilt-patterned covers made from wallpaper samples. The children also planned and drew illustrations to go along with their stories. Books were subsequently displayed in the classroom so students could enjoy reading each other's final Family Folklore Scrapbook (see Figures 27.1 and 27.2).

The Storytelling Process

During the sixth week of the experience, the class explored the storytelling process to prepare for their storytelling presentations. Tips on how to prepare, learn, and present their stories were brainstormed, discussed, and recorded on chart paper. In order to help students concentrate on the meaning of their stories and to downplay mechanical memorization, students brainstormed, for example, all the words they could think of to describe one of their special memories and created cluster diagrams with the words (see Figure 27.3). This sorting and categorizing helped them realize that many words, not just one, can provide visual pictures for listeners.

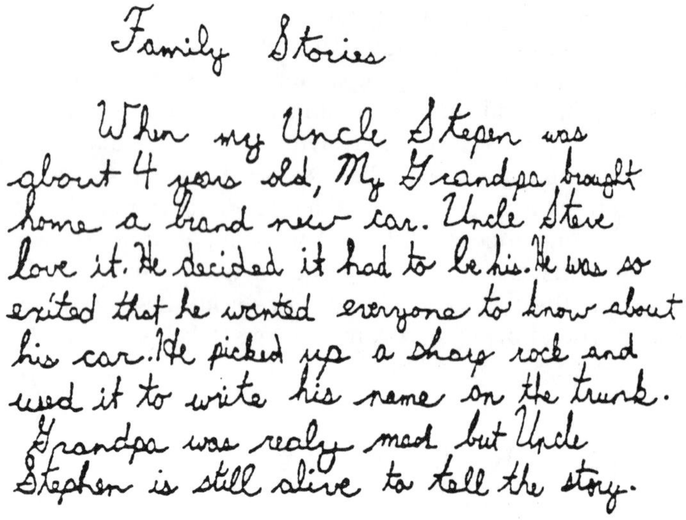

Family Stories

When my Uncle Stepen was about 4 years old, My Grandpa brought home a brand new car. Uncle Steve love it. He decided it had to be his. He was so exited that he wanted everyone to know about his car. He picked up a sharp rock and used it to write his name on the trunk. Grandpa was realy mad but Uncle Stephen is still alive to tell the story.

FIGURE 27.1   First Example of One Student's Family Story

In this way, students focused on story sense and not memorization. Students were encouraged to practice telling their stories aloud at least four or five times. They were permitted to write down key transitional sentences and a few key words if they felt they needed to.

To help students prepare for their final presentations, Mrs. Taylor modeled several poor storytelling techniques and styles that detracted from the telling. Students were quick to point out how these interfered with presentations. Students

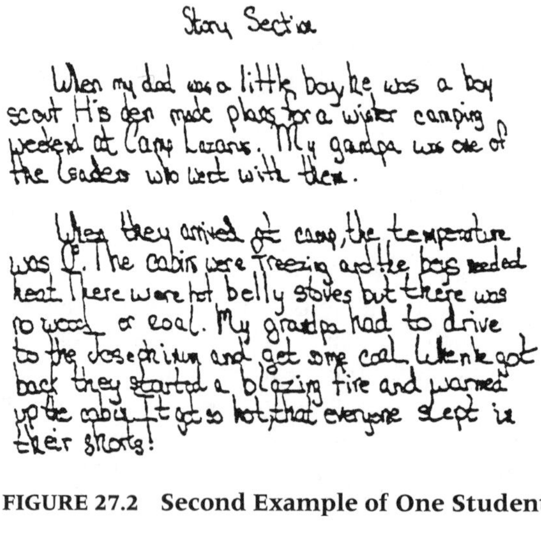

Story Section

When my dad was a little boy he was a boy scout His den made plans for a winter camping weekend at Camp Lazarus. My grandpa was one of the leaders who went with them.

When they arrived at camp, the temperature was 0. The cabins were freezing and the boys needed heat. There were pot belly stoves but there was no wood or coal. My grandpa had to drive to the Josephinum and get some coal. When he got back they started a blazing fire and warmed up the cabin It got so hot that everyone slept in their shorts!

FIGURE 27.2   Second Example of One Student's Family Story

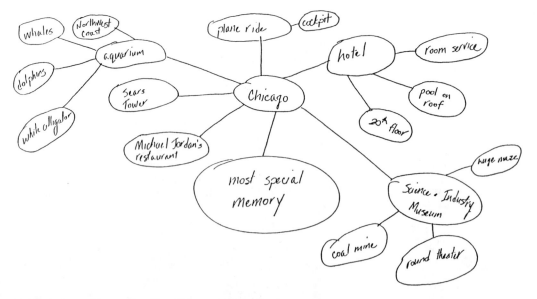

FIGURE 27.3   Example of a Cluster Diagram

then discussed key points of a presentation that make for a polished performance and generated a list of criteria: reasonable volume and rate, prepared opening and closing sentences, a sequence of events that was easy to follow, and good character development.

The Storytelling Experience

With much encouragement, support, and praise from Mrs. Taylor and each other, students were finally ready to tell their stories. Week seven found the students nervous but eager and excited. Students critiqued each other's stories, giving specific praise for each person's story and recommendations for making their next effort even better. Nobody was prouder than the students themselves. All of their work was well worth the effort. The following week, seventeen intrepid fourth graders trooped up to the fifth-, seventh-, and eighth-grade classes to tell their stories to other students.

What did the students learn through this project? They discovered that learning can be fun and interesting in a rich social environment that promotes individual and group interaction. Capitalizing on children's family and cultural heritage by collecting, researching, writing, and telling family folklore stories made the experience meaningful and relevant for children. History became a living, breathing event for these children, and the experiences they shared will long be remembered.

REFERENCES

Brooke, P. (1986). Exploring family folklore. *Instructor, 96,* 114–118.

Dembar, J. (1986). *Nathan's Hanukkah bargain.* Rockville, MD: Ken Ben Copies.

Flournoy, V. (1952). *The patchwork quilt.* New York: Dial.

Hazer, B. S. (1979). *Tight times.* New York: Viking.

Langner, N. (1979). *Freddy my grandfather.* New York: Four Winds Press.

Miles, M. (1971). *Annie and the old one.* Boston: Little, Brown.

Rylant, C. (1982). *When I was young in the mountains.* New York: Dutton.

Rylant, C. (1985). *The relatives came.* New York: Bradbury Press.

Smithsonian Institute. (1982). *A celebration of America family folklore.* New York: Pantheon Books.

Weitzman, D. (1975). *My backyard history book.* Boston: Little, Brown.

Williams, V. (1982). *A chair for my mother.* New York: Greenwillow.

Yoder, M. (1979). *Storytime with grandma.* Harrisburg, VA: Christian Light.

28 Making History Memorable

CAROLYN JOHNS
Teacher, Klein (TX) Independent School District

Elementary classrooms are filled with children eager to learn, but frequently this enthusiasm fades as they become overwhelmed by the nature and amount of requirements as well as materials they have to read. As a fifth-grade teacher, I often observe this frustration on their faces. The underlying question, therefore, may be: As teachers, do we help students brainstorm, predict, and rehearse before tackling expository text or do we merely make assignments and expect students to read and remember for tests?

Comprehension is an interaction between what the author has written and the reader's own background experiences. When educators neglect this and inadvertently foster students who memorize history facts for a day, view science experiments as entertainment, and become "polite readers" (Newkirk, 1982), the students find little meaning or few relationships to their real lives. The New Jersey Writing Institute I attended carried the theme, "If I can think it, I can say it; if I can say it, I can write it; if I can write it, I can read it; and if I can read it, I can share it." This theme can be applied productively across the curriculum.

The subject area I will focus on is history because it is here that I see the most frustration among fifth-grade students. Historical facts are often abstract and easily forgotten unless students can relate new information to something they already know. Through literature and writing, teachers can make learning history a memorable experience for students.

Employing Children's Literature to Make History Memorable

The Upstairs Room (Reiss, 1972) and its sequel, *The Journey Back* (Reiss, 1976), are examples of historical fiction I find useful. These books provide rich descriptions

[From "Making History Memorable," by Carolyn Johns, 1989, *Journal of Language Experience, 10*(1), pp. 16–18. Copyright 1990 by the Language Experience Special Interest Group. Reprinted and revised with permission.]

of people, events, and situations so that readers can get a sense of the times and imagine the realities associated with the Nazi regime. The personal tribulations the Jewish people endured are exemplified as two girls go into hiding. The circumstances the girls encounter as they strive to stay alive help students comprehend historical facts, events, and issues associated with this era. As readers become immersed in the girls' flight and plight, they become emotionally involved with them and feel compassion because they have been denied the freedom to engage in the fun and playful activities identified with young people of that age.

Another book to aid in understanding the effects of war is *Sadako and the Thousand Paper Cranes* (Coerr, 1977). By reading Sadako's story, students get a sense of the emotional upheaval and tragic events that followed the dropping of the atomic bomb on Hiroshima. Children easily share and express their empathy for her and the thousands of Japanese children who helped support and encourage Sadako's valiant struggle to survive the leukemia she was infected with as a result of the radioactive fallout. The books described here and others can help students develop a perspective on war. The teacher can encourage students to ask questions, express feelings in writing, and share ideas orally. History begins to come alive!

Using fictional books such as *The Indian in the Cupboard* (Banks, 1980), *The Castle in the Attic* (Winthrop, 1986), and *Island of the Blue Dolphins* (O'Dell, 1960) provides a sense of place and time. Rather than providing readers with boring historical facts, these books can take the reader on vicarious adventures to far-off places he or she might not otherwise visit or experience. Readers' imaginations are stirred and different perspectives are obtained as they read about characters and their lives.

Employing Journal Writing to Enhance Understanding of Historical Events

Journal writing and journal reading are another idea for making history memorable. The diaries and journals of the explorers enhance understanding of "days gone by" and provide information for students to investigate, examine, and question. Explorers recorded what happened as well as their feelings, happenings, and ideas just as students do in their own journals. Journal writing encourages students to observe and experience things around them that can be associated with the historical information in their textbooks. They can add more information or write reactions in their journals that help them to envision historical events. The name Anne Frank takes on new meaning as students compare her diary notations during the war with the recently discovered letters she wrote to a pen pal in Iowa before the war (Anne Frank's pre-diary, 1988, p. 16.). Comparisons like these help children understand how political decisions are made, how these decisions influence our lives, and how freedom is something to be cherished.

Creating Original Scripts for Reader's Theater Presentations Based on Historical Fiction Books

Using reader's theater activities with historical fiction books is beneficial because they provide a focus for the event that is being studied. Children begin by discussing their favorite chapters in small groups. After a brainstorming session, they write their own versions of episodes from the book. These scripts can then be performed as a reader's theater before an audience. Students not only enjoy history, they gain greater insight into our historical past through the recreation and enactment of the historical event.

Enlivening History by Combining Discovery and Writing Projects

Discovery projects can serve as culminating activities. For example, following reading about the westward movement and studying expository texts associated with frontiersmen, the gold rush, and wagon trains, my students are invited to design a ranch. Descriptions of frontier life, as in Laura Ingalls Wilder's books, are particularly helpful for understanding the full context of life at an earlier time. Groups of four or five students become a family on a ranch. It is suggested that each family choose a name for their ranch, design a brand, and write a fictional history of their ranch's discovery. Next, they write about how their ranch has changed from its beginning to the present day, create lyrics for a song that symbolizes the ranch, and finally, construct a ranch mascot with a full description as to why it was chosen. The students enjoy brainstorming, expressing their individual ideas, and working as a family as they investigate many resources from literature and textbooks, as well as share their personal experience stories. As a culminating activity, the families plan and present information about their ranch before an audience. Sometimes audiences are invited to vote for their favorite ranch. Enthusiasm runs high throughout the project and best of all, everyone learns a lot about the Expansion Period of the United States.

Adapting Language Experience Activities to Other Content Areas

This chapter described how reading and writing connections were used to help students vicariously experience history as well as develop their own inquiry projects so that history could become more personal and memorable. This same approach can be used in all subject areas. Content areas may differ, but the conceptual processes are basically the same. Once classroom teachers, such as myself, realize that all areas of learning are related and that students need to be active participants, then our teaching will be more innovative and our students will be more informed and motivated to discover the world around them while learning more about themselves. Most important, students and teachers will not be subjected to a boring "read the text and answer the questions" curriculum.

REFERENCES

Anne Frank's pre-diary Iowa pen pal releases historic letters for auction. (1988, July 22). *New York Times News Service*, p. 16.

Banks, L. R. (1980). *The Indian in the cupboard*. New York: Doubleday.

Coerr, E. (1977). *Sadako and the thousand paper cranes*. New York: Putnam.

Newkirk, T. (1982). Young writers as critical readers. *Language Arts, 59*, 550–554.

O'Dell, S. (1960). *Island of the blue dolphins*. Boston: Houghton Mifflin.

Reiss, J. (1972). *The upstairs room*. New York: Crowell.

Reiss, J. (1976). *The journey back*. New York: Crowell.

Winthrop, E. (1986). *The castle in the attic*. New York: Bantam.

29 LEA

A Framework for Assessing Students' Higher-Level Thinking Skills

MARY ELIZABETH KLINE
Teacher, Plain Center Elementary School (OH)

The basic premise of the Language Experience Approach (LEA) is to integrate reading instruction with language arts activities and to build on students' personal experiences and knowledge. Assessment of prereaders and emergent readers needs to be consistent with their developmental level and knowledge of the world around them. Middle-grade students, however, face considerably more complicated and challenging communication and assessment tasks because expectations are higher because of the age, maturity, and developmental level of the students.

No longer limited by an egocentric view of the world, middle-grade students are challenged to become critical thinkers and comprehend information in various sophisticated forms. Exposure to literature, trade books, content area texts, and other media sources allows students to vicariously experience global events that span centuries. Students, however, need to read and listen critically to the interpretations and opinions of others so that they can determine how these various perspectives fit with their own knowledge and beliefs.

Students learn best in an integrated curriculum with content that is relevant to their own lives (Vacca, Vacca, & Gove, 1987), with activities that are meaningful, and with materials that are authentic, natural, and functional (Goodman, 1989). An appropriate way to design instruction then is to connect the known to the unknown when incorporating new knowledge about language and literacy and to ensure that reading and writing activities are purposeful and meaningful as well as enjoyable (Vacca & Vacca, 1989).

The challenge for teachers then is to integrate all of these tenets and still effectively explore personal, local, and world issues; meet state and district proficiency mandates and regulations; and maintain a child-centered curriculum. LEA provides a framework to help students assimilate difficult concepts and ideas in thoughtful ways that are relevant, informative, and interesting. Through activities that build on students' prior knowledge, students are able to make connections with unfamiliar concepts and ideas. At the same time, teachers can easily integrate communication skills and assess students' performance and growth.

Assessing Higher-Level Thinking Skills in the Context of Social Studies

My goal is to move students to more sophisticated, mature language skills. These language skills involve critical thinking; making inferences; differentiating fact from opinion; comparing and contrasting accounts from various sources; recalling information from one time period or situation and applying it to new situations; and locating, evaluating, and applying researched information to their personal lives. In order to have students become aware of their own biases and consider the perspectives of others, I use writing, reading, and discussions to encourage group interaction and respect.

Our social studies textbook on the American colonization period provided the perfect opportunity to meet my overall goals and explore prejudice within a specific context. I like to have students in my fifth-grade classroom investigate the concept of prejudice as we study historical times and events. I usually start by having students talk about what they already know about prejudice, generate a list of things they would like to change as a result of what they learn from reading historical accounts, and provide ideas on how they could change future generations' perceptions and prejudices. As students are engaged in activities, I make observations and write anecdotal notes.

Comparing and Contrasting Historical Accounts and Perspectives

In explaining the reasons for slavery and the roles of the slaves and the masters of the plantations, our social studies textbook presents an overly simplified view. In fact, many students disagreed with the authors' perspectives and questioned the text's accuracy. Through discussion it soon became apparent that students had a different view based on what they had learned in previous classes. To provide students with more background knowledge, historical accounts, perspectives on slavery, and information on that period in history, as a class we read *Slave Dancer* (Fox, 1991). This historical fiction book is a story of a young cabin boy's experiences on the triangular trade route that brought slaves to the colonies.

It is important to understand that LEA is a strategy that allows ongoing evaluation as part of the learning and teaching process. For me, evaluation is an integral

2-1-95   Mari   Lit. Discuss Group
                Slave Dancer - Marian Anderson

"Jessie had some feeling for the slaves in the hold
but he didn't do anything about it. At least Eleanor
Roosevelt had the guts to resign from the Daughters
of the American Revolution, when they wouldn't let
Marian sing in Washington D.C."

2-1-95   Joe   Lit. Discuss Group

"What do you expect—that was in 1939—a hundred
years later—of course you would see less prejudice."

2-1-95   Jen   Lit. Discuss Group

"Not necessarily! Captain Cawthorne was like Ray
who killed Martin Luther King Jr.— he was as
heartless and cruel at the end of the story as the
beginning. At least Jessie changed. He went from
staring at blacks on the streets of New Orleans to
realizing they were people just like him."

2-1-95   Meagan   *Slave Dancer* p. 43

Slow rate—little expression
significant miscues—initial sounds—ignores punctuation
    —"carried" himself to sleep vs. "cried"
    —"seemed" in agony vs. "screamed"

**FIGURE 29.1   Anecdotal Notes Showing Individual Student's Ability to
Compare and Contrast Accounts of *Slave Dancer* and a Biography**

part of my curriculum and not a separate entity. To assess students I made individual anecdotal notes that focused on each student's fluency, rate, and expression when students read orally. During group discussions, I wrote anecdotal notes on each student's ability to compare and contrast accounts from *Slave Dancer* with the biographies they were each reading and with the textbook (see Figure 29.1). Students used Venn Diagrams to organize and sort details between the three sources.

Debating the Issues and Implications
Concerning Prejudice

At the same time the class was reading *Slave Dancer*, students selected another book for independent reading that provided more information and accounts of prejudice, sometimes in contemporary contexts, such as *Meet Addy* (Porter, 1993) and *Nettie's Trip South* (Turner, 1987). Students wrote personal reactions to these books in their learning logs and cited incidents from their readings during literature discussion groups.

The purpose of the literature discussion groups was to have students understand the roots of prejudice, learn new vocabulary to help them express their thoughts clearly and intelligently, and discover the complicated and moral issues and implications underlying prejudice. Each day teams of five or six students each began with an essential question to discuss. For example, all groups debated the need for slavery—one group taking the plantation owners' perspective and the other group that of the slaves.

Each day during group discussions I focused on one team. I listened and made notes on content understanding, use of prediction and clarifying strategies, explanations of how literature reflects various periods of time, and the students' ability to extend their understanding into modern-day situations. I also observed their group dynamics and noted cooperative team strategies, such as valuing everyone's ideas and opinions.

Sometimes discussions were formally scored using a rubric designed by Zola (1992) that indicates specific communication skills (see Figure 29.2). Positive points were given for items such as taking a position on a question, making relevant comments, using evidence to support a position, presenting factual information, drawing another person into the discussion, and recognizing irrelevant comments. Negative points were given for not paying attention, distracting others, creating interruptions, making irrelevant comments, monopolizing, and making personal attacks. Opinions were accepted only when accompanied by supporting facts. This was an accurate form of evaluation, not only of content but of the students' critical thinking and communication skills. Students who may have been limited by their ability to communicate through written language successfully discussed, evaluated, and applied key concepts to their own lives and other situations in history.

Other Opportunities to Assess Students' Thinking, Performance, and Growth

As the year progressed, students did research about famous people who had made significant contributions to our nation. Their written and oral reports reflected sophisticated reading and language skills such as gathering and evaluating material related to a topic and condensing that material into a final presentation. Rubrics were designed to reflect the writing process skills that were important in both research and presentation (see Figure 29.3). Before their research began, students brainstormed specifics that would indicate a quality process for this type of project. Both teacher and students worked together until we reached a consensus about the criteria for evaluation. This helped students have ownership of the goals and expectations for their learning, rather than putting the sole responsibility on me to tack on some arbitrary grade at the end of the process.

Points	Positive		Points	Negative	
(2)	Taking a position on a question		(−2)	Not paying attention or distracting others	
	Meagan			*Meagan*	*−2 −2*
	Jen	*2, 2, 2*		*Jen*	
	Joe	*2*		*Joe*	
	Mari	*2*		*Mari*	
(1)	Making a relevant comment		(−2)	Interruption	
	Meagan	*///*		*Meagan*	*−2 −2 −2 −2*
	Jen	*//// ////*		*Jen*	*−2*
	Joe	*//// //// /*		*Joe*	
	Mari	*////*		*Mari*	*−2*

*Actual score sheet contains all categories

Student Totals:

Meagan ____
Jen ____
Joe ____
Mari ____

Individual Discussion Score Sheet

Points	Positive		Points	Negative	
(2)	Taking a position on a question	____	(−2)	Not paying attention	____
(1)	Making relevant comments	____	(−2)	Interruption	____
(2)	Using evidence to support a position or presenting factual information	____	(−1)	Irrelevant comment	____
(1)	Drawing another person into the discussion	____	(−3)	Monopolizing	____
			(−3)	Personal attacks	____
(1)	Asking clarifying question or moving discussion along	____		Total	____
(2)	Making an analogy	____		Grade	____
(2)	Recognizing contradictions	____			
(2)	Recognizing irrelevant comments	____		Name _____ Room _____	

FIGURE 29.2   Master Discussion Score Sheet

Criteria for Biography Project

You will receive your best score if you have completed each of the following sections by the due date specified:

Biography of _____

Date started _____   Midpoint reading check _____   Date completed _____

RESEARCH:

Fact cards including at least three sources and:
- Famous person when young (family, hardships, special circumstances, etc.)   _____
- Interesting events in person's life   _____
- What this person is most famous for   _____
- What impact (important contributions, etc.)   _____
- What impact this person has on our lives today   _____

ROUGH DRAFT ESSAY:

Rough draft:
- Thesis statement
- Paragraphs that include: _____
  - Topic sentence for each main idea in thesis statement   _____
  - Supporting details   _____
  - Closing and transitional sentences   _____
- Closing paragraph that restates main ideas in thesis and draws a conclusion   _____

Revising and editing:
- Changes to clarify meaning   _____
- Editing that corrects grammar and spelling errors   _____
- Evidence that I'm aware of my goals   _____

FINAL DRAFT ESSAY:

- Neat and complete—Claris Works skills evident   _____
- If written—includes picture
- If oral—use of costume or props to enhance presentation   _____
  - See Writer's Express for Oral Report expectations   _____

FIGURE 29.3   Rubric for Research and Writing Process Skills

Assessing Student Writing and Thinking

A unit of study on the author Mildred Taylor introduced students to the classics *Roll of Thunder Hear My Cry* (1976), *Song of the Trees* (1975), *The Gold Cadillac* (1987b), and *The Friendship* (1987a). Students were inquisitive as they searched for truths, reflected on the past, discussed current examples of prejudice, and suggested ideas of how to free future generations from this terrible problem. Throughout the process, I wrote anecdotal notes about students' understanding of vocabulary in context, story analysis, and group sharing following daily reading. Student writing, specifically critiques and summaries, provided opportunities to assess their critical thinking, content, organization, development, rationales for their views, and mechanics. My notes provided rich descriptive information about students over time for assessment of changes in specific areas and overall growth.

Social studies tests were short-answer essays; students had to organize and construct coherent answers and provide details and data to show understanding (see Figure 29.4). Figure 29.4 is an example of some of the test questions. All stu-

---

Short Answer Essay Section:

You will receive your best score if you support all opinions with facts. Credit will be given for organizing your thoughts in the margin before you respond. Be sure to answer in complete paragraphs.

1. Choose two famous black Americans that were discussed in your literature discussion group. Compare their struggles for equality. Be sure to note their significant contributions.

Could be combined – similar ideas

Thurgood Marshall 1954 S.C. judge Separate is not equal

M.L.King Jr 1963 peaceful rights

(Thurgood Marshall and Martin Luther King Jr were black Americans who fought for equality. Both men fought for equal rights and tried to stop injustice.) King didn't believe in violence, so he tried peaceful ways to make changes like sit ins and (marches) Marshall tried to make changes as a Suprem Court Judge. He said that separate was not equal and King tried to prove it. Marshall still worked for this even after King got (killed) Both men worked hard to make our world a better place for blacks everybody. *Maybe* *give example – be specific*

assassinated

2. Why do you think that prejudice against blacks persisted for such a long time in our nation's history? (Be sure to support your opinion with facts from at least two sources.)

Need plantation economy

misunder standings

hate

prej. grows

hard to stop

200 yrs.

Once people are used to doing something a certain way, its hard to change. This is especially true of (bad habits.) In colonial times slave traders made a deal with plantation owners that was too hard to pass up. No one was thinking of blacks as people – just a way to have cheap labor and more profits. They didn't think about their feelings then or many years after. Even when some people wanted blacks to have equal treatment as the constitution guaranteed, it took a lot of killing and fighting to make it happen. Probably because of misunderstandings and hate built on hate! Prejudice is hard to stop – it's like cancer cells – you might want to kill them and be healthy but sometimes they get out of control. It took generations to stop the prejudice. I think that if even one prejudice cell is alive our hole nation is in danger. That's why ever person needs to fight against prejudice! wow! *Well stated!*

Explain your thoughts! *how is prejudice bad?* *its habit?*

You write well

New book! *New thoughts!*

Good! your ideas

Your feeling!

FIGURE 29.4 Examples of Short-Answer Essay Test Questions

dents' answers to the test questions were evaluated using the following criteria, which were shared with students before they studied for the test:

- Support your opinions with facts.
- Organize your thoughts before you write.
- Write complete paragraphs (topic and closing sentences).
- Use correct grammar and spelling.
- Make connections from the past to the present.

Assessing Specific Technical Skills

Spelling banks were composed of new words and specific vocabulary we encountered in social studies and other content areas. Students began to realize how important using specific terms were to communicate their ideas to one another. They discovered that the exact meaning of words is dependent on context and that many word concepts span several curricular areas. For example, students learned that a perspective or point of view could be presented artistically, be very explicitly grounded in historical data, or have a subjective and personal tone.

Assessing Final Projects

At the end of the year, students chose how to present their final projects. Their goal was to express their thoughts about prejudice with a depth of understanding referring to particular details or information they had learned from various sources and activities. Presentation formats included poetry, visual/graphic arts, video productions, short historical fiction stories, letters to the editor, editorials, and personal narratives. In this way, students learned to develop language and creative power, not just reading and writing skills.

Since effectively communicating thoughts and ideas was the major goal of these presentations, it was easy to assess growth in proper use of grammar, spelling, and skill areas. For example, students expanded their vocabularies and learned to effectively express their ideas as they became more proficient writers and risk takers. Not only did students grow in reading and language skills, they also developed a deeper understanding, tolerance, and respect for all people by participating in language experience activities.

Grading and Communicating Students' Progress with Others

I live in a real world with real demands from the state, local school district, and community. My students need to be proficient not only in language arts skills, but in content areas. As a teacher, it is my responsibility to take what I see in the classroom and explain it to a diverse audience. The power of LEA, however, speaks for itself because students who have experience using graphic organizers and opportunities to think critically do extremely well on state proficiency tests.

Our local school district requires traditional report card grades of A, B, C, and N (needs improvement). At the beginning of each nine weeks, students set goals for learning. Their goals might include the following: to more effectively communicate in their group, to choose more challenging spelling words, to read a new genre for the outside reading requirement, and to include more specific or descriptive vocabulary and details in writing. Individual students conference with me about their progress each grading period. At our conferences, it is their responsibility to convince me as to what grade should be placed on their report card. Sources of proof from their portfolio include scored discussion sheets, learning logs, and graphic organizers. The conference and data they present, combined with my anecdotal records, help us mutually determine the grade each student earns.

Student-led parent conferences are held in the fall and spring. Each student meets with their families and teacher to share their work and show their progress. Students' final projects are a major focus at conferences with peers, parents, and the teacher. At the end of the school year, we have a portfolio celebration in which family members are invited to participate. This is a powerful time for students to share their learning with a broader audience. Family members are not only amazed at the volume of content the students know, but at the sophisticated communication skills within their groups.

Conclusion

Language is power! The experience of receiving and expressing ideas in meaningful contexts is a powerful teaching and learning tool. Language—whether written, recorded, or oral—and experiences—whether personal, group, or vicarious—provide a connection to those around us as well as a link with the past and future. Thus, LEA is not just about reading and writing instruction, it is about empowering students to learn, to experience, to reflect, and to share their knowledge and lives with one another. What we communicate, how we communicate, and how we become literate is what teaching and learning are all about.

REFERENCES

Fox, P. (1991). *Slave dancer*. New York: Dell.
Goodman, K. (1989). *The whole language evaluation book*. Portsmouth, NH: Heinemann.
Porter, C. (1993). *Meet Addy*. Middleton, WI: Pleasant Co.
Taylor, M. (1975). *Song of the trees*. New York: Dial Press.
Taylor, M. (1976). *Roll of thunder hear my cry*. New York: Penguin/Puffin.
Taylor, M. (1987a). *The friendship*. New York: Bantam.
Taylor, M. (1987b). *The gold Cadillac*. New York: Dial Books for Young Readers.
Turner, A. W. (1987). *Nettie's trip south*. New York: MacMillan.
Vacca, J. L., Vacca, R. T., & Gove, M. K. (1987). *Reading and learning to read*. Boston: Little, Brown.
Vacca, R. T., & Vacca, J. L. (1989). *Content area reading* (3rd ed.). New York: HarperCollins.
Zola, J. (1992). Middle and high school scored discussions. *Social Education, 56*(2), 121–126.

30 Is Anybody Really There?

Developing Voice in Student Writing

WILLIAM J. ROMEO

Teacher, Parma (OH) City Schools

What language arts teacher has not had to suffer through reading what Ken Macrorie (1985) refers to as "Engfish," that affected, pompous language that has all the personality of a computer-synthesized voice? It is understandable that one of the terms that receives a great deal of attention from writing teachers these days is "voice," an elusive quality that provides personality to a piece of writing. For those who want to get a feel for what this term means, here is a simple experiment: Take a handful of your students' written work with their names concealed in some way. Read the papers and attempt to determine the author of each one from the way the writing sounds, or at least judge whether the papers sound different from one another. If this is an easy task, your students are probably writing with strong, distinctive "voices." If the papers all sound similar, you probably need to address voice in your writing instruction in order to eliminate the bland, character-less, safe writing that characterizes such a large percentage of what students turn out at school. Are kids capable of writing with lively, unique voices? Just ask them for a peek at those notes they send across the room when they think your back is turned, and you may be surprised at the quality of what you read!

Nurturing Individual Voice in Students' Writing

It seems strange that there should be so much voiceless writing going on in our classrooms. The process approach to writing, which has become a part of the language arts curriculum in so many schools, aims at student ownership of the writing and, consequently, a strong personal voice in the students' work. However, in too many cases, the process has been reduced to a formula or series of steps that students are required to follow, regardless of their own writing styles. When writing instruction neglects the central role of the student as author, the result becomes little more than a stilted exercise aimed at pleasing the teacher and earning a letter grade, the sort of writing that has that anonymous, voiceless quality, devoid of personality—in other words, "Engfish." If you have read more of this stuff than you care to admit, you'll be pleased to know that the development of voice in student writing is fairly easy to nurture.

Nurturing Self-Expression and Personal Style

The first step is to allow students to write with a natural, personal style. This may sound pretty obvious, but it requires the teacher to allow the student to have more control of the writing. To begin with, the choice of writing topic, and in many cases, even format, must be the student's; in other words, genre and style requirements should be flexible enough to offer the kind of latitude that allows the student to find his or her own voice. Writing, however, cannot happen without lots of talking, which leads to the second step.

The second step is to encourage a great deal of talking as part of the writing process, especially at the earliest stages. Prewriting and initial drafting should involve the ear as well as the mind. Some students already have well-developed internal ears that enable them to hear the words they are committing to paper, but others may actually need to say their ideas aloud as they write in order to hear how they sound. Allowing students to work with classmates who are able to take dictation from them and write their ideas down as they think aloud frees these writers from some of the inhibiting factors that can stifle their natural writing voices. A related technique uses a tape recorder to gather ideas that may later be transcribed. The initial draft of some writing need not be on paper at all!

Discerning the Author's Voice

As the drafting process continues, students should be encouraged to read their ideas aloud or have a classmate read the writing to them. Part of the drafting then becomes listening with a discriminating ear, accepting what sounds natural and right, and rejecting what does not. Of course, effective communication must be one of the criteria used to critique the writing. For example, if the writer's goal is to communicate ideas to a wide-ranging audience, the listener should decide whether the writing does so. This can be accomplished by trying the draft out on a variety of people, whose responses should indicate whether the writing is clear or confusing, as well as whether it sounds like the writer or not.

Dialogue in stories or plays also may be critically appraised by classmates to determine whether the speaking parts sound like real characters' voices or like generic, indistinguishable lines. As Macrorie (1984) writes, "You can tell quickly when a written conversation is phony" (p. 54). For example, if two characters having a conversation cannot be easily distinguished from one another on the basis of their speaking parts, the writer will need to inject into their speech whatever mannerisms, vocabulary, or ideas are necessary to bring the characters to life.

Strategies to Help Students Develop a Sense of Voice

An issue at this point concerns how voice is developed. The debate is whether voice should actually be taught or allowed to develop naturally with guidance from the teacher. There are exercises that allow students to experiment with different voices with little or no actual instruction necessary.

Point of View

One exercise involves writing about an object from the viewpoints of three different people. Notice in this student example how Heather, an eighth-grade writer, makes subtle changes to distinguish among her three speakers:

> *Heather's own point of view:*
> I highly value my new flute . . . I would be absolutely horrified if someone came into my room and started to fool around with it. I would be panic strucken [sic] if it would ever be stolen. In twenty years I will still be playing and loving my flute . . .

> *Little brother's point of view:*
> My big sister keeps this neat, shiny thing in her room on weekends. On the other days she takes it to school. Every night after we eat she goes down in her room and plays it. I wish she would let me play with it someday. I want to make pretty music too . . . . The next time she goes out to baby-sit, I'm gonna sneak down in her room and look at it . . .

> *Mother's point of view:*
> Last year, in February, my husband and I bought our daughter a brand new $600 flute. I know it's a lot of money, but she is musically enclined [sic]. She deserves it. She is first chair in 2 bands. She's doing quite well, I'd say . . . . We love to listen to her exquisite music every time she practices . . .

Heather creates different voices by shifting her vocabulary, changing the subjects addressed, and varying the degree of sophistication—evidence that even prior to any actual instruction in voice, she possesses a repertoire of different voices and knows how to use them appropriately.

Any classroom teacher can develop similar exercises; the aim should be to give students the opportunity to try on voices in much the same way they would try on costumes, having fun being someone else. For example, a familiar situation is presented, such as being called out of class to speak with the principal. Students take the role of either the student or the principal, working in pairs and writing the conversation that could result in such a confrontation. During the writing time, the students switch roles and attempt to continue writing with the same voice until the conversation has reached some sort of conclusion. These conversations are then shared with the class by having the writers read them aloud. Each reading is followed by a discussion of how effective the voices were in developing believable dialogue. The writers and their audience may also discuss which techniques, vocabulary, mannerisms, etc., were successful in creating the voice of each character.

Once this exercise has been done successfully in class, it becomes a tool that students can use when they are inventing dialogue for stories and plays, and these skills will enable them to write with distinctive voice in nonfiction situations as well. What we can give to our students is the "freedom of speech" they need to write their ideas without the fear of reprisal that often stifles their communication. The license to use one's own voice shifts the writer's focus from trying to be safe to trying to say something worthwhile.

Role-Playing

Role-playing is another excellent way to create realistic speech for story or play dialogue. Allowing students to tape record role-playing situations for later transcription fosters the development of three-dimensional characters whose speech reveals unique personalities through word choice, pronunciation, slang, sentence length, etc. Reading these transcriptions aloud to critical listeners provides the writer with a measurement of the success the writing achieves in portraying the characters. Whether the student actually decides to use role-playing or simply write dialogue without help, the important thing is to listen for the sound of a real voice speaking. Again, Ken Macrorie (1984) says it well: "Sit still a moment and listen to yourself speaking inside. If you hear a voice that takes on a clear tone . . . listen as you write and get it on paper" (p. 161).

The role of the teacher at this point should be that of critical listener as well as a technical adviser who helps the student develop ways of representing dialogue in print. The student retains responsibility for the actual ideas and writing while the teacher becomes more of a consultant whose intervention in the student's writing process is minimal.

Recognizing Student Ownership

Although exercises in voice may motivate students to experiment with it in their writing, a better source of voice awareness is student writing itself. Tom Liner states, "The longer I teach writing the more exercises like these ring hollow" (Kirby, Liner, & Vinz, 1988, p. 152). Elliot Wigginton, formerly of *Foxfire*, agreed that actual writing was the best way to develop voice. Wigginton's students were the actual writers of the *Foxfire* publications, which dealt with Appalachian life and lore in rural Rabun Gap, Georgia. Their writing incorporated their own voices as well as the distinctive voices of the local people they interviewed for their articles. According to Wigginton (1988), this control of voice was not the result of any direct formal instruction in techniques; rather, it was the result of students' ownership of their writing and the opportunity they had to build on the natural quality of their own expression.

Foxfire writers also were taught to transcribe interviews from taped recordings, taking care to use the actual words and speech patterns of their subjects. This involved careful listening to speakers and developing orthography that faithfully reproduced the speech in print. These techniques, which resulted in articles that conveyed the local flavor of Rabun Gap along with the individual personalities of its people, are easily incorporated into any language arts class.

Employing Voices across the School Curriculum

Whatever techniques are used to foster the development of voice, it's important to allow students freedom to find their own voices and learn to use them on a regular basis. From exercises and fictional conversations, this voice awareness should be allowed to expand to all phases of the student's writing, including that which is done in other subjects. This does not imply that the conventions of writing, such as strong, complete sentence structure or standard punctuation, should be abandoned in favor of an "anything goes" policy. Rather, it refers to writing instruction that teaches the student to speak in his or her own unique, personal voice when communicating in writing, to express freely what it is that needs to be said without pandering safe but empty answers to the holder-of-the-red-pen in exchange for satisfactory grades.

If we want kids to produce vibrant writing, we must give them room to do so, exchanging the traditional role of grader for a more useful role of mentor or coach. Language arts teachers also need to inform their colleagues in other departments that writing need not retain the bland quality that has characterized it for so long. If we encourage other teachers to abandon the exclusive use of third-person detached point of view requirements on essays and reports in favor of more dynamic, lifelike writing, we will be rescuing teachers from the agony of reading stacks of bland, voiceless reports and rescuing students from the agony of having to produce them.

By consistently encouraging students to use their own voices, the entire school day could become a real writing workshop in which kids could learn to write appropriately in authentic writing situations. What better way to develop strong, distinctive voice as a writer than to practice using that voice to write about science or social studies as well as the topics encountered in the language arts class! It's time we replace "Engfish" with real language that can hold readers' attention and delight them while it communicates effectively. Imagine never having to suffer through a stack of papers covered with dead, voiceless writing again. That alone is reason enough to give voice a chance!

REFERENCES

Kirby, D., Liner, T., & Vinz, R. (1988). *Inside out: Developmental strategies for teaching writing.* Portsmouth, NH: Boynton/Cook.

Macrorie, K. (1984). *Writing to be read.* Portsmouth, NH: Boynton/Cook.

Macrorie, K. (1985). *Telling writing.* Portsmouth, NH: Boynton/Cook.

Wigginton, E. (1985). *Sometimes a shining moment: The Foxfire experience.* Garden City, NY: Doubleday.

Wigginton, E. (1988). [Telephone interview].

31 Writing Workshop

The Power of Language Experience in the Middle Years

N. SUZANNE STANDERFORD

Associate Professor, Northern Michigan University

I remember early adolescence as one of the worst times of my life, as do many other adults. It was a time of awkward physical changes, confusing emotional changes, and self-doubt. Middle schoolers today face the same challenges of growing up. In fact, these "middle years" may be even more challenging today as students must negotiate an array of societal changes every day that often leave adults feeling confused and uncertain. Middle school teachers face unique challenges to help young people make sense of their experiences and develop as confident and capable young adults. Having students explore their experiences in written language is one excellent way to meet this challenge.

A writing workshop (Atwell, 1987; Calkins, 1986) is ideal for middle schoolers who are experiencing the challenges of growing up because it employs the principles of the Language Experience Approach (LEA) (Tompkins & Hoskisson, 1991). LEA is particularly appropriate for middle school students because it meets their unique socio-emotional and educational needs by valuing their experiences and recording them in written language. LEA uses the experiences of the students as topics and uses their language for the text, thereby creating optimum conditions for success.

Language Experience and the Writing Workshop

The writing workshop parallels LEA in four basic ways: (1) use of experience-based text; (2) active reading, writing, and responding; (3) need for substantial class time; and (4) publishing texts.

Use of Experience-Based Text

LEA begins with the students' experiences. In a writing workshop, text is also based on the experiences of the students. The freedom and the responsibility to choose the topic, the writing approach, and the language for the text result in student ownership of the writing, similar to the group ownership of language experience stories. Moving from the teacher as scribe to the student as author encourages the natural evolution of literacy skills.

Active Rereading, Responding, and Revising

LEA uses rereading, responding, and revising to develop accurate and interesting texts. In a writing workshop, students continually reread and revise their written drafts. They share their writing with peers and teachers, who respond with comments and questions. These conferences offer ideas to help the authors improve their pieces. Response is a second key principle of writing workshop, which enables authors to clarify and improve their intended meaning. Drafting, responding, and revising texts produces higher-quality writing and provides opportunities for students to explore their ideas more thoroughly.

Need for Substantial Class Time

LEA requires substantial class time. A writing workshop also requires a significant investment of class time. The students need daily time to spend with their writing. They must consider topics, research ideas, compose drafts, share their work, revise the texts, and edit final copies. Providing time for writing is a third principle of writing workshop, which parallels the need for class time in the language experience approach.

Publishing Texts

Language experience texts are often published in book formats, which students personalize and share. In a writing workshop students publish personal texts and share them within the classroom and beyond. Students can personalize and extend their texts with illustrations, author pages, and specialized shapes and print styles. These books then become part of the classroom library, the school library, or the family library.

Deepening Writing Experiences in the Middle School

Writing becomes more sophisticated as students move into the middle grades because they go beyond remembering and retelling experiences—they begin to reconsider and analyze their experiences through writing. They often embed ideas in a variety of genres, such as poetry, fiction, and essays. By honoring the power of using students' experiences as a basis for written text, a writing workshop can enable older students to write about their experiences and ideas in thoughtful and powerful ways. Opportunities to reconsider their personal experiences enables them to connect with the experiences of others and begin to generalize their thinking to broader life issues.

Meeting the Unique Needs of Middle School Students

Middle school students are in one of the most difficult developmental stages of life. They go through enormous and confusing physical and socio-emotional changes (Slavin, 1994). They begin to develop "reflectivity," an ability to consider and study oneself. They come to realize that their beliefs may not always agree with their actions, and they struggle to understand why they behave as they do. They compare themselves to others and often desire to change who and what they are. The increased awareness that they are separate and unique is coupled with a strong need to belong, to be like everybody else. "The issue of who and what one 'really' is dominates personality development in adolescence" (Slavin, 1994, p. 100). As middle school students attempt to define themselves, reactions from others are woven into their own self-concepts. Their self-definitions are revised as they learn about their own and their family histories, try on a variety of roles and ways of behaving, and express beliefs and feelings, which may strongly influence their actions. Middle schoolers are in an almost constant state of change as they seek to figure out who they want to be, to strongly exert their independence, and at the same time, to be accepted by others.

Middle school girls face additional developmental challenges in many of today's societies because they begin to lose their sense of worth, identity, and confidence during the middle school years (Barbieri, 1996; Gilligan, 1988; Sadker & Sadker, 1994; Orenstein, 1995). Adolescent girls face societal messages and expectations to become the "perfect girl," one who displays "good" female behavior such as "having no bad thoughts or feelings . . . the girl who speaks quietly, calmly, who is always nice and kind, never mean or bossy (Brown & Gilligan, 1992, p. 59). Yet, at the same time, these young women hear that to be mature adults, one must be self-sufficient and independent (Taylor, Gilligan, & Sullivan, 1995). Females, who often use language to connect and build rapport with others by sharing experiences and feelings (Tannen, 1990), find in early adolescence that their ideas, ways of communicating, and experiences are not always valued because they differ from a more accepted, male-oriented societal view (Taylor et. al., 1995). Thus, young women come to see their own experiences as lacking and often begin to dissociate from themselves as they seek to gain acceptance by pursuing the perfect girl myth (Bishop, 1996). Bishop contends that writing about personal experiences in journals provides a way for middle school girls to use language to develop their own thoughts and ideas and to strengthen their sense of voice, a way to prevent this dissociation from self. Writing workshop can also meet this need of young women as they use their experiences to construct texts that are shared and valued within a supportive community of writers.

The writing workshop can be an excellent way to meet both the socio-emotional and the educational needs of middle school students. Barbieri (1966) states, "I am renewed in my conviction that writing remains our best hope of self-discovery and reading our clearest way to encounter human experience beyond our own" (p. 9). She suggests that thinking and writing about their experiences offer students opportunities to consider and practice for decisions that they will encounter in their lives. Writing about their experiences provides the opportunity for students to consider the significance of those experiences, to find the "threads of meaning" (p. 149) that can help them better understand who they are. Literacy skills are developed, applied, and refined as students read and write extensively about topics that are of interest and that matter to them.

The Challenge of Scheduling

The middle school schedule can make it difficult for teachers to fit in a writing workshop. If students spend less than one hour per day with a teacher, it some-times seems impossible to cover the required curriculum and to provide extended time for talking, thinking, and writing. Some schools are changing schedules and providing longer blocks of time within which teachers can collaborate and team teach their subjects. This "block scheduling" can provide ways for teachers to con-nect their subjects, integrate topics and units that fit well together, and use their time more flexibly. As teachers begin to plan together, they often find aspects of the curriculum that could be taught more effectively in an integrated program than in separate, short class periods, thus providing time for other approaches such as writ-ing workshop. Other teachers have found that using writing as a vehicle for con-sidering subject matter enhances student learning, and these teachers teach subject matter within their workshops. However teachers make time, for a writing work-shop to be effective, students must have time each day to work with their writing.

Defining Student and Teacher Roles

Calkins (1991, 1994) cautions that writers seldom find the writing process a nice, neat linear progression in which they brainstorm topics, compose a draft, revise, edit, and then publish, but this has been the most common interpretation of the writing process in schools. Calkins suggests that instead, a writer must "live a writerly life"; a writer must be more aware of his or her life and begin to see ordi-nary events as significant. Calkins has her students keep notebooks in which they record events, thoughts, feelings, and questions throughout the day. She believes that these notes eventually develop into writing topics; the writing grows from these seemingly insignificant experiences of the students. This view of how stu-dents select and develop topics is somewhat different from many earlier books on writing (e.g., Calkins, 1986).

Students have both choices and responsibilities for their writing in an effec-tive workshop. Some teachers have interpreted this to mean that teachers take a laissez-faire attitude toward student writing. However, in the workshop, teachers still have a powerful role in helping students improve their writing. Listening to students carefully in conferences provides the teacher with many opportunities to stretch the students' thinking and writing abilities. Comments such as "I liked the part where you said . . ." and questions such as "Can you tell me more about . . . ?" allow the student to retain ownership of the writing while providing support and guidance for revision (Atwell, 1987). Teachers can also feel comfortable requiring students to try writing about a topic of their choice, but in a required genre to help them try out new ways to write. Or, teachers might assign a general topic, such as the Civil War, while leaving it to the students to select one aspect of that topic to pursue in their writing. Teachers who use writing workshop constantly balance freedom and guidance.

Student authors also need responses to their writing; however, it would be a mistake to assume that students new to writing workshop automatically know how to respond in helpful ways to their peers' writing. The teacher needs to help students develop ground rules for conferring, including ways to honor the author's ideas and ways to ask questions that are helpful. Peer conferences can be the most tricky part of the workshop. Some researchers have begun to document incidences of children using their writing and their choice of peers with whom they conference to exclude or hurt others (Lensmire, 1994). Teachers must spend time in the beginning developing a climate of respect and trust among the students and must remain watchful for incidents that violate that respect and trust. A writing workshop requires safety and honor for all voices.

Writing in the Lives of Middle School Girls

I recently interviewed a group of middle school girls and listened to pieces of their writing. Each of them told me that they began writing in elementary school and have continued in middle school.

Terry

One student, Terry, talked about writing as "something we do in English class" and stated that she did not write much outside of class. Terry said that in middle school she has begun writing about more complicated things and that she usually chooses poetry over stories. Terry's poem describes writing time in her English class (see Figure 31-1).

Terry captures the feel of writing in class while making the point that once class ends, students put aside their writing for the day. She commented, "I'm never afraid of writing. I like to write." However, this writing is something she does as a requirement and continues to be a description of her experiences and feelings. Even though Terry likes to write, she does not yet see writing as a powerful way to consider who she is and what she wants. I suspect many middle schoolers' experiences with writing mirror Terry's. One challenge for middle

English Class

English class is almost silence.

You hear the clock ticking, papers rustling, pencils scribbling.

Everyone thinking their own thoughts, in their own words,

deeply absorbed in writing.

Everyone writing something different,

Stories, poems, lists, thoughts, words, ideas.

The bell rings.

People talking, backpacks thumping, books closing.

No one cares about writing

Until next English class.

FIGURE 31.1 Terry's Poem about English class

school teachers is helping students such as Terry become more able to use writing as a means to think about their lives.

Marie

Marie, another prolific writer, seems to have moved further in her development as a writer. She uses writing to examine her own and her peers' experiences, to express her thoughts, to puzzle over issues of concern to her, and to deal with her own emotions. Her writing shows the value of friendships, struggle for independence, daily successes, and life in and out of the classroom.

Sierra

Sierra perceives writing more from the role of an aspiring professional writer. She says, "I think writing is one of my main roles in life." She writes short stories and plays. Some of her plays have been performed by local community children's theater groups. Rather than writing stories as a way to reconsider troubling issues in her own life, Sierra likes to write stories for others to read and enjoy.

One of Sierra's stories, entitled "Baby," is about Brianna, a teenager, who has self-doubts and faces childbirth alone. The baby's father dumps her and begins a relationship with her sister, Cara. Sierra builds sibling rivalry between the sisters by portraying Cara as the more beautiful sister. She describes Brianna's disturbing recurrent dream using foreshadowing to pique the reader's interest. Her writing demonstrates other techniques, such as shifts in setting and dialogue, that experienced writers use to craft interesting stories. Sierra shares her writing with her father, a professional writer. This experience has helped Sierra to gain confidence and skill as a writer.

All three of these writers bring unique needs, approaches, perspectives, experiences, and aspirations to the writing workshop. The risk-free environment provided in the workshop enables these young women to explore their own unique situations and needs. The value placed on their ideas, feelings, and experiences as they compose and share their writing enables each to feel confident in who she is and to explore who she wants to be.

Conclusion

Middle school is a tumultuous time in the life of a young person. Physical and emotional changes are often overwhelming. Academics frequently take a backseat to personal doubts and concerns. Middle school teachers have the opportunity to positively influence the lives of these young people by providing structure, support, and time for them to record and reconsider their lives through writing. Writing, sharing, and revising texts based on their experiences develops the communication and thinking skills necessary for success. These reflective writing experiences enable them to develop as confident, literate individuals as they move toward adulthood. Writing can provide a means to express their feelings, try on different roles, offer fictionalized accounts for solving real-life dilemmas, and examine their own beliefs and ideas.

REFERENCES

Atwell, N. (1987). *In the middle: Writing, reading, and learning with adolescents*. Portsmouth, NH: Boynton/Cook.

Barbieri, M. (1996). *Sounds from the heart: Learning to listen to girls*. Portsmouth, NH: Heinemann.

Bishop, M. (1996). Preserving voice: Girls and their journals. *Voices from the Middle, 3*(1), 11–15.

Brown, L. M., & Gilligan, C. (1992). *Meeting at the crossroads: Women's psychology and girls' development*. Cambridge, MA: Harvard University Press.

Calkins, L. M. (1986). *The art of teaching writing*. Portsmouth, NH: Heinemann.

Calkins, L. M. (1991). *Living between the lines*. Portsmouth, NH: Heinemann.

Calkins, L. M. (1994). *The art of teaching writing* (2nd. ed.). Portsmouth, NH. Heinemann.

Gilligan, C. (Ed.). (1988). *Mapping the moral domain: A contribution of women's thinking to psychological theory and education*. Cambridge, MA: Harvard University Press.

Graves, D. H. (1983). *Writing: Teachers and children at work*. Portsmouth, NH: Heinemann.

Lensmire, T. J. (1994). *When children write: Critical re-visions of the writing workshop*. New York: Teachers College Press.

Orenstein, P. (1995). *School girls: Young women, self-esteem, and the confidence gap*. New York: Anchor Books.

Sadker, M., & Sadker, D. (1994). *Failing at fairness: How America's schools cheat girls*. New York: Scribner.

Slavin, R. (1994). *Educational psychology: Theory and practice*. Boston: Allyn and Bacon.

Tannen, D. (1990). *You just don't understand: Women and men in conversation*. New York: William Morrow.

Taylor, J., Gilligan, C., & Sullivan, A. (1995). *Between voice and silence: Women and girls, race and relationships*. Cambridge, MA: Harvard University Press.

Tompkins, G., & Hoskisson, K. (1991). *Language arts: Content and teaching strategies*. Englewood Cliffs, NJ: Merrill.

32 LEA and Students with Special Needs

HARVETTA M. ROBERTSON

Assistant Professor, Texas A&M University, Commerce

Few would argue that the ability to communicate with others is a critical component for achievement and success. Through communication and personal effort, relationships are built and maintained, and goals are set and achieved. It follows then, that if specific interventions are not implemented, limited possibilities and options exist for an individual who has difficulty participating in the communication process. The Language Experience Approach (LEA) offers a viable means of enhancing the communication abilities and literacy competencies of all students, including those with special needs—both in actively communicating and in understanding the oral and printed messages of others. Perhaps these "special needs" result from a difference in language, a disability, or a different learning style. Whatever the origin, direct attention must be given to planning, implementing, and evaluating the effectiveness of instruction if these students are to experience success.

A key component of effective teaching is considering the individual needs of all students when selecting curricular materials and instructional approaches that are most likely to affect positive educational and personal outcomes in students. The selection of these materials and approaches is directly influenced by one's philosophical beliefs. Mercer and Mercer (1993) propose that there is a "substantial gap . . . between what is known about effective teaching and what is practiced routinely" (p. 4). It is unreasonable to expect different results when the same ineffective practices are implemented. Chapters in Section 1 highlight the theory, principles, and research that demonstrate the efficacy of LEA. It is for all the reasons cited that this philosophical approach is recommended for use with students who have been identified as having special needs.

Several reasons why LEA can be considered a philosophically and instructionally sound emphasis for students with identified special needs are that LEA builds on students' interests and self-expression, uses students' oral language and backgrounds, and attempts to build classroom communities for learning. An overview of each of these and other aspects of LEA will be discussed briefly here and in greater detail for specific groups in the chapters that follow in this section.

Building on Students' Interests and Self-Expression

Bruning, Schraw, and Ronning (1995) stress that "learning to read is not a skill separate from a child's language experience, but rather is one growing naturally from it" (p. 240). As discussed in previous chapters, skill building is not separated from thinking in LEA. Instead, there is pronounced influence and impact between the students' ability to think and reason and their ability to gain new skills. Experiences are based on the children's own spoken language, capitalizing on the children's interest in communicating their thoughts with others. These efforts to communicate are natural—from early development when immediate needs and desires are commonly expressed, to later years when more complex issues become the focus of communication efforts. LEA provides a logical vehicle for self-expression for students with special needs who find themselves experiencing "outcast" status in traditional educational settings.

Using Students' Oral Language and Background

New emphasis is being put on the importance of bridging children's learning—making obvious the connections between students' prior knowledge and new learnings (see Stokes, Chapter 33). In LEA, vocabulary and sentence patterns flow from the child's own speech. The child becomes the source, rather than simply the recipient, of curricular content (see Casement, Chapter 34 and Duling, Chapter 36). For many students with special needs, unsuccessful experiences in school settings are common. These unsuccessful experiences are natural consequences of learning environments where materials and programs are not considerate of student needs. LEA builds directly on the words of the student. Immediately, students are engaged in the learning process, and engaged learners experience greater achievement (Mastropieri & Scruggs, 1994). Because the oral language background of the student is of critical importance in LEA, all students can benefit from this approach, even those who have a language other than English as their primary language (see Mohr, Chapter 35 and Lewis-White, Chapter 37). Chapters in this section all support this philosophy.

Building Classroom Communities for Learning

The importance of building a sense of community in learners cannot be overemphasized. Falvey, Givner, and Kimm (1995) stated it well:

We believe that each child can learn and succeed, that diversity enriches us all, that students at risk for failure can overcome that risk through involvement in a thoughtful and caring community of learners, that each child has unique contributions to offer to the community of learners, that each child has strengths and needs, and that effective learning results from the collaborative efforts of us all to ensure the success of each student. (p. 9)

LEA uses a variety of reading materials and allows time to listen to the student. It allows each student, no matter what his or her special need, to make contributions to the immediate classroom community. Granted, the creation and maintenance of such a community takes time and concerted effort, but educators can "structure learning activities that encourage positive social interaction . . . [and students can be] taught to be caring . . . and supportive of one another" (Sapon-Shevin, 1996, p. 37). With LEA, students' individual contributions impact the success of the community's effort as a whole.

Conclusion

LEA employs a variety of materials, provides ongoing, meaningful activities, and allows all students to express themselves orally and in writing. It builds connections between speech and print and promotes the interaction between oral and written language. LEA considers and builds on students' individual needs, provides opportunities for students to be effective contributors to their classroom communities, and enhances both the academic and social proficiencies of all students.

REFERENCES

Bruning, R. H., Schraw, G. J., & Ronning, R. R. (1995). *Cognitive psychology and instruction* (2nd ed.). Englewood Cliffs, NJ: Merrill.

Falvey, M. A., Givner, C. C., & Kimm, C. (1995). What is an inclusive school? In R. A Villa, & J. S. Thousand (Eds.), *Creating an inclusive school*, pp. 1–12. Alexandria, VA: Association for Supervision and Curriculum Development.

Mastropieri, M. A., & Scruggs, T. E. (1994). *Effective instruction for special education* (2nd ed.). Austin, TX: Pro-ed.

Mercer, C. D., & Mercer, A. R. (1993). *Teaching students with learning problems* (4th ed.). Englewood Cliffs, NJ: Merrill.

Sapon-Shevin, M. (1996). Ability differences in the classroom: Teaching and learning in inclusive classrooms. In D. A. Byrnes & G. Kiger (Eds.), *Common bonds: Anti-bias teaching in a diverse society* (2nd ed.), pp. 35–47. Wheaton, MD: Association for Childhood Education International.

33 Empowering Students with Learning Disabilities through Language Experience

SANDRA M. STOKES

Associate Professor, University of Wisconsin, Green Bay

A child with learning disabilities typically demonstrates difficulties in one or more of the following areas: metalinguistic awareness, organization, auditory processing, word retrieval, generalizing information, and making connections between new information and what is already known (Lerner, 1997). Most intervention for readers with learning disabilities aims to strengthen their areas of weakness, usually through workbook exercises and skill sheets in combination with a basal reader (National Institute of Education, 1985). The instructional goal of these activities seems to be rote memorization of vocabulary, phonics rules, and spelling.

The skills approach to reading instruction with students who have learning disabilities (LDs) is based on the belief that language develops in sequentially fixed steps and that learning to read can occur only when all the sequential skills have been mastered. Thus, word, phrase, and sentence-level activities are usually selected for use in remediation (Griffith & Ripich, 1984). When students appear to have problems with word recognition, especially recognizing and pronouncing letters and sounds or whole words, they generally have difficulty reading whole sentences. In a skills approach, this lack of carryover from smaller units of discourse (letters and words) to larger ones (phrases and sentences) indicates that lower-level skills were not completely mastered in the first place (Griffith & Ripich, 1984). Therefore, the typical recommendation is to reteach lower-level skills in the same manner as before.

[From "LD Students and Language Experience," by Sandra M. Stokes, 1989, *Journal of Language Experience, 10*(2), pp. 19–23. Copyright 1989 by the Language Experience Special Interest Group. Reprinted and revised with permission.]

Goodman (1991) describes this as a scenario for failure:

> The less well [students] do, the more intensively the teacher applies worksheets, flash cards, skill drills, and remedial exercises . . . . If the usual amount of time spent on such activities is not paying off, then more time is provided for them, either at the expense of other, more meaningful aspects of the reading period, such as free reading time, or other aspects of the curriculum, such as social studies, science, music, or art . . . in the name of helping readers in trouble overcome their deficits. (p. 129)

As Goodman further pointed out, this student misses out on activities, such as building concepts, as well as reading, writing, and doing. It should be no surprise then, that when instruction is approached in this manner, the gap between grade level and reading performance usually widens. Lower-level remedial activities very rarely result in improvement of overall performance (Tuch, 1977).

Thus, many experts advocate for more realistic and holistic approaches to effectively teach and assess students with learning disabilities (Bloom & Lahey, 1978; Stires, 1991). Falk-Ross (1997) states that, in order to assist students with learning disabilities to develop the metalinguistic awareness they need to fully participate in all the activities in a regular classroom, it is paramount that the necessary scaffolding be provided or introduced first. Since the traditional skills approach does not produce the gains needed, using the Language Experience Approach (LEA) is a very logical alternative.

Why Use LEA with Students Who Have Learning Disabilities?

As the National Institute of Education (1985) pointed out, "reading is a constructive process . . . [in which] readers draw on their store of knowledge about the topic . . . to . . . 'construct' the meaning" (p. 9). LEA provides a way of implementing this definition of reading fluency: LEA values, incorporates, and extends the students' prior knowledge while providing the perfect avenue for ongoing individualized assessment. Language experience activities help students develop positive reading/writing attitudes and habits as they strengthen identified weaknesses. Assessment of students' strengths, weaknesses, academic progress, and personal growth can all be accomplished within the context of instruction.

Students who participate in language experience activities are encouraged to create their own texts through dictation or writing. It has been recognized for some time that when students choose and compose their own topics, their writing is better in both quality and quantity (Routman, 1991; Stires, 1991; Zarnowski, 1981). Seeing what they have dictated or written helps students with learning disabilities make connections between words in print and meaning (Hall, 1981). Sharing their writing with classmates allows students to improve their reading and oral communication skills (Gaskins, 1982). Dictation and writing activities can also provide a framework for addressing organizational skills, particularly in regard to text organization, which is often a problem for students with learning disabilities (Lerner, 1997).

When students with learning disabilities read what they themselves and their classmates have written, they can easily use context clues to identify unknown words. Since students with learning disabilities often have difficulty with auditory processing, phonics instruction is not as profitable as having students focus on context clues to identify words. Thus, language experience activities provide opportunities for teachers to capitalize on the visual abilities, strengths, and/or memory common among students with learning disabilities, as an avenue to improve the students' ability to decode and encode words.

Reading research has consistently shown a relationship between vocabulary and comprehension (Davis, 1968; National Institute of Education, 1985; Spearitt, 1972). Since this relationship has often been the justification for teaching lists of words and their meanings to students, it is common for students with learning disabilities to have word lists to memorize. However, as Vygotsky (1962) noted, words do not have meaning for children until those words can be incorporated into what children already know. Seeing and using words in contexts that have no meaning for a child will not result in true understanding or learning of those words. When students dictate and write from their own experiences, they increase their vocabularies because the words have meaning for them (Gaskins, 1982).

Improving Listening, Reading, and Writing Skills with Literature

Reading aloud from quality children's literature should be a part of daily activities. Children's literature often features language rhythms and vocabulary not typically found in basal readers. These rhythms and words can become incorporated into the students' own sense of language when they hear them. Favorite stories can be read and reread, thereby improving memory skills and students' knowledge of what to expect in stories as well as improving reading fluency. Since prediction is the foundation of comprehension (Smith, 1988), these rereadings encourage students with learning disabilities to anticipate and predict events in the next reading of the same story. These experiences build background that can be used for future predictions, thereby improving comprehension.

The term *schema* refers to one's organized knowledge of the world (Anderson, 1985; Bartlett, 1932). Rumelhart (1977) hypothesized that schema provide networks of interrelationships on generalized topics. Schema play an important role in directing incoming information toward a particular spot in memory (Anderson & Pichert, 1977). Children's knowledge of stories, for example, and the stories' particular syntactical language patterns, character and plot development, as well as sequence of events, emerges early (Roth & Spekman, 1986; Stein & Glenn, 1975, 1979). As a child matures, his or her schema or knowledge of stories become more elaborate and specific, due to increased experiences (Schallert, 1982). Children who have opportunities over time to listen to quality children's literature, and to dictate and write stories and personal narratives, improve their knowledge, retention, and elaboration of story structures. Thus, comprehension of new material becomes more efficient.

Nurturing Creative Expression

Drama activities can also be an effective part of a language experience program for students with learning disabilities. Acting is a creative way for children to breathe life, energy, and expression into written and oral texts. In this way, language becomes more than words printed on a page when students realize the power they bring to the play/acting event. This creative process reinforces the fact that words in print have a purpose, a meaning, and serve other functions. Repeating lines can be effective in creating, refining, and improving students' memory, reading fluency, and knowledge of elements related to stories, plays, acting, pantomime, and play production.

Children with learning disabilities generally need help improving their metalinguistic awareness, especially their knowledge about language (Falk-Ross, 1997; Van Kleeck, 1984). Early metalinguistic awareness begins in nonverbal communication, which is important for socialization as well as for language acquisition and development (Knott, 1979). Poor verbal or nonverbal communication may negatively affect a child's interpersonal relationships in the early years. The foundation for the child's language awareness, which is shaky to begin with, is thereby further weakened (Wiig & Semel, 1984). Therefore, a language experience program that emphasizes all facets of language and includes such reading, writing, and dramatic arts activities as described here, can promote language awareness. This improved awareness of language can increase the learning disabled student's reading abilities.

Using Ongoing Assessment for IEP Documentation

The document that guides instruction of students with learning disabilities, as well as that of all students needing special education services, is the Individualized Education Plan (IEP) (Lerner, 1997). Teachers can easily observe and write anecdotal notes recording students' performance and growth during instruction as part of their routine activities. These assessment strategies can easily be adapted for use with most IEPs (see Table 33.1). In fact, students can keep track of their own performance and growth in portfolios, which can be used for documentation.

TABLE 33.1

Present Levels of Performance	Annual Goals	Instructional Objectives	Evaluation Procedures
Kelly comprehends at the fourth-grade level.	Kelly will increase her reading to at least the fifth-grade level.	Given instruction, Kelly will develop a larger vocabulary; be able to write a cohesive paragraph; improve her oral communication skills with her peers; use context clues; be able to make and evaluate predictions about stories.	80% accuracy on teacher-made tests

Conclusion

A well-planned program of language experience activities with ongoing assessment, such as the ones described in this chapter, can be an effective approach for students with learning disabilities and for teachers who are frustrated with the traditional skills approach. Language experience activities provide opportunities for students to create texts and construct meaning at the same time they improve their language development. LEA consistently encourages the use of context clues, assists students in using and building on their knowledge base, and contributes to the retention of stories and their common elements. At the same time, use of LEA sparks students' interests and improves their attitudes toward listening, speaking, reading, and writing. These benefits can transfer to beliefs about learning in school and hopefully spearhead positive, effective habits for life.

REFERENCES

Anderson, R. C. (1985). Role of the reader's schema in comprehension, learning, and memory. In H. Singer & R. B. Rudell (Eds.), *The theoretical models and processes of reading* (3rd ed.), pp. 372–384. Newark, DE: International Reading Association.

Anderson, R. C., & Pichert, J. W. (1977). *Recall of previously unrecallable information following a shift of perspective.* Tech. Rep. No. 41. Urbana, IL: Center for the Study of Reading, University of Illinois

Bartlett, Sir F. C. (1932). *Remembering: A study in experimental and social psychology.* Cambridge, England: The University Press.

Bloom, L., & Lahey, M. (1978). *Language development and language disorders.* New York: John Wiley & Sons.

Davis, F. B. (1968). Research in comprehension in reading. *Reading Research Quarterly, 3,* 499–545.

Falk-Ross, F. (1997). Developing metacommunicative awareness in children with language difficulties: Challenging the typical pull-out system. *Language Arts, 74,* 206–216.

Gaskins, I. W. (1982). A writing program for poor readers and writers and the rest of the class, too. *Language Arts, 59,* 854–861.

Goodman, K. (1991). Revaluing readers and reading. In S. Stires (Ed.), *With promise: Redefining reading and writing for "special students,"* pp. 127–134. Portsmouth, NH: Heinemann.

Griffith, P. L., & Ripich, D. (1984). *Story structure, cohesion, and propositions: Story recall by learning disabled and nondisabled children.* Paper presented at the American Speech and Hearing Convention, San Francisco.

Hall, M. (1981). *Teaching reading as a language experience* (3rd ed.). Columbus, OH: Charles E. Merrill.

Knott, G. P. (1979). Nonverbal communication during early childhood. *Theory Into Practice, 18,* 226–233.

Lerner, J. (1997). *Learning disabilities: Theories, diagnosis, and teaching strategies* (7th ed.). Boston, MA: Houghton Mifflin.

National Institute of Education (1985). *Becoming a nation of readers: The report of the Commission on Reading.* Washington, DC: US Department of Education.

Roth, F. P., & Spekman, N. J. (1986). Narrative discourse: Spontaneously generated stories of learning disabled and normally achieving students. *Journal of Speech and Hearing Disorders, 51,* 8–23.

Routman, R. (1991). *Invitations: Changing as teachers and learners K–12.* Portsmouth, NH: Heinemann.

Rumelhart, D. E. (1977). Understanding and summarizing brief stories. In D. LaBerge & S. J. Samuels (Eds.), *Basic processes in reading,* pp. 265–303. Hillsdale, NJ: Erlbaum.

Schallert, D. L. (1982). The significance of knowledge: A synthesis of research related to schema theory. In W. Otto & S. White (Eds.), *Reading expository material,* pp. 13–48. Hillsdale, NJ: Erlbaum.

Smith, F. (1988). *Understanding reading.* Hillsdale, NJ: Erlbaum.

Spearitt, D. (1972). Identification of subskills in reading comprehension by maximum likelihood factor analysis. *Reading Research Quarterly, 8,* 92–111.

Stein, N. L., & Glenn, C. G. (1975). *A developmental study of children's construction of stories.* Paper presented to the Biennial Meeting of the Society for Research in Child Development, New Orleans, LA.

Stein, N. L., & Glenn, C. G. (1979). An analysis of story comprehension in elementary school children. In R. O Freedle (Ed.), *New directions in discourse processing,* Vol. 2, pp. 53–120. Norwood, NJ: Ablex.

Stires, S. (Ed.). (1991). *With promise: Redefining reading and writing for "special students."* Portsmouth, NH: Heinemann.

Tuch, S. (1977). The production of coherent narrative texts by older language-impaired children. *The South African Journal of Communicative Disorders, 24,* 42–60.

Van Kleeck, A. (1984). Assessment and intervention: Does "meta" matter? In G. P. Wallach & K. G. Butler (Eds.), *Language learning disabilities in school-age children,* pp. 179–198. Baltimore, MD: Williams & Williams.

Vygotsky, L. S. (1962). *Thought and language.* Cambridge, MA: MIT Press.

Wiig, E. H., & Semel, E. (1984). *Language assessment and intervention for the learning disabled* (2nd ed.). Columbus, OH: Charles E. Merrill.

Zarnowski, M. (1981). A child's composition: How does it hold together? *Language Arts, 58,* 316–319.

34 ZPD + LEA = Reading for Special Needs Children

A Formula for Success

ROSE ANNE CASEMENT
Doctoral Candidate, University of Maine

Working within what Vygotsky (1986) has named the zone of proximal development and using a comprehensive Language Experience Approach (LEA) to teaching reading and writing has brought success to a group of children previously excluded from academic expectations. The personally meaningful reading program that I have developed with my students is an experiential reading program in which we create our own shared text daily. Using this approach, we have gradually created more complex writing products, integrated writing into each student's program, and created an archive of our work. The integral component of this meaningful and successful reading program is incorporating the students' own language into their reading materials and teaching within a child's zone of proximal development. With this approach, each student is able to be included in literacy.

It is not uncommon in our schools, in special education or in the regular classroom, to find students who have not learned to read. These students learn to see themselves as failures in this crucial academic area. Since reading is an integral part of their school day, they not only feel like failures in reading but they are also overwhelmed by the school experience, in which reading plays such an important role.

Too often, for the student with special needs, the goals and objectives that have guided their reading program have been repeated year after year with the report that they are "in progress." Most reflect a reading theory that children learn reading from the ground up: that small units of phonic or word recognition form the basis of the reading. The Dolch word lists are studied and, one after another, phonics drill programs are tried. The goals have remained the same, the approach remains the same, and the continued lack of success begins to be blamed on the student. Behavior problems begin to emerge and become the focus of the child's experience with school. What does not seem to occur to those who are becoming exasperated with the student is that most people, under similar circumstances, would begin to develop anti-behaviors if, on a daily basis, they were to enter a world of failure where all of their peers could witness their struggle.

The work I am currently doing began three years ago in a composite classroom for children identified with a variety of handicapping conditions, including the labels *learning disability, multi-handicapped, mental retardation,* and *attention deficit disorder.* My work with them began with these expectations:

1. Each student could and would learn to read.
2. Developing language skills would be an integral part of that experience.
3. The reading that we did would be meaningful to the students' lives.
4. We would need to spend a significant part of our day on developing language skills, and we would take that time.
5. All of the students needed to look at learning as a behavior and develop an understanding of the focus needed to create a successful learning opportunity for themselves.
6. This would be done in a social environment as much as possible.
7. Each child would see himself or herself as a successful reader.

The Theory behind These Expectations

These expectations were based on the underlying reading theory that an understanding of language is basic to reading. It is through an individual's understanding of the spoken word that he or she begins to relate to text. "A word without meaning is an empty sound, no longer a part of human speech" (Vygotsky, 1986, p. 6). This experience is best done in a social context since the purpose of language is interactive and difficulties that a student may be having with inner speech are revealed through talk. These expectations also reflect the concept that students can work with others beyond their mastery level but within their problem-solving area. Vygotsky refers to this area where learning takes place as the zone of proximal development (ZPD). This area is composed of multiple variables and requires ongoing assessment. When a teacher works with each student's zone of proximal development, students are more likely to be responsive to learning, and enthused about their work, and they perceive themselves as successful. Understanding that each student has a unique ZPD encourages teachers to accept different responses and to establish conducive social environments for learning to take place. Van Der Veer & Valsiner (1993) summarize that belief about learning well: "Speech is not only a tool of communication, but also a tool of thinking, consciousness develops mainly with the help of speech and originates in social experience" (p. 64).

Language: Conversation, the Roots for Literacy

Literacy is rooted in language, and language—both written and spoken—is the basis for communication. We use language to state, restate, and reflect both on our concrete experiences and on the abstract concepts that we are studying. For most students in school, the advancement to more complex language is a natural and uncomplicated process that, although certainly uneven among students, leads predictably to a more sophisticated vocabulary, syntactical awareness, and semantic understanding. This progression is so unstructured that as educators we are inclined to minimize conversation in the classroom, but for children who have not interacted successfully in reading and writing, their own language as a tool of communication is worthy of focus. Like any person with a skill that feels fragile, the individual who is uncomfortable with language is often less likely to explore, in this case with verbal communication and language-related activities. Furthermore, teachers who assume that students understand the purpose of subject-specific language and technical "school talk" place an added burden on students if they do not prepare or assist students' comprehension of unfamiliar concepts. In order to integrate content area language, students' knowledge and use of language, and their own unique ZPD in planning and conducting my instructional activities, I integrate students' interests, language, writing, and reading with conversation. Allen (1965) expressed this approach well when he said, "No matter what reading abilities are selected for emphasis or what experiences are introduced in the learning environment, they should fulfill the purpose of helping each child deepen the feeling that s/he can read successfully" (p. 6).

Conversation: A Catalyst for Learning

Students who have a long history of difficulty with language need to be active participants in social activities that include conversation. Allowing time for students to talk about familiar topics helps create a safe climate for students to practice taking risks, clarify thoughts, and communicate with others. When these critical ingredients are present in my classroom, I observe students who are excited and eager to communicate and who have increased confidence and self-esteem.

My role as the teacher in these conversations is, first, to help students frame their thoughts and words; second, to listen to the meaning of their message and help them structure and clarify their message; and third, to help them expand their vocabulary choices, correct inaccuracies or confusions, and elaborate on the content of their message. In preparing for these conversations, I explain that they need to be thoughtful and courteous, listen to others, share their ideas, and respond in appropriate ways. In other words, the role of the students is to listen carefully, serve as an authentic audience for their peers, and mirror an understanding as they listen for meaning when another student speaks or reads aloud. Students may also ask questions for clarification when they do not understand something. The responses of other students serve to make the speaker more aware of the need to use semantically and syntactically correct sentences or phrases. Therefore, shaping, reshaping, and clarifying thoughts and oral language are ongoing processes.

From Conversation to Text

Vygotsky stated that "written speech is considerably more conscious, and is produced more deliberately than oral speech" (1986, p. 182). Making that transition from conversation to written text should be deliberate, but it should also be seamless. The process of transition should be deliberately shaped by questions so that students identify what they want recorded in the shared text, but recognize the difference between conversation and written text.

Students' conversations preceding the writing of the shared text generate a lot of ideas, language, and vocabulary that students may choose to include in the shared text. During the writing of the shared text, students dictate, direct, and refine what is written as the teacher asks, "How should I begin this sentence?" or says, "Tell me what to write." As each student reports about his or her news, it is recorded. Next the teacher asks if what was written is accurate and reflects what the student wanted to share.

At times during the recording, the teacher may make suggestions or ask if the student would like to elaborate. Questions surface that deal with technical writing issues: "Where do we need a comma in this sentence?" "Do I need a capital letter here?" "Why?" During this process, it is crucial that students feel safe enough to take risks so that they will explore and learn. Students' responses, even when incorrect, are acknowledged: "Hold that thought and see if it checks out."

I have found using shared texts gives students the experience of taking turns, listening, and respecting others' ideas and experiences. It gives them an opportunity to be supportive of one another and to share and acknowledge the success and frustration of each other.

Reading Our Language

After the individual news items are written, each student reads his or her own news aloud. They may also read each other's if they choose. As each child reads, the teacher provides support to ensure success. For a child who is not experienced with reading, this support may include reading the text in phrases or short sentences and having the student repeat the text. For a more independent reader who has reached a puzzling word, the support may include pointing out the initial sound in the word or prompts to remember what that word might be in that context. Regardless of the support they require, the aim is to have each student experience success. The completed shared text is available for students to read again and again. Since the shared text is familiar to the students, they feel confident reading. Finally, copies of all the shared texts are filed in what we call "the archives." These files are saved for at least a year, and students who want to read them may do so. These files serve to chronicle the history, progress, and growth of our learners, and since they are comprised of our own students' negotiated and dictated news stories or events, students are interested in reading them.

Post Writing and Assessment

After reading the shared text, each child writes or dictates a paragraph about something that has not already been included in the shared text. This gives students an opportunity to compose and write their own thoughts. Working on the shared text provides a scaffold for students to construct their own news item later. The teacher and student conference one-on-one. Next, students make corrections, rewrite the work, and everyone reads what they have written with the whole group. Students who have physical limitations dictate their paragraph and practice their emerging writing skills by tracing a word or sentence.

It is my experience that standardized tests provide little more than a screening mechanism in assessing students because they measure isolated phonic and word recognition skills that are unrelated to meaningful context and do not offer an accurate reflection of students' comprehension. Therefore, the conversations and discussions that include questions and answers provide an opportunity for me to evaluate students as I take into consideration each individual's experience, cognitive stage, and motivation. It is only in this way that I can assess how the social interactions impact each individual's ZPD. Accurate assessment of each student's ZPD and knowledge of his or her developmental stage guide my instruction. For my needs, this kind of ongoing assessment within the classroom, including listening to the students' reading and using miscue analysis, is a far more helpful indicator of each student's reading progress. I keep samples of students' work in portfolios to provide evidence of their growth and accomplishments in reading, writing, and skill development. Looking through their own portfolios, students can see their progress, which in turn motivates them and boosts their self-esteem.

Expectations: Critical for a Learning Environment

One of the most difficult problems my students have in school is not their handicapping condition, but rather the expectations that accompany their label and undermine their growth. When we began working together, my students were conflicted about the expectations I had for them. On one hand, they were excited because they enjoyed being challenged and could see progress in the work that they were doing. On the other hand, they had become used to doing very little challenging work in school and behaved in ways that took the focus away from their academic problems/needs. We talked about focus being necessary for learning.

We talked about why they were in school, why I was with them, what I expected from them, and why I had the expectations I did.

Vygotsky (1986) observed that the impact of a person's handicap is secondary to an individual's social standing. Our classroom focuses on improving social behaviors. The program we use, "Making Better Choices" (Harris, 1984), is designed to take an intentional look at developing appropriate social behaviors. Individual students identify a behavior that is having a negative effect on their success in their schoolwork or in relationships with other students, and then the students and I develop a written plan that clearly specifies a different behavioral approach to that situation. Students are empowered because they make their own decisions to change, choose an alternative behavior, and review the outcomes of their changed behaviors. The written plans serve as another meaningful text for reading.

Challenge Leads to Confidence

There is no way we can give self-esteem or confidence to anyone, yet both are critical for acquisition of and love of learning. In my classroom, I have seen my students go from being intimidated by academic requirements to eagerly participating in academic activities. I have seen students go from not wanting to be at school to not wanting to miss a day. I have seen them strike out toward the library to find a book to read knowing that the world of books will take them to where they are motivated to go. I have seen their joy of accomplishment at reading and writing, and I have seen them love to learn.

Conclusion: Like Watching a River

The students I work with are unique, fascinating, courageous, and at times inspirational—as are all children. Their learning ebbs and flows, at times blocked by some internal log jam. As their logs are removed, sometimes gently, one at a time, and other times pushed by the force of collected energy, the learning hastens on its way. They learn to get around obstacles and avoid barriers, but the river is a long one and sooner or later the struggle begins at a different spot. The cycle of continued movement is as inherent in a child as it is in a river.

In my work with students, Vygotsky's research (1986) in the area of human development provides a realistic look at how the enculturation of stereotypes presents some of the greatest barriers and minimizes the expectations that surround the life of handicapped people. Their social standing as viable individuals and students, more than their physical and mental limitations, forms their educational path. This realization, along with an emphasis on the individual's own language, cognitive development, and the social nature of learning, has shaped my teaching with special needs children and young people.

Working in their zone of proximal development is critical to keeping the river flowing. Although this concept seems simple, the challenge is to assess the complex nature of the ZPD and adapt instruction to current educational practice. The social nature of learning is far too complex to provide us with the information we need in a standardized test package. We may find that our culturally and philosophically limiting definitions of learning that are reflected in standardized tests may ultimately be the biggest log jam in our search for a student's ZPD.

The assessment of a student's zone of proximal development is ongoing in all of the interactions I have with my students. LEA is ideal because it provides me with a framework to structure lessons, assess students, capitalize on students' experiences and knowledge and use of language, and to establish social learning environments. My observations of how a student interacts with me or other students, as well as how each one reflects on his or her own learning, all contribute to my instruction and assessment. Together, knowing how to employ what I know about students and using LEA have worked well for me and my students. Ultimately, for each student, their own enthusiasm for learning is a force that keeps them moving over, around, and through the obstacles in their path.

REFERENCES

Allen, R. V. (1965). *Attitudes and the art of teaching reading.* Washington, DC: Department of Elementary-Kindergarten-Nursery Education National Education Association of the United States.

Harris, W. J. (1984). The making better choices program. *The Pointer, 29,* 16–19.

Van Der Veer, R., & Valsiner, J. (1993). *Understanding Vygotsky: A quest for synthesis.* Cambridge, MA: Blackwell.

Vygotsky, L. (1986). *Thought and language* (rev. ed.). A. Kozulin, Ed. Cambridge, MA: MIT Press.

35

Variations on a Theme

Using Thematically Framed Language Experience Activities for English as a Second Language (ESL) Instruction

KATHLEEN A. J. MOHR

Assistant Professor, Kennesaw State University

Mrs. Jones has been assigned to teach English as a Second Language (ESL) at a struggling elementary school. She has tested and identified more than forty students who qualify for special instruction because of limited English proficiency, but there is no regular classroom available due to crowded conditions. Scheduling the students for instruction is difficult because they are in twelve different homerooms. Mrs. Jones has been allocated a very small budget and a hodgepodge collection of mostly teacher-assembled materials. Of the basal texts she does acquire, she has only four copies of each title, two titles per grade level. In addition to these realities, a variety of first languages are spoken by the identified students, who range from five to twelve years of age. As the ESL teacher, Mrs. Jones is expected to teach level-appropriate lessons, conducted for approximately forty-five minutes in the hall, on the stage, or in a corner of someone else's room. The administrators, teachers, and parents are hopeful that her special English instruction will expedite the oral fluency of the students and enable them to read and write on grade level as soon as possible.

Many ESL teachers will immediately identify with the variables stated above. Lack of materials, space limitations, too many students, and too little time for meaningful instruction are common factors currently facing most ESL teachers. When faced with any combination of these realities, a teacher must determine the best way to plan and conduct language lessons that will encourage limited-English-speaking students to acquire and use English successfully. How can a single teacher plan and conduct lessons for students who vary so greatly in language, age, grade, and motivation? Such an enormous challenge may, in part, be answered by a thematic approach to instruction with an emphasis on activities carefully designed to facilitate language growth.

Language Experience Approach (LEA) for Second Language Learners

LEA has long been heralded as an apt method for early literacy instruction, particularly for English-limited students (Garcia, 1974). One of the primary strengths of LEA is that it efficiently integrates listening, speaking, reading, and writing, and it promotes individual involvement, which can be very motivating for students. Additionally, although it requires much from the teacher, few materials are necessary to implement the procedures. LEA values the experiential and language backgrounds of the students and enables each student to participate from his or her own point on the continuum of language skills. Its emphasis on shared oral language that is used as a basis for reading and writing provides a strong platform for launching successful literacy development for ESL students of any age.

LEA includes the following basic procedures: a stimulus or experience is orchestrated to instigate oral discussion; the oral language of the students is then recorded; and then this written text becomes the source for reading activities. MaryAnne Hall (1978) defines LEA as a method for teaching reading. She states that in LEA

> instruction is built upon the use of reading materials created by writing down children's spoken language. The student-created reading materials represent both the experiences and the language patterns of the learner. (p. 1)

A comparison of LEA tenets with those of modern second language acquisition theory highlights common perspectives that strengthen LEA's value for language-divergent students. The work of language acquisition theorists, particularly Stephen Krashen (1987, 1988), and LEA advocates (Lee & Allen, 1963; Stauffer, 1980) substantiate the following:

1. **Language acquisition is a social activity.** Language is not developed except through interaction with other people. Thus, second language instruction should allow for dynamic conversation among its participants.
2. **Authentic communication is central to language development.** Second language instruction should facilitate real talk about real topics rather than solely providing drilled practice of isolated skills. Encouraging students to contribute what they already know about a subject uses their prior knowledge as a bridge to further their understanding of concepts.
3. **Shared experiences generate meaningful language interactions.** Shared language experiences connect students, giving them something in common, yet

allowing each individual to contribute his or her perspective. Such sharing allows students to assume a variety of communication roles, such as speaker, listener, questioner, explainer, audience, and critic. Communicating with others about common experiences enables students to negotiate meaning and refine their thoughts given a contextual framework.

4. Facilitated experiences and procedures promote comprehensible input for learners. Comprehensible input (Krashen, 1987) refers to messages that are understood. Incomprehensible input is mere noise to a language learner. Sharing a field trip or project, a book, or a film offers contextualized language input to learners. Such activities provide visual, aural, and tactile substance that can be represented by language. If the receiver has sufficiently similar experiences to identify with the content and adequate associated language the message is comprehended. With more identification and increased language acquisition, comprehension increases and the underlying knowledge base is enhanced.

5. Individual involvement is the key to personalized acquisition. When students are personally involved, experiences have more meaning. Language acquisition is personalized in that each individual builds a unique language repertoire. Language development is enhanced by motivated involvement in socialized settings that facilitate application, rather than passive observation.

6. A pragmatic focus on vocabulary development best guides instructional activities. Vocabulary is internalized only when it connects to enlarging schemata or scripts that the learner can then utilize in related situations. Terms learned without context are mere lists memorized but not necessarily ready for use. Students should be led to develop vocabularies and conversational patterns that can be used readily.

7. The four basic language skills (listening, speaking, reading, writing) are best developed when integrated. Discussing new concepts, then writing about them, and reading the dictated texts incorporates the four language skills and serves to reinforce the learning. ESL students benefit greatly from orally expressing their thoughts prior to writing them down. The opportunity to construct sentences in a conversational manner (listening and speaking) appears to greatly enhance the writing and associated reading process for ESL students.

8. Communicative content is to be valued over form of utterance. Getting the meaning across is preferred over focusing on the grammar of the language form. Good form certainly enhances the success of meaningful communication, but without substance, even grammatically correct verbiage is incoherent. If students worry too much about how they craft their speech, they are distracted from the intent of their communication.

9. Motivation to use and expand language elements expedites the acquisition process. Wanting or needing to communicate creates a strong desire to acquire and apply language successfully. Language use, however, is both pragmatic and creative. Providing reasons to communicate and supporting language efforts encourages students to take language risks that expand their competencies.

10. An honest concern for affective elements humanizes language instruction. Language learners are much more likely to interact in a second language when they feel comfortable and successful. Providing an appreciative environment helps lower anxieties and focuses the learner on meaningful communication, thus perpetuating the desire to interact.

It appears, then, that second language acquisition theory corroborates the basic tenets of LEA, and to its credit, LEA has been used successfully with ESL students for many years. However, given the common hardships of ESL teachers delineated earlier, it might be difficult for some ESL teachers to make use of LEA procedures. From a curricular perspective, ESL teachers should consider the use of themes in order to coordinate LEA activities. The use of specially selected and carefully organized thematic units of instruction may afford ESL students with LEA opportunities that increase communicative development.

Using a Thematic Framework for LEA Activities

A thematic approach to language arts lessons provides the teacher with a focus around which to plan a variety of lessons, including LEA activities for the wide array of ESL students. Once the focus has been determined, the teacher can direct his or her attention to what experiences to provide, what books to share, what writing activities to initiate, what specific skills to emphasize, and ways to assess growth. Using a theme extends the period of focus so that the acquired vocabulary can be used again and again and students can thus internalize the terminology, rather than simply memorize it. A focus on vocabulary is necessary for ESL students because contrary to a primary LEA tenet, these students cannot express in English everything that they think. ESL students need the words with which to express their thoughts.

A thematic framework, likewise, serves to balance narrative and expository texts read and written with students. Children have both factual and fictional ideas that they want to convey. Likewise, students are learning from both factual and fictional sources across their curricular programs. Well-chosen themes enable students to communicate about their real and imaginary worlds. For example, in a unit called Real and Unreal Pigs, younger students were asked to characterize in a Venn diagram what real pigs do and what make-believe pigs do. Older ESL students researched the uses of pigs and learned special pig terminology (e.g., *pork, swine, sow, bacon*).

With thematic instruction, students can build conceptual understanding because they revisit key concepts and add to their understandings from a variety of sources and activities. Random language arts lessons are less likely to build conceptual development or rehearse key vocabulary.

The choice of theme is an important consideration. It appears judicious to select themes based on language utility. In other words, choosing themes that equip ESL learners with the vocabulary, conversational patterns, and syntactical structures that students need and will apply outside the classroom is a good idea. Despite their perennial popularity, a unit on dinosaurs, teddy bears, or robots would probably yield less utility than clothing, relatives, machines, or occupations. It is possible for ESL teachers to select themes based on the magnitude of vocabularies found in academic concepts. Research (Marzano & Arredondo, 1986) provides a list of the categories that include the largest number of related terms. For instance, there are more words in elementary textbooks that deal with jobs and occupations than for events. Marzano and Arredondo's list of lexical categories provides a source for themes or instructional topics. Of course, choosing topics that facilitate students' curricular studies, such as plants, health matters, mathematical processes, and so on, helps them strengthen their academic performance in those areas.

A theme is not necessarily merely a topic, such as Halloween or Hearts or the Solar System. According to Sam Sebesta (1989), a theme entails exploring or expanding a topic. Sebesta proposes that theme-based instruction should explore "a topic to find issues, make inquiries, and arrive at judgments" (p. 2). Such a stance increases the potential value of thematically framed language instruction for students. If the goal is to explore a topic, students should be expected to ask questions, make connections to personal experiences, seek answers, and write and read about the concepts they are developing about the selected theme. Well-explored themes fuel discussion, and because the topic remains centered for a period of time, students have more opportunities to use their developing vocabularies and syntactical complexity. In others words, students' sentences tend to be longer, to be more elaborate, and to contain more precise word phrasing. It is recommended that theme studies continue for two or more weeks in most situations. A longer length of exposure reduces curriculum and resource changes. Layered encounters, that is, repeated and expanded exposure to elements in pragmatic themes or topics, allow for extended application of vocabulary and promote deeper conceptual development.

In order to maximize the potential for discoveries, connections, and insights during thematic instruction, teachers may choose to blend themes or present them as questions. For instance, double themes, such as Family Occupations, Insects in Springtime, or Winter Sports, encompass more concepts and include more vocabulary than singular topics. Thematic questions, such as, "How have machines changed?" or "What animals make good pets?" beg students to participate and respond with synthesis and evaluation.

LEA consists largely of providing shared experiences that yield dynamic discussion, which is then summarized in writing. The resultant text is used as reading material and the source for reading and language analysis activities. The written texts, whether narrative or expository, can be the product of thematic units that include trips, films, books, speakers, tasks, or experiences. Those interested in ways to extend the use of the dictated texts should refer to Lundsteen (1989) and Norton (1985).

Ways to Extend Thematically Framed LEA Activities

In addition to using dictated stories, ESL teachers can use the following generic activities to strengthen the value of thematic instruction. These activities can be used with most any theme study. They instigate discussion and can be done in groups with shared or independent follow-up. They are suited to ESL instruction because they serve as open-ended review activities that can be altered to match the limited, yet developing, reading and writing competencies of second-language learners.

Alpha Listing

During the study of a topic, students are encouraged to generate an alphabetical list of words relating to the theme. These words can then be used for spelling lists, sentence constructions, bingo games, and compositions. Older students can be challenged to look for special vocabulary in their theme-oriented lessons and keep individual lists in personal unit folders. Younger students can be encouraged to contribute to a group list kept as a chart in the classroom. Focusing on a variety of related terms strengthens conceptual understanding of the selected topic (see Figure 35.1). As an option, the list can include the English words and the same terms written in the student's first language. Such a list provides a source for cognate comparisons with older students. In conjunction with letter-sound-symbol correspondences, younger students could build a list of words that start with a selected

ALPHA LISTING

Topic: Water

a aquarium
b brook
c clouds
d dew, damp
e evaporate
f frost
g geyser
h hurricane
i icicle
j juice
k kayak
l lake
m monsoon

n nimbostratus
o ocean
p precipitation
q quicksand
r rain
s steam
t tears
u undulate
v vapor
w wave
x xebec
y Yangtze
z Zeebrugge

FIGURE 35.1   Alphabetical Listing of Selected Terms Related to Water

letter. For instance, if studying food, words could be collected that name food items and start with the letter I. Illustrations or cut-out pictures could reinforce the expanding food lexicon.

Word Wondering and Wandering

Word Wondering and Wandering is an adaptation of a prereading anticipation activity originated by Paula Hodges (Spiegel, 1981). This activity involves listing words that might be included in a text to be read. Based on what they already know, students are asked to generate words that they suspect might be included in a passage, or the teacher can list key vocabulary terms on a chart or the board and solicit student opinions as to whether they are likely to be found in the passage to be read. For example, students who may have studied insects are asked to anticipate the vocabulary included in a passage on bees. Rationales for choices and discussion of the terms can then precede the reading of the passage (see Figure 35.2). Students can place checkmarks next to the highlighted terms when reading, they can use the lists to check their comprehension, and, finally, they can employ the terms as a source for postreading discussion.

Semantic Grid

Semantic grids are used commonly as a means to summarize language learning. They are a general tool that can serve several purposes for ESL activities. The teacher can select key vocabulary that students have used in their dictated or self-composed LEA texts. These words become the items listed in the grid and the

WORD WONDERING AND WANDERING
Topic: _Ant Cities_

Text: _HBI Reader_

Words that might be:	Yes	No
1. work	✓	—
2. queen	✓	—
3. garden	✓	—
4. house	—	✓
5. cricket	—	✓
6. carry	✓	—
7. crystals	✓	✓
8. den	—	✓
9. hill	✓	—
10. dragonfly	—	✓

FIGURE 35.2   A Completed Word Wondering and Wandering Activity Related to a Text Passage on Ant Cities

SEMANTIC GRID

Topic: Folktales and Fairy Tales

Attributes:

Items:	BIG	POOR	YOUNG	EVIL	MAGICAL
1. GINGER-BREAD MAN	no	yes	yes	yes	?
2. LITTLE RED HEN	no	yes	no	no	no
3. GOLDILOCKS	no	?	yes	no	no
4. PAPA BEAR	yes	yes	no	no	no
5. WEE BABY BEAR	no	yes	yes	no	no
6. TROLL	yes	yes	no	yes	?
7. BIG... BILLY GOAT	yes	yes	no	no	no
8. JACK	no	yes	yes	no	no
9. OGRE	yes	no	no	yes	yes
10. OGRE's WIFE	yes	no	no	no	?

FIGURE 35.3   A Semantic Grid of Fairy Tale Characters and Selected Features

teacher or students can determine the features or attributes to complete the grid. Then the students can discuss and eventually respond orally or in writing with a simple yes/no, or plus/minus, to signify the validity of the attributes (see Figure 35.3). This activity builds vocabulary and concept development while enforcing comprehension of the theme students are studying. Students are called on to analyze what they know about terms in reference to related features.

Expectation Sentences

As a review of a selected theme, students are challenged to complete ten basic sentences about a particular group or class. Students must sort through their knowledge of topics and represent conceptual understanding in written form. This activity can be used as a pre- and/or postassessment of conceptual knowledge. Invalid sentences can be challenged to help clarify understanding. This activity can be done orally or shared with a group of younger students (see Figure 35.4).

EXPECTATION SENTENCES
Expectations we have about: _refrigerators_

1. **They are** _machines_ .

2. **They are not** _toys_ .

3. **They can** _keep food from turning bad_ .

4. **They can not** _move by themselves_ .

5. **Sometimes they will** _break_ .

6. **Sometimes they will not** _work_ .

7. **All will** _open and close_ .

8. **None will** _bite_ .

9. **With them,** _we put pictures up_

10. **Without them,** _food will get bad_ .

FIGURE 35.4   Completed Expectation Sentences about Refrigerators

"If I Were . . ." and Other Patterned Poems

Using poems, such as Kazue Mizumura's (1973) *If I Were a Cricket*, as a model, students select a noun relating to the theme or language experience activity and then describe it using their own language. When this activity is preceded with extended discussion about the selected topic, students can be encouraged to find appropriate phrases for describing and characterizing the topic (see Figure 35.5). There are many poems in the English language that feature specific syntax, such as "If I were . . ." (a subjunctive construction), that serve as a pattern for students to use in their own writing. The students can easily write pattern-based poems that the teacher can use to assess their knowledge and vocabulary in English.

Conclusion

These activities have been presented to encourage ESL teachers to meet the language needs of their students with thematically framed LEA activities. Carefully planned themes can serve a variety of grade levels simultaneously. In fact, thematic instruction is especially suited for cross-age groups. This type of instructional

If I were a cricket,

all through the autumn nights

I would sing for you,

a silver bell song

you would never forget.

IF I WERE

If I were a *honey bee*

with a body yellow and brown

I would *make a sweet treat*

and put it in a

box for you!

IF I WERE

If I were a *butterfly*

with many different colored wings

I would *dance in the air*

and above the flowers

to show you how to fly.

FIGURE 35.5   Child-Authored Poems Patterned after *If I Were a Cricket* **by K. Mizumura.**

Source: **Used by permission of HarperCollins Publishers.**

program is suited for diverse groupings and yet it is individualized because each student expands his or her own personal language repertoire; the activities allow individual students access to those elements that they are ready to acquire linguistically from the shared experiences.

Once teachers determine which theme to present, they can visit the school and public libraries to collect books and materials related to the theme. It is important to provide stimulating experiences that motivate the students and activate discussion. The recorded LEA texts that result from the interaction also add to the unit resources. Including additional activities, such as those presented here, reinforces students' learning by layering the theme-related vocabulary and concepts. In this manner, a teacher can meet the language needs of a variety of students, in diverse settings, with limited materials and resources. Perhaps the most important benefit of LEA is that the thematic activities provide teachers and students with engaging opportunities for meaningful social interaction. As Krashen (1987) recommends:

> The solution to our problems in language teaching lies not in expensive equipment, exotic methods, sophisticated linguistic analyses, or new laboratories, but in full utilization of what we already have, speakers of the languages using them for real communication. (p. 1)

It is via motivating experiences, shared dialogue, and supportive environments that students acquire a second language, because they are compelled to communicate, which is the purpose of language. An LEA perspective aligns with the goal of successful, authentic communication. Meshing language activities in a thematic framework enables ESL teachers to plan and provide a variety of experiences that facilitate second language acquisition. Effective ESL instruction is a complex task, but providing LEA activities within a thematic approach, rather than using a skills or basal approach to instruction, is an expeditious way to extend activities that synergize for meaningful interaction in English.

REFERENCES

Garcia, R. L. (1974). Mexican Americans learn through language experience. *The Reading Teacher, 28*(4), 301–305.

Hall, M. (1978). *The language experience approach for teaching reading: A research perspective*. Newark, DE: International Reading Association.

Krashen, S. D. (1987). *Principles and practice in second language acquisition*. New York: Prentice-Hall International.

Krashen, S. D. (1988). *Second language acquisition and second language learning*. New York: Prentice-Hall International.

Lee, D. M., & Allen, R. V. (1963). *Learning to read through experience* (2nd ed.). Englewood Cliffs, NJ: Prentice-Hall.

Lundsteen, S. W. (1989). *Language arts: A problem-solving perspective*. New York: Harper & Row.

Marzano, R., & Arredondo, D. E. (1986). *Tactics for thinking*. Aurora, CO: Mid-continent Regional Educational Laboratory.

Mizumura, K. (1973). *If I were a cricket*. New York: Thomas Y. Crowell.

Norton, D. E. (1985). *Language activities for children* (2nd ed.). Columbus, OH: Charles E. Merrill.

Sebesta, S. L. (1994). *The benefits of theme-based literature*. Celebrate Reading: Professional Resources. Carrollton, TX: Scott Foresman.

Spiegel, D. L. (1981). Six alternatives to the Directed Reading Activity. *The Reading Teacher, 34*(8), 914–920.

Stauffer, R. G. (1980). *The language experience approach to the teaching of reading* (2nd. ed.). New York: Harper & Row.

36 Literacy Development of Second Language Learners with Technology and LEA

VICKI PARSONS DULING

Teacher, Kings Glen Elementary School, Fairfax County (VA) Public Schools

Technology is revolutionizing and changing the way we teach language arts in our schools. For example, the use of computers, multimedia, and the Internet in our classrooms is an essential part of life today. Although technology has had a sizable influence on all students, the second language learner too can benefit from the increased and consistent use of all aspects of technology. Not only can the use of technology address methods of meeting the needs of various learning styles, it also can provide a vehicle for building students' knowledge of English through a very appealing medium. Although most ESL or second language students receive some special services from the school support programs, the vast majority still must function in the regular classroom (Penfield, 1987). Therefore, teachers who teach ESL students in regular classrooms, as well as qualified ESL teachers, need specific training. As Perez (1996) points out:

> The development of ESL is the responsibility of all the teachers a child encounters in school, rather than just the designated ESL teacher. Yet many regular classroom teachers feel, understandably, that they neither have the time nor the expertise to assist children in second language development. Part of their resistance is based in misconceptions about what the teaching of a second language involves. (p. 180)

The Importance of Connecting Language and Experience for ESL Learners

Both language and experience are critical to the physical, social, psychological, and educational growth of all children. The intimate relationship between experiences and language in social and personal communications is clearly apparent from the early days of human life. Therefore, when the young child begins school, language and experiences should be the foundation of all instruction. Building on existing schema is important in order to have learning be meaningful, relevant, and effective.

John Dewey (1938) provided a classic educational theory for twentieth-century America. His theory that learning will occur when children's previous life experiences are linked with new information is still relevant in today's classrooms (Carroll, 1995). Therefore, instructional methods for reading and writing should involve the fusion of new material with existing schema or knowledge rooted in children's experiences. In order to bring that kind of learning about, Dewey believed that teachers must match curriculum and instruction by taking into consideration students' physical, psychosocial, and intellectual developmental stages.

To help the ESL learner, classrooms must continually provide many avenues for success to support reading, writing, listening, and speaking. For example, using literature-based materials, teaching reading skills in the content areas, and immersing students in experiential activities invites true learning. Whether the students are using math manipulatives, discussing a book through literature circles, exploring social studies through simulations or reader's theater, or using hands-on science experiences, they must learn to construct their own meaning in each collaborative activity (Collier, 1995; Daniels, 1994; Routman, 1991; Sturtevant, 1996). As students experience each learning activity, they connect with their prior knowledge (schema) and assimilate the content information as well as receive daily experience in the oral use of the English language. This supports Krashen's (1985) natural approach theory, which states that students must receive comprehensible input that is understood, natural, interesting, meaningful to the student, and one step beyond the student's present level of competence in the second language. This theory embodies the belief that if the content information is understood and if there is enough language input, then the grammar aspects of language will be acquired automatically (Collier, 1995: Lightbown & Spada, 1993; Perez, 1996). Seemingly, Vygotsky's theory of the zone of proximal development also supports this approach (Good & Brophy, 1995). Experiential learning can provide these kinds of opportunities for students to work collaboratively in small groups, which provides further daily second language oral exposure.

In the upper elementary and middle school grades, the language experience approach (Stauffer, 1970) naturally complements the whole language philosophy for teaching second language learners as it encourages the interaction of the students' schemata. Using such techniques as K-W-L charts (Ogle, 1986), the Directed Reading-Thinking Activity (Stauffer, 1970), Venn diagrams, and data retrieval charts can help students organize their language experience story or information in the content area. Once the background knowledge is activated, individual stories and writing can take place (Burns, Roe, & Ross, 1996; Spangenberg-Urbschat & Pritchard, 1994).

Using Technology and Language Experience Activities with ESL Learners

Computer technology can provide an exciting method for fostering literacy through language experience. The use of technology allows students to learn at their own speed in a nonthreatening and intrinsically motivating environment. It allows each student flexibility, choice, and a feeling of success. Change is a constant as more schools connect to the Internet and equip classrooms with appropriate hardware and software that can be used daily.

Improving Math Concepts with Educational Software

For the past several years, I have utilized many computer programs with my regular upper-elementary classes as well as with the fifth- and sixth-grade ESL students at Kings Glen Elementary School in Fairfax County, Virginia. Technology was infused with the curriculum through a wide variety of popular educational software and CD-ROMs. For example, when a sixth-grade girl from Somalia arrived in my class, I needed to provide meaningful mathematics instruction for her in a classroom of thirty-two students. This child had no English speaking skills and was illiterate in her own language. In addition, she had never experienced any kind of formal school setting. Fortunately, another sixth-grade Somalian student was able to translate and provide a vital link for early communication. I found myself creating lessons with my own children's early math materials from home and supplies from the nearby K–3 school. Before long the student discovered the computer and was able to transfer the manipulative addition/number concepts quickly to the *Number Munchers* computer game (1992). If time did not permit one-on-one daily instruction for this student, meaningful activities and practice took place using the computer.

Composing Texts

Another technology method used for the beginning language learner includes composing at the computer. Fran Dixon, an ESL teacher at Kings Glen Elementary School, utilized wordless cartoon strips that could be easily understood by looking at the pictures. First, she encouraged students to orally describe each picture or story with a sentence or two. The purpose of this activity was to develop students' vocabulary, oral expression, and risk taking. This activity served as a rehearsal for students' writing. Fran then encouraged students to write their explanation or story. Students could either type their explanation on the computer or dictate their explanation, depending on each student's abilities and English language proficiency.

Using the computer to write their stories eliminated the need to physically print or write in cursive. Since some students are still not comfortable forming the letters using a pen or pencil, using the computer worked best for them, allowing them to concentrate on constructing meaning and writing for a purpose. As students became more proficient in describing the cartoons orally and in writing, Fran introduced longer and more complex cartoon strips. In fact, some students still returned to their initial explanations and refined and improved their explanations over time as they gained more understanding and experience, and improved their English language proficiency. Students' progress and literacy growth have been most positive employing this method to have students compose short texts.

As students have become more successful and comfortable using the computer, other pronunciation and word recognition games have been introduced, such as bingo, matching lotto, and word code games.

The Immigration Project: Writing and Designing Personal Stories

One of the units we study in social studies focuses on explorers and immigration. Since many of our students have experienced the immigration process personally or heard family stories, we wanted to validate them and their experiences. Therefore, we decided to have our students start by interviewing their parents or other relatives about their immigration experiences and then report the details in writing to the class.

Students' Language and Cultural Backgrounds

At the time of this project, our class was composed of five children who spoke Vietnamese, four who spoke Spanish, and one each who spoke Korean, Indian, Persian, Portuguese, or Uzbekistanian as their first language. Students were mostly categorized as somewhat proficient, although one young man from India spoke no English upon his arrival to the United States and could be categorized as an emergent speaker. Therefore, most of the children interviewed their parents in their first or native language and then translated the information into English, their second language. This activity served multiple purposes: it created a bond between students and parents; generated a wealth of familiar information for students to read and write about; highlighted personal and unique qualities and contributions; and affirmed each students' sense of self, family history, and culture.

Using a Computer to Create a Class Slide Show

To expand this activity, each student then wrote their own arrival stories. Although the majority of our students were recent immigrants, experiences were different. This project turned out to be the most exciting language experience project we did. It involved creating a class slide show utilizing Broderbund's *Kid Pix* software (1992), which enables children to create original drawings and paint, as well as use a choice of commercially produced and copyright-free stamps. In addition, the *Kid Pix* software has the capability to generate slide shows with voice overlay. Students designed their own slide, including their names, birthdays, favorite items, pets, and information about their home countries. The program allowed them to access ready-made stamps or pictures, to draw freehand using drawing and drafting tools included in the program, and to design their entire slide. After the students created their slides, they saved the slides on classroom floppy disks. These could be edited at any time, so students continued to revise their pictures. Next, they used writing skills to plan the oral explanation about themselves to accompany their slide. Some students wrote out a paragraph introducing themselves while others made lists or notes of things they wanted to say. Many students grew through the trial-and-error process. Several thought they knew exactly what to say from their notes, only to find out that when it actually came time to speak into the computer microphone, they hesitated. It was a new experience, and they did not feel confident speaking without practicing exactly what they were going to say. Many were enamored with the sound of their own and others' voices. In the first few days of this project, students often listened when other students were editing their audio segments.

Within a very brief time, students noticeably improved their spoken English fluency. It seemed the excitement of hearing their own voices coming from the computer was a motivational factor. Several students were never satisfied with their recording and continued to revise and rerecord. Since *Kid Pix* is particularly user friendly, students could manipulate the controls easily. The entire project took about three weeks for each student to complete a slide and record the voice overlay. The latter part of the activity could be accomplished in a shorter amount of time if necessary. Since there was only one computer in the classroom and students had to find time between other activities to use it, we were not concerned about how long it took to complete the project. The focus was on the writing process and each student's success.

Final Production Phase   Individual student slides were organized into a classroom slide-show presentation. This process took about two hours and required some technical expertise. In the future, however, I would direct students to complete this part of the project with my guidance and direction. The versatility of producing slide shows is that it is appealing to children, it can be student directed, it is portable, and it may be used for various purposes in the curriculum (Grabe & Grabe, 1996).

The following writing samples exemplify the diversity of students' cultural and educational backgrounds and emphasize their personal history. Each student designed and developed a slide separately. First, they shared information by talking about themselves with their peers, then they wrote facts and information they wanted to include in their slide, and finally they recorded their personal stories:

FIGURE 36.1 Jimmy Le's Computer-Generated Slide

Hi! I'm from Vietnam. My name is Jimmy Le and I am eleven years old. I have one sister. My mom works at a factory and my dad works at a print shop. I am in sixth grade and my sister is in first grade. I have two angel fish. They laid eggs but the eggs didn't hatch.

Hi. My name is Jung-Ah and I am from South Korea. I am twelve years old. I like to play with my dog. His name is Gom-Jee which means kinda like stupid in Korean. He is a Siberian Huskie. That's all.

FIGURE 36.2 Jung-Ah's Computer-Generated Slide

FIGURE 36.3   Mihir's Computer-Generated Slide

Hello. Hello. My name is Mihir. I am coming to America in May. [Mihir had spent only four months in the United States before completing this task.] My father's name is Chandrakant Patel. I have one brother and two sisters. I am eleven years old. My country's name is India. Bye.

Hi. My name is Tamara Nunes and I am from Brazil. I have been here for one year and two or three months. I am twelve years old and am going to be thirteen on November 2nd. I like playing video games and riding my bike and watching TV. I really miss my family that is left in Brazil. Here I just have my dad and some of my cousins. I want to go back to Brazil to see my family.

FIGURE 36.4   Tamara's Computer-Generated Slide

As the varied examples show, the students quickly made the slide show personal and meaningful. More extensive individual slide shows could be constructed that include more details about immigration experiences and life in America. Allowing students to expand their family immigrant stories and connect them with their own personal stories would be the natural avenue for improving and expanding this project in the future.

The Value of the Language Experience Classroom Approach

The value of tapping into each student's individual immigrant experience developed ownership, motivated the learner, incorporated students' experiences, and provided multiple opportunities for students to engage in meaningful reading, writing, listening, and speaking activities. Stauffer (1970) stated:

> The Language-Experience Approach . . . take[s] advantage of the wealth that children bring with them to school—linguistically, intellectually, socially, and culturally. By focusing on language as a means of communication, the transfer from oral language usage to written language is made functionally. Reading does become talk written down. (p. xi)

By incorporating technology software that appealed to many different learning styles, students were motivated and able to write and share their individual histories.

Ownership of the material and an immediate validation of their past experiences helped to facilitate learning in our ESL classroom. The software program provided important accessible and user-friendly hands-on experiences with technology and increased the technological comfort zone for many students. The ease and comfort experienced by the ESL students with this project transferred to other technology uses in other teaching settings. The pride, interest, fun, and learning achieved through this project were exciting and fulfilling for all students. Expanding and increasing the use of classroom technology in the future can only enhance the learning and language experience for all students.

REFERENCES

Burns, P. C., Roe, B. D., & Ross, E. P. (1996). *Teaching reading in today's elementary schools*. Boston: Houghton Mifflin.

Carroll, P. S. (1995). John Dewey for today's whole language middle school. *Middle School Journal, 27*, 62–68.

Collier, V. P. (1995). *Promoting academic success for ESL students: Understanding second language acquisition for school*. Elizabeth, NJ: Teachers of English to Speakers of Other Languages-Bilingual Educators (NJTESOL-BE).

Daniels, H. (1994). *Literature circles*. York, MN: Stenhouse Publishers.

Dewey, J. (1938). *Experience and education*. Kappa Delta Pi Lecture Series. 1963 edition, New York: Collier Books.

Good, T. L., & Brophy, J. (1995). *Contemporary educational psychology*. White Plains, NY: Longman.

Grabe, M., & Grabe, C. (1996). *Integrating technology for meaningful learning*. Boston: Houghton Mifflin.

Kid Pix. (1992). Novato, CA: Broderbund Software.

Krashen, S. D. (1985). *The input hypothesis*. New York: Longman.

Lightbown, P., & Spada, N. (1993). *How languages are learned*. Oxford, England: Oxford University Press.

Number Munchers. (1992). Minneapolis: The Learning Company, MECC.

Ogle, D. (1986). K-W-L: A teaching model that develops active reading of expository text. *The Reading Teacher, 39*, 564–570.

Penfield, J. (1987). ESL: The regular classroom teacher's perspective. *TESOL Quarterly, 21*, 21–29.

Perez, B. (1996). Instructional conversations as opportunities for English language acquisition for culturally and linguistically diverse students. *Language Arts, 73*(3), 173–181.

Routman, R. (1991). *Invitations: Changing as teachers and learners K–12*. Portsmouth, NH: Heinemann.

Spangenberg-Urbschat, K., & Pritchard, R. (Eds.). (1994). *Kids come in all languages: Reading instruction for ESL students*. Newark, DE: International Reading Association.

Stauffer, R. G. (1970). *The language-experience approach to the teaching of reading*. New York: Harper & Row.

Sturtevant, E. G. (1996). Content literacy and experiential learning: A winning combination for secondary curriculum. NASSP. *Curriculum Report, 25*(3), 1–4.

Walker, B. J. (1992). *Supporting struggling readers*. Markham, Ontario: Pippin.

37 Negotiated Language Experience and Content Area Instruction in the Bilingual Classroom

LINDA LEWIS-WHITE

Assistant Professor, Eastern Michigan University

"Who can tell me the stages of the water cycle?"

Like lightning the classroom is filled with the sounds of English and Spanish chatter as the students turn to one another to negotiate the concepts from their science lessons. Discussion may last from five to ten minutes but soon the room quiets, and hands are thrust high, signaling the students' readiness.

Pointing to a large diagram of the water cycle that has been drawn on butcher paper, I ask, "What is the first stage of the water cycle?"

"Evaporation," comes the answer as I nod at Martita.

"Great! Now can you explain what happens during this stage?" I continue writing *evaporation* on the diagram.

As Martita begins to explain what she understands of the process of evaporation, she relies on her classmates for words or parts of the sequence that give her trouble. She and her classmates negotiate the information using both English and Spanish. When she has formulated her reply, Martita directs her answer to me and I write it in note form on the chart. Then the class and I read the notes and add any information that is missing. So begins the negotiated language experience process on the water cycle.

What Is a Negotiated LEA Text?

Traditionally, the Language Experience Approach (LEA) uses shared experiences such as field trips, speakers, demonstrations, and so forth as the catalyst for writing. Students participate in the activity and then as a group write about their experience. This written text, which is referred to as the "negotiated LEA," becomes part of the reading material for the class.

Language experience activities in the content area classroom are taught in the students' native or primary language in conjunction with English as a Second Language (ESL) instruction. These negotiated texts then become the starting point for the writing experience in English. Students use primary language textbooks to read about the subject, participate in experiments and demonstrations, and develop English vocabulary for the concepts being taught. The negotiated LEA text is used in content area instruction to teach language concepts such as conventions of written English, spelling, and phonics during ESL instruction.

Why Use Negotiated LEA Texts?

In bilingual classrooms students are taught in their native or primary language at the same time they are acquiring English or their secondary language. Students' progress is measured in terms of the development of their language proficiency. Language proficiency is the ability to use language to negotiate meaning. Cummins (1979a, 1979b, 1980) suggests that there are two types of proficiencies, Basic Interpersonal Communications Skills (BICS) and Cognitive/Academic Language Proficiencies (CALP). BICS refer to a person's communicative ability to function in everyday interpersonal activities. CALP refers to the communicative ability needed in any language to learn and manipulate new ideas or information. Research findings indicate that immigrant children achieve conversational proficiency (BICS) in their secondary language with their peers within about two years of their arrival in the classroom; however, they take five to seven years to approach the academic language skills (CALP) in their secondary language, which is necessary to be successful in school (Cummins, 1984).

Cognitive/Academic Language Proficiency in primary or native language and secondary language are interdependent (Cummins, 1981), so that in order for students to be successful in their secondary language, they must have foundational skills and concepts in their primary language first. Once students understand the foundational concepts in their primary language, instruction in the secondary language can build on those concepts, beginning with vocabulary. Students learn the concept once and transfer that concept into English after they acquire the new labels.

Using what Breen and Candlin (1979) have called the "communicative methodology of language," the teacher facilitates the communicative process between the students and the content of the lessons. The students negotiate between themselves and the content in order to redefine their knowledge of a concept or skill in the secondary language.

By using negotiated LEA strategies to facilitate the communicative process, the teacher sets up instructional activities in psychological and social contexts in which the students become both learners and teachers (Breen and Candlin, 1979). Within the instructional setting, students recognize the knowledge they possess and through negotiation confirm what they know. The students engage in monitoring their own communicative proficiency as well as providing feedback to their classmates.

Vygotsky (1978) said that what we know corporately is more than the sum total of what we know individually. For bilingual students, the negotiated LEA activity provides opportunities for them to develop the academic language skills and abilities in their secondary language through repetitive and group interaction within the content area. It also provides for the integration of literacy development in the secondary language within the context of real-world learning.

How Do I Structure Negotiated LEA Activities?

All negotiated LEA activities begin with instruction in the content areas (mathematics, science, social studies, health) in the students' native language. These lessons follow a typical lesson cycle and use native language textbooks and other instructional materials.

During ESL instruction the students and I begin to build the English vocabulary through a thematic instructional approach. Utilizing bilingual vocabulary charts with words grouped by category and word maps with illustrations, students are soon able to recognize English labels for concepts they have already learned in Spanish.

In addition, the students listen to or read English language texts that are instructionally appropriate for their level of language proficiency. They engage in other activities that facilitate the acquisition of the new vocabulary, such as music, art, and drama. These activities also expose the students to a variety of linguistic expressions and styles using the same core content vocabulary. According to Sanchez-Sadek (1995), students must be exposed to a new vocabulary item at least seventy-five times before it becomes part of their usable vocabulary.

The Writing Process

Once the students are familiar with the English labels for the concept, we are ready to begin the negotiated LEA text. Because I have a writing workshop classroom, the process for writing the negotiated LEA closely follows the writing process—prewriting, writing, conferencing/negotiating, editing, and publishing.

Prewriting

I begin the prewriting session by calling the students to sit on the floor in front of the board. On the board, I place a graphic organizer that is appropriate to the subject. For example, to introduce the water cycle, I used a diagram of the water cycle. To explain how to regroup in subtraction, I used a math problem written in three-inch-high numbers. The visuals help students clarify the questions for themselves and offer contextual support for their answers.

Students are asked to explain what they know about a given subject. After the question is asked, students spend from five to ten minutes discussing it among themselves. They are encouraged to use both Spanish and English as needed to clarify their knowledge. Then I ask a question that assists the students in breaking the subject down into manageable parts. For example, the first question might be "What do you know about the water cycle?" and the second question would be "What is the first stage of the water cycle?"

A student called on to answer the question may begin to answer and then confer once again with classmates as needed or may answer the question completely before asking classmates for confirmation of the answer. Either way, all students are responsible for the accuracy of the answer. As the student speaks, I write notes on the chart paper, and the students are also encouraged to take notes. When the student is finished answering, the class and I read the notes orally together and I ask them if there is anything that is left out or that needs to be added. Prewriting continues until the class has notes for the entire negotiated LEA text.

Writing, Negotiating, and Editing

Once the prewriting is complete, students then dictate the LEA text using the notes. As students dictate, they negotiate for accuracy in content as well as grammar. When the draft is completed, we read the text together and edit it for clarity. Depending on the topic, the actual process of writing the negotiated LEA text may take anywhere from two to five hours during the course of a week.

Publishing

When the students have said that the LEA text is complete, I type it up on the computer and print it so each student has a copy. The original is posted in the room. As a class, we read the text chorally and students are encouraged to read the text for practice by themselves. Occasionally I check a student's reading fluency in English by having the student read the LEA text aloud. Other language lessons and activities such as grammar, writing conventions, or spelling are conducted using the negotiated LEA text. This text is also used to evaluate the students' acquisition of the core vocabulary for the subject.

I encourage my students to keep their notes, the negotiated LEA text, and any vocabulary list all together in content area folders to use as reference materials in the future. In addition to benefiting from the folders' value as reference materials, students can look at their folders in each subject area and see the amount of knowledge they have gained during the year.

What Do My Students Know about the Water Cycle?

The depth of knowledge and the quality of language usage varies with each class from year to year. What follows is a sample negotiated LEA on the water cycle from my current third-grade class.

> The earth and its atmosphere form a closed system. This means that all the gasses that make up the atmosphere and all of the water for the earth are already in the earth's environment and we can not add to them.
>
> The water cycle is a closed system within the earth's atmosphere. The water cycle has three parts evaporation, condensation, and precipitation.
>
> Evaporation occurs when energy from the sun or moving air (wind) causes a body of water to heat up. When this happens, molecules of water begin to move faster and spread out. The water is now a gas called water vapor. The water vapor moves with the air above the body of water.
>
> The warm air rises carrying the water vapor with it. As the water vapor goes higher into the atmosphere, it begins to cool. The water molecules begin to move more slowly and come closer together, or condense. They mix with dust and other particles in the air to form clouds. This stage of the water cycle is called condensation.
>
> Winds in the upper atmosphere move the clouds over land masses. The clouds continue to collect water until they are too heavy. When the water molecules are too large and heavy to remain suspended in the air, they fall in the form of mist, rain, sleet, snow or ice. This stage is called precipitation.

Together, a group of sixteen bilingual third-grade students, whose language proficiency ranges from non-English speaker to fluent English speaker, was able to produce this concise but scientifically accurate informative piece on the water cycle. Individually, not one of these students could have produced this piece of writing. However, in writing this and other negotiated LEA texts, the students gained more than the academic skills and concepts taught. They also developed confidence in their own knowledge and skill in the content area, increased their oral fluency, and became active participants in their own learning.

Conclusion

The negotiated language experience activities in my classroom establish an environment in which my students and I become learners together. It provides multiple opportunities for students to actively interact with the language and content of the subject, in order to transition their communication abilities in their native language, Spanish, to their secondary language, English. Additionally, it provides opportunities for us to engage in purposeful literacy development activities that are integrated with the content area materials.

REFERENCES

Breen, M., and Candlin, C. (1979). Essentials of a communicative curriculum. *Applied Linguistics, 1*(2), 90–112.

Cummins, J. (1979a). Cognitive/academic language proficiency, linguistic interdependence, the optimum age question, and some other matters. *Working Papers on Bilingualism, 19*, 121–129.

Cummins, J. (1979b). Linguistic interdependence and the educational development of bilingual children. *Review of Educational Research, 49*(2), 222–251.

Cummins, J. (1980). The entry and exit fallacy in bilingual education. *NABE Journal, 4*, 25–60.

Cummins, J. (1981). The role of primary language development in promoting success for language minority students. In *Schooling and language minority students: A theoretical framework*, pp. 3–49. Office of Bilingual Bicultural Education, California State Department of Education, Sacramento. Los Angeles: Evaluation, Dissemination and Assessment Center, California State University.

Cummins, J. (1984). *Bilingualism and special education: Issues in assessment and pedagogy*. San Diego: College-Hill.

Sanchez-Sadek, C. (1995). *Basis for the development of an integrated curriculum*. Keynote address at the Third Annual Summer Institute, New Visions 95: Fusion of School and Culture. Arlington, TX: July 28.

Vygotsky, L. (1978). *Mind in society*. Cambridge, MA: Harvard University.

38 The Language Experience Approach

Yesterday, Today, and Tomorrow

MICHAEL R. SAMPSON

Professor, Texas A&M University, Commerce

MARY BETH SAMPSON

Assistant Professor, Texas A&M University, Commerce

The wisest man of all time is best remembered for his exclamation "There's nothing new under the sun!" Solomon was indeed an insightful man, and his adage is more true today than ever—despite all that appears to be new in education as we move into the twenty-first century.

Today's bookshelves are overflowing with books of new theories and philosophies. The last decade has seen a proliferation of books, articles, and conference presentations on topics such as multiple intelligences, learning styles, whole language, literature-based instruction, process writing, and "balanced literacy." Many consider these to be the most exciting times in the history of education. But a true student of history realizes that the years 1950 to 1970 were an age when the giants of the Language Experience Approach (LEA) left a legacy of philosophy and practice that were the launching pads from which today's practices emerged. A new generation of teachers have almost forgotten the names—Roach Van Allen, Russell Stauffer, Sylvia-Ashton Warner—as well as others (MaryAnne Hall, Doris Lee, Jeanette Veatch) who defined LEA through their focus on children and the language of the learner. But even these greats refuse to take credit for inventing something "new"; instead, they refer back to Edmund Huey's work in 1908, to Horace Mann's work, and to teachers in their one-room schoolhouses of the nineteenth century (Allen, 1994). But certainly three educators—Allen, Stauffer, and Ashton-Warner—developed the procedures and practices for what became know as the Language Experience Approach. Two of these vanguards—Allen and Stauffer—

were the organizers of the Language Experience Special Interest Group (LESIG) of the International Reading Association.

Yesterday

Roach Van Allen

The primary classroom is filled with the litter of literacy. Charts of children's language, favorite poems, and sentence strips are everywhere—taped to the window, draped over a chart, even hanging from the ceiling. Tempera paints, brushes, glue, and papers of many colors cover a table in the art center. Masks, puppets, costumes, and reader's theater scripts adorn the drama center. Excited voices chime in as children read a story together. Is this a process classroom of 1998? No, the year is 1956 and the classroom in San Diego is implementing the ideas of their young superintendent for instruction, Roach Van Allen. Allen had learned through his work with children in the border town of Harlingen, Texas, that language development is the key to reading development. And he found that the key to language development was a broad curriculum that was based on the arts. Hence, in the curriculum guide he developed for the San Diego County Schools, he wrote "EXPERIENCE is the foundation of all language development" (Allen, 1956). During his eight years as superintendent (1955–1963), Allen developed and researched his Language Experience Approach. His major contribution was a major research study that asked, "Of all the language experiences available for study in the elementary years, which ones have the greatest contribution to reading?" (Allen, 1976). His factorial analysis design served to identify twenty essential language experiences that have the greatest impact on literacy development. Thus, Allen moved LEA from practices that had obvious face validity to recognition by researchers that LEA had a research base of support. These twenty experiences were grouped into three strands of activities (Sampson, Sampson, & Allen, 1996), which included activities for self-expression (writing, singing, painting); activities for impression (reading, listening, assimilating); and activities for development of conventions or skills in context (spelling, language structure, graphophonic cueing system). For Allen, LEA was much more than dictation, its best-known feature. He truly broadened the approach by placing its foundation in the language arts. In spite of this, Allen will be forever remembered for his often quoted, and so clearly stated, definition of the link between thought, oral language, and reading: "What I can think about, I can talk about; What I can say, I can write; What I can write, I can read; I can read what others write for me to read" (Sampson, Sampson, & Allen, 1995, p. 33).

Sylvia Ashton-Warner

As Allen was finishing his LEA research in San Diego, an equally important work was underway half a world away in New Zealand. Ashton-Warner, faced with the difficulty of teaching New Zealand and Maori children to read, developed her own LEA through what she called "Organic Reading" (Ashton-Warner, 1958). Her views were classic LEA: (1) learning should start within the child and from the child's expressions (intrinsic); and (2) outside information is only learned when it becomes important to the learner (extrinsic). This philosophy led her to develop her organic vocabulary approach as a bridge from the known to the new—a bridge to help children move from their personal experiences to relating to the written experiences shared by others.

In her classic book, *Teacher* (Ashton-Warner, 1963), she presented the story of how she related to culturally diverse children and helped them to become readers through experience. In essence, she started with children's "organic, instinctive" reaction to reading. This led to children selecting daily words that were "organically" connected to the children, words that were "already part of the child's being" (Ashton-Warner, 1963, p. 30).

Ashton-Warner moved children through four stages or "Movements" as the students moved from learning and reading their own, internal personal vocabulary words in the first movement to writing stories in the fourth movement. She believed it would be foolish to ask a child to read a book that was outside his or her realm of experience, and stated "First books must be made of the stuff of the child himself" (Ashton-Warner, 1963, p. 35).

The trademark of her LEA approach was in the word cards she created for her students. Children would name a word they wanted to add to their collection, and Sylvia would write it on a card for the student. Students studied and reviewed their words each day.

Unfortunately, what most people remember about Ashton-Warner's LEA is negative—she destroyed word cards when students could not read the word. She defended the practice by saying "I take them from her and destroy because the word has failed as a one-look word and cannot have been of much importance to her" (Ashton-Warner, 1963, p. 47). However, she knew her children and their culture, and her methods had phenomenal results as children moved from intrinsic to extrinsic expressions and understandings.

Russell Stauffer

Russell Stauffer made invaluable contributions to the field of literacy through his language-experience approach. Although different from Allen's LEA (starting with the small point that Stauffer hyphenates *language-experience* and Allen does not), he shared many similarities in philosophy with Allen and Ashton-Warner. Stauffer wrote "Reading, writing, speaking and listening occur within the context of purposeful communication" (1970, p. 13). Stauffer believed that wise teachers must take advantage of the child's culture and language in order to facilitate the transfer from oral language to written language. Like Allen, Stauffer took dictation from children. Like Ashton-Warner, Stauffer made word cards of children's words (1970, p. 55). Children kept these words in Word Banks and used them for word study and creative writing activities. Stauffer was once again ahead of his time as he suggested "Creative writing topics may be suggested, but students should be encouraged to write about anything they wish" (1970, p. 83).

In conjunction with his LEA work, Stauffer left us with two major legacies: (1) spelling instruction (Stauffer, 1969); and (2) comprehension instruction. Much of today's spelling instructional practices may be traced to the work of Stauffer, his graduate students, and their graduate students. Stauffer's Directed Reading-Thinking Activity (DR-TA) became the cornerstone for comprehension instruction, and the model through which active reader involvement with text through predictions was delivered.

Today

Today's teachers owe a huge debt of gratitude to the LEA pioneers: Allen, Ashton-Warner, and Stauffer. But do we really realize to what extent these pioneers contributed to today's child-centered curricula? Let's examine some current practices and their roots.

Whole Language

By definition, whole language means "all of language." The term grew out of the lack of whole instruction that was a product of the 1960s and 1970s. Instruction tended to be focused on skills, developed out of context. In many ways, whole language is a throwback to the LEA days of the 1950s, and reflects the LEA pioneers' view of child-centered, whole-child instruction.

Multiple Intelligences

Decades before Gardiner's Seven Intelligences became labeled and popular, Roach Van Allen was writing about them. Allen referenced the work of J. P. Guilford (1959) and his structure of the intellect, and discussed how children demonstrated their intelligence through art, music, drama, physical activities, spatial activities, verbal activities, and so on (Allen, 1976 p. 395).

Predictable Books

Roach Van Allen made wide use of predictable books in his LEA, and was one of the first educators to embrace a young writer of predictable books, Bill Martin, Jr. A key meeting occurred between the two in 1958, when Allen invited Martin to come to San Diego County Schools to share his books. Martin left San Diego very impressed with Allen's work, and Allen became a lifelong supporter and user of the genres of books that Bill Martin, Jr., wrote (Allen, 1994). Predictable books are popular today, and so are the works of Bill Martin, Jr.

Dictation

In classrooms across America, primary teachers continue to take dictation from young children—in spite of warnings from today's process writing leaders. These process writing advocates don't understand LEA and its history. They don't understand that dictation involves different processes and has different goals than independent writing. Or, as stated by Sulzby, Teale, and Kamberelis (1989), teachers don't take dictation "because children can't write, they are using dictation as another form of writing" (p. 75). Dictation is important because the process allows students to see and develop insights into the relationships among language, reading, and writing.

Process Writing

Writing instruction has never been better for children in the United States than it is now, thanks to the research and work of current-day leaders Donald Murray, Donald Graves, Nancy Atwell, and others. However, their work is not unique—it too is founded in LEA history. Stauffer's children were heavily engaged in creative writing; Allen's children wrote every day; Ashton-Warner's students wrote from their "organic experiences." Allen, as early as 1976, discussed children's spellings and labeled their early spellings "exploratory spellings," which perhaps is an even better name than today's favorite—invented spellings! In addition, he engaged children in the refinement of their work. Children collaboratively engaged in the "editing" process as they explored and polished pieces of their writing for publication and celebration.

Tomorrow

At the turn of the century, we must decide if we will move forward or backward in our instruction of children. Many would have us move back to the days of out-of-context instruction—back to the days of skill learning as an end in itself. Yes, there is a renewed cry for teachers to move "back to the basics." Yet, nothing is more basic than reading, writing, and thinking. Thus, why not move "backwards" to LEA practices of the 1950s? In the founding days and the golden days of LEA, children received excellent, child-centered instruction. Let us carry on the legacy of Russ Stauffer, Sylvia Ashton-Warner, and Roach Van Allen, and keep the focus of instruction on experiences—and, most important, on our children.

REFERENCES

Allen, R. V. (1956). *Reading—Grades one through eight*. San Diego: Office of the Superintendent of Schools.

Allen, R.V. (1976). *Language experiences for communication*. Boston: Houghton Mifflin.

Allen, R. V. (1994). Speech given by Roach Van Allen at the International Reading Conference as he was named one of the "Greats of the 20th Century."

Ashton-Warner, S. (1958). *Spinster*. New York: Simon and Schuster.

Ashton-Warner, S. (1963). *Teacher*. New York: Simon and Schuster.

Guilford, J. P. (1959). *Personality*. New York: McGraw Hill.

Sampson, M, Sampson, M. B., & Allen, R. V. (1995). *Pathways to literacy: Process transactions*. Fort Worth: Harcourt Brace.

Stauffer, R. (1969). The effectiveness of language arts and basic reading approaches to first grade reading instruction. *Reading Research Quarterly, 4*(4), 468–499.

Sulzby, E., Teale, W. H., & Kamberelis, G. (1989). Emergent writing in the classroom: Home and school connections. In D. S. Strickland & L. M. Morrow (Eds.), *Emergent literacy: Young children learn to read and write*. Newark, DE: International Reading Association.

A Chronology of the Language Experience Special Interest Group

BONNIE C. WILKERSON

Director of Research, Evaluation and Assessment, Elgin, IL

Firsts

First Officers

Russell G. Stauffer, Chair
MaryAnne Hall, Secretary/Treasurer
First Annual Business Meeting: Anaheim, 1970

First Steering Committee
(predecessor of the Executive Board) 1970–71

Roach Van Allen
John Downing
Harry Hahn
Ed Henderson
Eleanor Roberts

First Preconvention Institute: Atlantic City, 1971

"the major effort of the group during its first year of existence"
(MaryAnne Hall, Minutes of the Annual Business Meeting, 1972)

First Forum: San Diego, 1976

The first forum was proposed by Dorsey Hammond at the Annual Business Meeting, 1975, for the purpose of "sharing ideas and raising questions." Jane L. Davidson was in charge of the program; Barb Evans handled local arrangements. Members who shared research were Ed Henderson, John Calvert, Harry Hahn, Jerry Treadway, Rich Vacca, Annette Guenther, and Jane Davidson.

First Newsletter: 1976

Publishing a newsletter was first discussed at the Annual Business Meeting, 1971, but was determined to be "not practical at the present time." Ed Henderson suggested at the Annual Business Meeting in 1976 that a newsletter be activated, and a committee for that purpose was appointed. Members of the committee were Harry Hahn, Annette Guenther, and Roach Van Allen.

First *Journal of Language Experience*: 1979, Vol. 1, No. 1

Editors: Annette Guenther, Dorsey Hammond, Rich Vacca
First Editorial Advisory Board: Appointed at the Annual Business Meeting, 1979; first advisory board input in Vol. 2, No. 1. The members of the editorial advisory board and their terms of office were:

V. Andree Baylis (1 year)
Ron Cramer (1 year)
Everest Green (2 years)
Annette Guenther (1 year)
MaryAnne Hall (3 years)
Dorsey Hammond (3 years)
Ed Henderson (2 years)
Eleanor Kirkland (2 years)
Gerry Williams (1 year)
Rich Vacca, Editor (2 years)

It was determined that the term of office of editor would be two years and that in terms of the advisory board, "hereafter expired terms will be replaced with people selected from the membership roster and terms will be for three years" (Minutes of the Annual Business Meeting, 1978).

Then and Now

Officers

1970–72. Russell G. Stauffer, Chair; MaryAnne Hall, Secretary/Treasurer
1972–74. Edmund Henderson, Chair; MaryAnne Hall, Secretary/Treasurer
1974–76. John Downing, Chair; Jane L. Davidson, Secretary
1976–78. R. Van Allen, Chair; Jane L. Davidson, Secretary/Treasurer
1978–80. Jane L. Davidson/Chair; Barb Evans, Secretary/Treasurer
1980–82. MaryAnne Hall, Chair; James Beers, Secretary/Treasurer
1982–84. Donna Ogle, Chair; Eunice Schmidt, Secretary/Treasurer
1984–86. Jerry Zutell, Chair; Bonnie C. Wilkerson, Secretary/Treasurer
1986–88. Charlene Gill, Chair; *1987–92.* Rich Healy, Secretary/Treasurer
1988–89. Sharon Arthur Moore, Chair
1989–92. Timothy V. Rasinski, Chair
1992–94. Nancy Padak, Chair; Donald Bear, Secretary/Newsletter; Wayne Linek,
   Treasurer/Membership
1993–   . Olga Nelson, Publications Committee
1994–96. Wayne M. Linek, Chair; Bonnie C. Wilkerson, Secretary/Treasurer
1996–98. Betty Sturtevant, Chair; Gary Padak, Secretary/Treasurer

The Executive Board

Functions of the Executive Board are to serve in an advisory capacity to the Chair and to plan or delegate responsibility for planning preconvention institutes and forums. Members are elected to serve two-year terms of office.

1970. R. Van Allen, John Downing, Harry Hahn, Ed Henderson, Eleanor Roberts
1972. R. Van Allen, John Downing, Harry Hahn, Eleanor Roberts, Russell Stauffer
1974. Annette Guenther, Ron Cramer, Barb Evans, Dorsey Hammond, Jerry
   Bailey
1976. MaryAnne Hall, Bob McCracken, John Downing, Annette Guenther, Ron
   Cramer
1978. Cynthia Homer, Mazie Bristow, Rich Vacca, Eleanor Kirkland, R. Van Allen
1979. David Tucker, Donna Ogle, Cynthia Homer, Mazie Bristow, R. Van Allen
1980. David Tucker, Donna Ogle, Jane Davidson
1981. Jane Davidson

1982. Carol Beers, William Stratton, Steve Hansell, Jerry Zutell, MaryAnne Hall
1983. Barb Kiefer, Steve Hansell
1984. Charlene Gill, Mary Alyce Lach, Barb Kiefer, Steve Hansell
1985. Sharon Arthur Moore, Nigel Hall, Charlene Gill, Mary Alyce Lach
1986. Dorsey Hammond, Nancy Padak, Sharon Arthur Moore, Nigel Hall
1987. MaryAnne Hall, Jim Beers
1988. Jack Barshinger, Timothy V. Rasinski
1989. Olga Nelson, Karen Pinter, Kathy Roskos
1990. Bill Henk, Wayne Linek
1992. Jerry Zutell, Betty Sturtevant, Donald Bear, Sally Nathenson-Mejia
1993. Peggy Moore, Mary Beth Sampson
1994. Robin Campbell, Gary Padak
1995. Ana Lado, Mary Jo Fresch

Annual Business Meetings

1971. Atlantic City.
1972. Detroit.
1973. Denver.
1974. New Orleans.
1975. New York City.
1976. Anaheim.
1977. Miami Beach.
1978. Houston.
1979. Atlanta.
1980. St. Louis.
1981. New Orleans.
1982. Chicago. Speakers: Martha King, Donald Graves
1983. Anaheim. "Research on Beginning Reading." Speakers: William H. Teale, Edward Chittenden
1984. Atlanta. "Spelling, Words, and Meaning: A Research Update" Speakers: Edmund Henderson, Marcia Invernizzi, Shane Templeton, Sharon Arthur Moore, Ron Cramer
1985. New Orleans. "Research in Beginning Literacy." Speakers: Denny Taylor ("The Home Connection") Diane DeFord ("The School Connection")
1986. Philadelphia. Speakers: Harold Rosen ("A Socio-Cultural View of Writing Development") Moira McKenzie ("Apprenticeship in Writing")
1987. Anaheim. Speaker: Angela Jagger ("Teachers as Observers")
1990. Atlanta. Speakers: Lee Galda, "Children's Literature as a Language Experience" Diane DeFord, "Reading Recovery as a Language Experience"
1991. Las Vegas.
1994. Toronto, Canada.
1995. Anaheim. Featured Speaker: Bill Martin, Jr. Theme: Celebrating the 25th Anniversary of IRA's First Special Interest Group
1996. New Orleans. Featured Speaker: Gloria Houston, author of *My Great Aunt Arizona*. Theme: The Integration of Language and Experience for a Lifetime of Learning

Preconvention Institutes

1971. Atlantic City. Program: Roach Van Allen, John Downing, Harry Hahn, Ed Henderson, Eleanor Roberts, Russell Stauffer
1972. Detroit. Program: Harry Hahn, Dorsey Hammond, John Downing
1973. Denver. Program: Ed Henderson. Theme: "Psycholinguistic Theory and Language Experiences." Presenters: Gill Schiffman, Ron Wardhaugh, Russell Stauffer, R. Van Allen, Harry Hahn
1974. New Orleans. Program: John Downing, Ron Cramer
1975. New York City. Program: Dorsey Hammond, Annette Guenther

1976. Anaheim. Program: Jane L. Davidson, Barbara Evans. Presenters: Wilson Rawls, Robert McCracken, Marlene McCracken, John Downing, Diane Arrigo, Gail Guth, Rich Vacca, Elizabeth Hunter

1977. Miami. Program: MaryAnne Hall, Evelyn Spache. Presenters: Yetta Goodman, George Spache

1978. No Preconvention Institute

1979. Atlanta. Program: Eleanor Kirkland, Charles Temple, Charlene Gill, Millie Lindell, Selma Wasserman, John Merritt, Norma Heiman, Alice Yardley, Irene Darvemza

1980. St. Louis. Program: Cindy Homer. Theme: "Language Experience: Focus on Research and Practice." Presenters: Cynthia Homer, Carolyn Burke, Irene Athey, MaryAnne Hall, Robert McCracken, Marlene McCracken, David Doake, Margaret Kratzer, Nora Walker, Joan Clark, Lucy McCormick Calkins, Jane L. Davidson, Edmund Henderson.

1981. No Preconvention Institute

1982. Chicago. Program: V. Andree Bayliss. Theme: "Language-Experience at All Levels: Holistic Approaches to Classroom Instruction." Presenters: V. Andree Bayliss, Moira McKenzie, MaryAnne Hall, Pauline Barker, Bonnie Greenslade, Marge Sauer, Jane L. Davidson, Donna Ogle, Jean Schultz, Judy Washburn, Rich Vacca, JoAnne Vacca, Lynn Strong, Nancy Padak, Bob Barton, David Booth, Dorsey Hammond

1983. Anaheim. Program: William Stratton, Carol Beers. Theme: "Language Experience for Students of Diverse Cultural Backgrounds." Presenters: William Stratton, James Beers, Carol Beers, John McKinnes, John Ryckman, Marie Clay, Kathryn Au

1984. Atlanta. Program: T. Stevenson Hansell, Barbara Keifer. Theme: "Thinking, Language and Reading." Presenters: Eliot Wiginton, Lois Lee Kaylor, Voncille Mallory, Kathleen Visovatti, Steve Hansell, Barbara Kiefer, Timothy V. Rasinski, Susan Semler

1985. No Preconvention Institute (Proposal not accepted by IRA)

1986. No Preconvention Institute (Proposal not accepted by IRA)

1987. No Preconvention Institute (Proposal not accepted by IRA)

1990. Atlanta. Theme: "Language Experience and the Integrated Curriculum."

In 1994 the LESIG board, faced with an IRA requirement that Special Interest Groups have only one entry on the conference program, recommended that LESIG keep its guaranteed spot on the program rather than submit Preconvention Institute proposals. The recommendation was unanimously approved at the 1994 Business Meeting.

Forums

1976. San Diego Sheraton-Harbor Island. Members shared research

1977. Sarasota, The Buccaneer Inn. Program: John Downing. Local Arrangements: Evelyn Spache

1978. San Antonio, The Menger Hotel. Program: Russell Stauffer. Local Arrangements: David Tucker and Fran Rhodes. Speakers: Rosie Barrera, Jim Califf, Jane L. Davidson, Norma Heiman

1979. St. Simons Island, The King and Prince Hotel. Program: Jim Beers. Local Arrangements: MaryAnne Hall. Speakers: Richard Anderson, Ronald Deadman

1980. Lake of the Ozarks, Missouri, Rock Harbor Resort. Local Arrangements: V. Andree Bayliss. Speakers: Lucy Calkins, Michael Halliday

1981. Biloxi, Mississippi, The Biloxi Inn. Program: William Stratton. Local Arrangements: MaryAnne Hall. Speakers: Robert Barton, David Booth

1982. Chicago, The Bismarck Hotel. Program: Eunice Schmidt and Jerry Zutell. Local Arrangements: Donna Ogle. Speakers: John Chapman, Hans Grundin, Morgen Jansen ("Language Experiences: Crossnational/Crosslingual Research")

1983. LaJolla, California. Forum Arrangements: Jerry Zutell, Bill Teale. Speakers: Peg Griffin ("Ways to Marshall Background Experiences for Use in Reading, Teaching, and Learning"), Kathryn Hu-Pei Au ("Micro-Ethnographic Research on Reading Comprehension and Young Children"), Edward Chittenden and Anne Bussis ("Longitudinal Study of Children Learning to Read: Inquiry Into Meaning")

1984. Callaway Gardens, Georgia, May 4–5. Forum Arrangements: MaryAnne Hall. Speakers: Judith Greene, Elizabeth Sulzby, JoAnne Vacca, Tom Gill

1985. Pensacola Beach, Florida, May 9–11. Program: Barb Kiefer. Local Arrangements: Bill Barnes, Bob Schlagel. Speaker: Jerry Harste ("Examining Our Assumptions About Literacy"). Panel discussion: "Perspectives on Specifics of Classroom Instruction." Moderator: Jerry Zutell. Panel: Jane Davidson, Nigel Hall, Steve Hansell, Jerry Harste, Barbara Kiefer

1986. St. Michael's, Maryland, Martingham Harbourtowne Inn, April 17–19. Program: Jerry Zutell. Local Arrangements: Charlene Gill. Speaker: Harold Rosen ("The Role of Child Language and Sense of Narrative in Learning to Read and Write"). Research Presentations: LESIG members. Panel Discussion: "Reflections on Forum Presentations, Implications for Future Directions."

1987. San Diego, Sheraton Grand Hotel on Harbor Island, May 1–2. Speaker: Linnea Ehri. Research Presentations: Donald Bear, Jane Davidson, Cheryl Troyer, Bonnie Wilkerson

1990. Athens, Georgia, May 4–5. Speakers: JoBeth Allen, Donna Alvermann, Carl Glickman, David Hayes, Sharon Merriam, David Reinking

In 1994 an effort was made to reinstitute forum, but through a general consensus the decision was made to focus attention on the 1995 regular program and continue to consider the issue of reinstituting forum, based on member interest.

Publications

Newsletter. 1976.
Committee: Harry Hahn, Annette Guenther, Roach Van Allen
Newsletter. 1977 (3 were published).
Committee: Rich Vacca, Dorsey Hammond, Annette Guenther
Newsletter. 1978 (3 were published).
Committee: Dorsey Hammond, Rich Vacca, Annette Guenther
Journal of Language Experience, 1979, Vol. 1, Nos. 1 & 2. Editors: Rich Vacca, Annette Guenther, Dorsey Hammond
Journal of Language Experience, 1980, Vol. 2, Nos. 1 & 2. Editor: Rich Vacca. Editorial Advisory Board: V. Andree Bayliss, Ron Cramer, Everest Green, Annette Guenther, MaryAnne Hall, Dorsey Hammond, Ed Henderson, Eleanor Kirkland, Geri Williams
Journal of Language Experience, 1981, Vol. 3, Nos. 1 & 2. Editor: Rich Vacca. Editorial Advisory Board: V. Andree Bayliss, James Beers, Ron Cramer, Jane L. Davidson, Everest Green, MaryAnne Hall, Dorsey Hammond, Ed Henderson, Eleanor Kirkland
Journal of Language Experience, 1981–82, Vol. 4, Nos. 1 & 2. Editor: Rich Vacca. Editorial Advisory Board (same as above)
Journal of Language Experience, 1982–83, Vol. 5, Nos. 1 & 2. Editor: V. Andree Bayliss. Editorial Advisory Board: David W. Booth, Jane L. Davidson, MaryAnne Hall, James R. Layton, Russell G. Stauffer
Journal of Language Experience, 1983–84, Vol. 6, Nos. 1 & 2. Editor: V. Andree Bayliss. Editorial Advisory Board: Jane L. Davidson, MaryAnne Hall, James R. Layton, Sharon Arthur Moore, Russell G. Stauffer, JoAnne Vacca
Journal of Language Experience, 1985, Vol. 7, No. 1. Editor: T. Stevenson Hansell. Editorial Advisory Board: James Beers, Jane L. Davidson, MaryAnne Hall, Sharon Arthur Moore, Russell G. Stauffer, JoAnne Vacca
Journal of Language Experience, 1986, Vol. 8, No. 1. Editor: T. Stevenson Hansell.
Journal of Language Experience, 1988 (Spring and Fall), Vol. 9, Nos. 1 & 2. Editor: Nancy D. Padak. Editorial Advisory Board: Brenda Church, Jane L. Davidson, MaryAnne Hall, Dennis Kear, Betsy Pryor, Kathy Roskos
Journal of Language Experience, 1989, Vol. 10, No. 1. Editor: Nancy D. Padak. Assistant Editor: Olga Nelson. Technical Assistance: Karen Brothers. Editorial Advisory Board: Brenda Church, Jane L. Davidson, MaryAnne Hall, Dennis Kear, Betsy Pryor, Kathy Roskos
Journal of Language Experience, 1990, Vol. 10, No. 1. Editor: Nancy D. Padak. Technical Assistance:

Karen Brothers. Editorial Advisory Board: Kathy Barclay, Andree Bayliss, Connie Sorenson, Cheryl Troyer, Bonnie Wilkerson, Jerry Zutell
Journal of Language Experience, 1992, Vol. 11, No. 1. Editor: Olga Nelson. Editorial Assistance: Nancy Bristol. Editorial Advisory Board: Kathy Barclay, Karen Pinter, Connie Sorenson, Jerry Zutell

Volume 11, No. 1 represented the final publication of the *Journal of Language Experience* and the end of its thirteen-year history. Members chose to change some aspects of the organization's activities, including publications. Subsequent publications efforts were to include a membership newsletter and occasional monographs. The membership newsletter was published as the *Language Experience Forum*.

Language Experience Forum Volume 25, No. 1, July 1994. Nancy Padak and Tim Rasinski, Editors
Language Experience Forum Volume 25, No. 2, February 1995. Nancy Padak and Tim Rasinski, Editors
Language Experience Forum Volume 26, No. 1, June 1995. Nancy Padak and Tim Rasinski, Editors

Policy

The Language Experience Special Interest Group operates under guidelines established by the International Reading Association. Additional policy developed by the membership of the Language Experience Special Interest Group is as follows:

1. Forum expenses should be covered within the Forum.
2. Members of the Executive Board are elected for two-year terms of office.
3. Members of the Editorial Advisory Board are appointed for three-year terms of office.
4. The Executive Board plans or appoints persons to plan preconvention institutes and forums.

Purposes

At the Tenth Annual Business Meeting of the Language Experience Special Interest Group (Atlanta, 1979), Ron Cramer read a paper written by Ed Henderson entitled "The Language Experience Special Interest Group in Its Second Decade—A Perspective." Group discussions followed, with focus on principles and practices of language experience. It was decided at that meeting that a statement should be written to express the basic principles and practices of the Special Interest Group. The statement of commitment was presented at the Annual Business Meeting, 1980, in St. Louis by Jane L. Davidson as a synthesis of the previous year's discussion. The statement was adopted at the 1980 meeting. (See Padak & Rasinski, Chapter 1, for LESIG's Statement of Commitment.)

INDEX

Ability grouping, 44–45
Activities, 4–5, 12–14
  assessment. *See* Assessment
  computer, 57, 250–255
  DR-TA. *See* Directed Reading-
    Thinking Activity
  DSTA. *See* Directed Spelling
    Thinking Activity
  environmental print, 50–51, 54–57
  ESL. *See* ESL instruction
  extended learning, for beginning
    readers, 44
  family folklore unit, 189–194, 192f
  group mapping, 142–147,
    143f–145f
  guided imagery, 68–72
  integrated. *See* Integrated
    curriculum
  math simulation unit, 183–188
  negotiated language experience, 259
  nursery rhyme, 83–85
  play-story connections, 73–81
  responsive, 78–79
  science nutrition unit, 174–182
  scrapbooks. *See* Scrapbook projects
  social studies, 189–198, 192f, 193f,
    201f, 204f, 205f
  with song picture books, 87–92
  for special needs students. *See*
    Special needs students
  story discourse, 64–67
  storytelling, 189–194
  word sorting, 157–160
  writing workshop. *See* Writing
    workshop
Activity Movement, 26–27
Allen, R. V., 4, 5, 6, 29–30, 232
Alpha listing, 242–243, 242f
Alphabet, writing. *See* Beginning
    writers; Writing process
Alphabet method, 26
Altwerger, B., 8, 33
Anecdotal notes/records, 106–107,
    201, 201f, 204–205
Arredondo, D. E., 241
Ashton-Warner, Sylvia, 13, 14,
    264–265
Assessment
  in DR-TA, 150
  in DSTA, 168–169, 168f
  of higher-level thinking skills in
    middle grades, 199–207. *See
    also* Middle grades
  in nutrition unit, 179–180

in primary grades, 102–108. *See also*
    Primary grades
  of special needs student
    at-risk for reading, 110–117
    learning disabled, 227, 228t
Assisted word sorting, 166, 167f
At-risk student, 110–117. *See also*
    Reading clinic profile; Special
    needs students
Author's voice, 209–210. *See also*
    Voice
Awareness
  in DR-TA, 149
  of written language, 15, 42, 49–50.
    See also Written language

Bank cards, 159–160
Bank simulation, 185–186
Barbieri, M., 217
Basal readers, 26, 27, 28, 29
Basic Interpersonal Communications
    Skills, 258
Beginning readers, 41–47. *See also*
    Preschoolers
  advantages of LEA for, 46–47
  assessing. *See under* Primary grades
  diversity of experiences, 42–43
  environment and, 15, 42, 53–54.
    See also Written language
  extended learning activities, 44
  First Grade Studies research project,
    8–9, 14
  grouping techniques, 44–45
  nursery rhymes for, 83–85
  song picture books for, 87–92
  teacher's role with, 45
  written language and. *See* Written
    language
Beginning writers, 93–101, 93f
  activities for, 50–51, 54–57
  assessing. *See under* Primary grades
  letter formation, 94–95, 95f, 96f
  phrase and sentence formation,
    97–99, 98f, 99f
  story sense, 99–100, 100f
  word formation, 95–97, 97f
  written language learning. *See*
    Written language
BICS (Basic Interpersonal
    Communications Skills), 258
Big Books, 56–57
Bilingual students, 257–262. *See also*
    Negotiated language
    experience

Biography project, 202, 204f
Block scheduling, 217
Blum, I. M., 15
Books
  picture, story discourse and,
    65–67
  predictable, 57, 266
  resource lists. *See* Resource books
  scrapbooks, 59–63, 61f–63f, 191,
    192f
  song picture books, 87–92
  time for, 78, 226
Breen, M., 258
Britain, 14, 19
  classroom practice, 20–21
  government initiatives, 21–22
  theory and practice, 22–23
Britton, James, 22
Brown, E., 64
Bruning, R. H., 222
Budget simulation, 184
The Bullock Report, 22
Burke, C. L., 15
Burrows, Alvina Treut, 29
Burwell, Vicki Matthews, 181
Butler, D., 64

Calkins, Lucy, 217
CALP (Cognitive/Academic Language
    Proficiencies), 258
Cards, for word sorts, 159–160
Chandlin, C., 258
Charting
  in edible science unit, 177t, 179t
  experience charts, 14, 27, 29–30,
    54–55
Children's literature
  creating scripts from, 197
  discussion groups, as assessment
    tool, 202, 203f
  generating story ideas from, 190
  integrating into social studies,
    195–196
  learning disabled students and,
    226–227
Children's Nutrition Research Center,
    174
Choice, play-literacy connections and,
    78
Chomsky, C., 33
City hall simulation, 185
Classroom
  British practices, 20–21
  as LEA environment, 4–6

Classroom *continued*
    as learning community. *See*
        Learning community
    organization, 6
    reading clinic methods and, 121
Clay, Marie, 16, 49, 64, 94, 157
Clinton, Bill, 174–175
Closed word sort, 118, 158–159
Cluster diagram, 191–192, 193f
CNRC (Children's Nutrition Research
    Center), 174
Cognitive/Academic Language
    Proficiencies, 258
Communicative methodology of
    language, 258–259
Community of learners. *See* Learning
    community
Comprehension
    developing, in DR-TA, 150–151
    questioning and, 148–149
Computers
    ESL students and, 248–256. *See also*
        ESL instruction
    preschoolers and, 57
Conversation, special needs students
    and, 232–233
Cooke, Flora, 25–26
Cooperative word sorting, 166–168
Creative expression, LD students and,
    227
Critical thinking. *See* Thinking
    skills/strategies
Cummins, J., 258
Curriculum
    focusing on, 102–103
    integrated. *See* Integrated
        curriculum
    LEA, advantages of, 46–47,
        138–140
    student voice in writing and,
        212–213

Davidson, J. L., 5, 6
Decision making, of classroom
    teacher, 127–128
    and students, 130–131
Department of Education (U.S.)
    First Grade Studies project, 8–9, 14
    forum on education reform, 181
Dewey, John, 249
Dictation, 266–267
Directed Reading-Thinking Activity,
    29, 31–32, 148–155
    developing comprehension,
        150–151
    DSTA and, 162–163
    history lesson transcript, 151,
        151t–153t
    identifying purposes for reading,
        150
    observing student reading, 150

rate of reading, 150
    skill training activities, 154
Directed Spelling Thinking Activity,
    161–173
    assessment and record keeping,
        168–169, 168f
    conceptual framework, 163–164
    DR-TA and, 162–163
    older students and, 169–170, 169f
    practice activities, 168
    prediction and discussion, 165
    student writing samples, 170–171,
        170f, 171f
    word hunting, 166
    word sorting, 166–168, 167f
Discovery projects, 197
Discussion
    in DSTA, 165
    literature discussion groups,
        assessing, 202, 203f
    of play-story connections, 75–76, 76f
Dixon, Fran, 250
Documentation
    anecdotal notes/records, 106–107,
        201, 201f, 204–205
    IEP, ongoing assessment and, 227,
        228t
    necessity of, 106
    reading clinic assessment, 112t,
        115t–116t
    of words learned, in DSTA,
        168–169, 168f
Donaldson, M., 64
Downing, John, 38, 40, 49
DR-TA. *See* Directed Reading-
    Thinking Activity
DSTA. *See* Directed Spelling Thinking
    Activity
Dual coding theory, 69

Eastern Michigan University Reading
    Clinic, student profile, 110–117.
    See also Reading clinic profile
Edelsky, C., 33
Edible science unit, middle grades,
    174–182
    activities, 178–179, 179t
    assessment in, 179–180
    engaging learners, 176
    explaining concepts, 177–178
    exploring flavors and ingredients,
        176–177, 177t
    integrating language arts, 175
    Learning Cycle Framework,
        175–176
Education, U.S. Department of. *See*
    Department of Education
Educational software, 57, 250
Engfish, 208
English as second language. *See* ESL
    instruction

Environmental print. *See* Written
    language
ESL instruction
    computers, use in, 248, 250
        class slide show, 252–255, 253f,
            254f
        for composition, 250–251
        immigration project, 251–255
        math software, 250
    LEA and, 238–240, 249–250
    technology and, 248
    thematic activities, 240–241
        alpha listing, 242–243, 242f
        expectation sentences, 244, 245f
        patterned poems, 245, 246f
        semantic grid, 243–244, 244f
        Word Wondering and
            Wandering, 243, 243f
Essay tests, 205–206, 205f
Evaluation. *See* Assessment
Expectation sentences, 244, 245f
Experience-based text, 215
Experience charts, 14, 27, 29–30,
    54–55
Experience story, 76–77, 77f
Experiential learning, 13
Extended learning activities,
    beginning readers, 44

Falk-Ross, F., 225
Falvey, M. A., 222
Family folklore unit, 189–194, 192f
Female students, middle grades, 216,
    218–220
First grade
    First Grade Studies research project,
        8–9, 14
    teaching experiences in, 123–125,
        126–136
First Grade Studies research project,
    8–9, 14
Flexibility
    grouping techniques and, 44–45
    in rate of reading, 150
Flores, B., 33
Folklore, family history unit, 189–194
Framework(s)
    for assessing higher-level thinking
        skills in middle grades,
        199–207. *See also* Middle grades
    DSTA, 163–164
    Language Cycle Framework, 175
    for learning, 1–10
    organizational, for instruction, 6
    thematic, for ESL students,
        237–247. *See also* ESL
        instruction

Gardner, Dorothy, 21
Giard, Mary, interview, 126–136
Girls, middle grades, 216, 218–220

Givner, C. C., 222
Goal-setting, by classroom teacher,
127–128
and students, 135–136
Goddard, Nora, 20
Goodman, K., 15, 32–33, 225
Goodman, Yetta, 8, 15
Government initiatives
U.K., 21–23
U.S. *See under* United States
Grades. *See* First grade; Middle grades;
Primary grades
Graves, Donald, 16
Great Britain. *See* Britain
Group Mapping Activity, 142–147,
143f–145f
Groups
grouping techniques, 44–45
literature discussion, assessing, 202,
203f
mapping activity, 142–147,
143f–145f
SIG. *See* Language Experience
Special Interest Group
Guided imagery experience, 68–71

The Hadow Report, 21, 22
Hahn, Harry, 38
Hall, MaryAnne, 3, 5, 6, 9, 38, 238
Halliday, Michael, 48
Hansche, L. N., 50
Harp, Bill, 87
Harste, Jerome, 15
Henderson, Edmund, 38, 40
Herse, R., 49
Historical overviews
of Ashton-Warner, Sylvia, 264–265
of British primary school
curriculum, 19–23
of LEA, in U.S., 14, 25–34, 263–266
of LESIG. *See* Language Experience
Special Interest Group
of Stauffer, Russell, 265–266
of Van Allen, Roach, 264
History. *See* Social studies
Hodges, Paula, 243
Holdaway, D, 15
Huey, E. B., 25–26

IEP documentation, 227, 228t
Imagination, guided imagery, 68–71
Immigration project, 251–255, 253f,
254f
Individual word sorting, 166–168
Individualized Education Plan, 227,
228t
Individualized Reading, 27–29
Instruction. *See also* Activities
availability of materials, 6
ESL. *See* ESL instruction
linking assessment to, 103–104

for at-risk reading clinic student,
111–113, 112t
reading clinic methods, classroom
use, 121
organizational framework for, 6
principles, first grade, 126–136
reading clinic strategies, 113–114,
117–119
reading methods, historical
overview, 26–34
of special needs students. *See*
Special needs students
strategy instruction, 6–7
Integrated curriculum
edible science unit, 174–182
environmental print experiences,
50–51, 54–57
family history unit, 189–194
LEA as, 16
Williamsville simulation, 183–188
Intelligences, multiple, 266
International Reading Association
LESIG. *See* Language Experience
Special Interest Group
research review, 9, 17
Invented spelling, 95–99, 96f–99f
Isaac, Susan, 21

Jett-Simpson, M., 64
Johnston, P. H., 102
The Journal of Language Experience, 38
Journal writing
in DSTA, 170–171, 170f, 171f
in history units, 196

Kalmes, Pat, 114
Kamberelis, G., 267
Karnowski, L., 87
Kimm, C., 222
Krashen, Stephen, 238

Language
acquisition, theory of, 238–240
English as second language. *See* ESL
instruction
knowledge, assessing in primary
grades, 105
reading mastery and, 231–233
written. *See* Written language
Language Cycle Framework, 175
Language experience approach
activities. *See* Activities; Integrated
curriculum
advantages, 46–47
for beginning readers. *See*
Beginning readers
British, 14, 19–23
defined, 2–4
effectiveness, 8–9
historical overviews. *See* Historical
overviews

language acquisition theory and,
238–240
in middle grades. *See* Middle grades
negotiated, 257–262. *See also*
Negotiated language
experience
organizational framework, 6
rationale, 1–2
for special needs students. *See*
Special needs students
tenets, second language acquisition
and, 238–240
whole language and, 1, 7–8, 33–34,
266
writing workshop parallels,
214–215
Language experience learning and
teaching, 12–18
current developments, 15–18
described, 12–14
historical perspective, 14
Language Experience Special Interest
Group, 32, 37–40, 269–276
annual meetings, 271–272
board members, past and current,
38, 40, 271
commitment, statement of, 10
firsts, 269–270
forums, 273–274
officers, past and current, 38, 40,
270–271
policy guidelines, 276
preconvention institutes, 272–273
publications, 274–276
purposes, 276
statement of commitment, 10
LD students. *See* Learning disabled
students
LEA. *See* Language experience
approach
Learner
classroom teacher as, 129
as user of language, 12–13
Learning. *See also* Language
experience learning and
teaching
Dewey's theory of, 249
experiential, 13
LEA as framework for, 1–10
special needs students and,
232–233
of written language, 15, 48–51
Learning community
goal-setting, 127–128, 135–136
of special needs students, 222–223
teacher and student roles, 130–132,
133–134
Learning disabled students, 224–229.
See also Special needs students
improving skills with literature,
226–227

Learning community *continued*
  LEA and, 225–226
  nurturing creative expression in, 227
  ongoing assessment for IEPs, 227, 228t
Learning how to mean, 48
Lee, D. M., 29–30
LESIG. *See* Language Experience Special Interest Group
Letters, formation by beginning writers, 94–95, 95f, 96f
Library simulation, 185–186
Liner, Tom, 211
Listening skills/strategies, LD students and, 226–227
Listing, alpha, 242–243, 242f
Literacy
  assessing. *See under* Primary grades
  development, song lyrics and, 87–92
  play-story connections, 73–80
Literacy environment, creating, 54–56
Literature, children's. *See* Children's literature
Literature webs, 57
Logsdon, D. M., 15
Lyrics, literacy and, 87–92

Macrorie, Ken, 208, 210, 211
Manzo, A. V., 149
Mapping, Group Mapping Activity, 142–147, 143f–145f
Marshall, Sybil, 20–21
Martin, Jr., Bill, 266
Marzano, R., 241
Materials, availability, 6
Mathematics
  educational software, 250
  Third International Math and Science Study, 174
  Williamsville simulation, 183–188
Meaning contrast, 169–170, 169f
Meaning-making processes
  assessing, in primary grades, 104–105
  learning how to mean, 48
  vs. learning skills in isolation, 7
Meek, Margaret, 78
Meltzer, N. S., 49
Mercer, A. R., 221
Mercer, C. D., 221
Middle grades, 137–141
  advantages of LEA in, 139–140
  assessing higher-level thinking skills in social studies context, 199–207
  anecdotal notes, 201, 201f, 204–205
  essay tests, 205–206, 205f

final projects, 206
  literature discussion groups, 202, 203f
  report cards and parent conferences, 206–207
  research reports, 202, 204f
  specific technical skills, 206
  edible science, 174–182. *See also* Edible science unit
  female students, 216, 218–220
  rationale for LEA in, 138–139
  writing workshop, 214–220. *See also* Writing workshop
Miller, Patricia, 9
Moeller, G. D., 15
Mountain, L., 64
Multiple intelligences, 266
Museum simulation, 185–186
Musical lyrics, literacy and, 87–90

Narrative charts, 30
National Assessment of Education Progress, 175
National Curriculum (U.K.), 23
National Institute of Education, 225
National Society for the Study of Education Yearbook, Part II, 26–27
National Standards, 140
Negotiated language experience, 257–262
  activities, 259
  defined, 258
  rationale, 258–259
  writing process, 259–261
Newspaper simulation, 185–186
Notes, anecdotal, 106–107, 201, 201f, 204–205
Nursery rhymes, 83–85
Nutrition unit. *See* Edible science unit

Open word sorts, 158–159
Oral language
  discussion. *See* Discussion
  special needs students and, 222
Organization, of LEA classroom, 6, 129–130

Paivio, A., 69
Paley, Vivian, 79
Pappas, C. C., 64
Parents
  partnering with, 132–133
  story discourse with preschoolers, 64–67
Patterned poems, 245, 246
Perez, B., 248
Phonics, 26, 46, 156, 157
  beginning writing and, 96
  song picture books and, 89

Phrases, formation by beginning writers, 97–99, 98f, 99f
Picture books
  of songs, literacy development and, 87–92
  story discourse and, 65–67
Picture cards, 159
Play experience, 75
Play-story connections, 73–80
  beyond LEA, 77–78
  from play to story, 74–75
  teacher role in, 78–79
The Plowden Report, 22
Poems, patterned, 245, 246
Point of view, sense of voice and, 210–211
Post office simulation, 184–185
Predictable books, 57, 266
Prediction
  in DSTA, 165
  predictable books, 57, 266
Preschoolers. *See also* Beginning readers; Beginning writers
  environmental print activities, 54–57
  literacy development, 53–54
  story discourse, 64–67
Primary grades. *See also* First grade
  assessment in, 102–108
  curricular and testing focus, 102–103
  documentation, 106–107
  of language knowledge, 105
  linking instruction to, 103–104
  of meaning-making processes, 104–105
  of personal attributes, 105–106
  reading clinic, 110–117. *See also* Reading clinic profile
  reporting, to parents, 107
  readers. *See* Beginning readers
  teaching experiences in, 123–125, 126–136
  writers. *See* Beginning writers
Print. *See* Written language
Process writing. *See* Writing process
Publications
  LESIG, 274–276
  science resource books, 181–182
  song picture books, resource list, 90–92
Publishing, in writing workshop, 215
  bilingual classroom, 260–261

Questioning, critical thinking and, 148–149

Reader's theater, 197
Reading clinic profile
  assessments
    affective, 113

following first semester, 115t–116t, 116
of letter-sound relationships, 113
ongoing, 119–120
at time of referral, 110–111
typing instruction to, 111–113, 112t, 121
instructional strategies, 113–114, 117–119
Reading instruction, historical overview
in U.K., 19–25
in U.S., 14, 26–34
Reading process. *See also* Children's literature
assessing. *See* Assessment
of beginning readers. *See* Beginning readers
defined, 3–4
DR-TA. *See* Directed Reading-Thinking Activity
Group Mapping Activity, 142–147, 143f–145f
instructional methods, historical overview, 26–34
song picture books and, 89
special needs students and
reading clinic process. *See* Reading clinic profile
reading instruction, ZPD and. *See under* Special needs students
in writing workshop, 215
Record keeping. *See* Documentation
Reflection, teacher as practitioner of, 128–129
Reid, J. F., 49
Report cards, 107, 207
Research
First Grade Studies project, 8–9
LEA effectiveness, 9
Research reports, biographical, 202, 204
Resource books
science, for inquiry projects, 181–182
song picture books, 90–92
Response
play-story connections and, 78–79
in writing workshop, 215
Revision, 215
Rhymes, nursery, 83–85
Roberts, Eleanor, 38
Rogers, Carl, 13
Role-playing, 211
Ronning, R. R., 222
Rumelhart, D. E., 226

Scheduling, of writing workshop, 217
Schraw, G. J., 222

Science
edible. *See* Edible science unit
Third International Math and Science Study, 174
Scrapbook projects, 59–60
activities, 60–61, 61f, 62f
benefits, 61–63, 63f
family folklore scrapbook, 191, 192f
Scripts, creating, 197
Sebesta, Sam, 241
Self-improving system, 157
Semantic grid, 243–244, 244f
Sense of story
beginning writers and, 99–100, 100f
development, 50
parental tips for developing, 64–67
play and, 74
use in storytelling unit, 189–190
Sentences
expectation, 244, 245f
formation by beginning writers, 97–99, 98f, 99f
SIG. *See* Language Experience Special Interest Group
Sight vocabulary, development, 46, 89
Slide show, computer generated, 251–255, 253f, 254f
Smith, F., 33
Smith, Frank, 87, 149
Smith, N. B., 27–28
Snow, C. E., 64
Social studies, 189–198
activities, 196–197
assessing higher level thinking in, 199–207. *See also* Middle grades
DR-TA transcript, 151, 151t–153t
family folklore unit, 189–194, 192f, 193f
integrating children's literature into, 195–196
Software, 57, 250
Song picture books
linking literacy and lyrics through, 87–90
resource list, 90–92
Sorting. *See* Word sorting
Special interest group. *See* Language Experience Special Interest Group
Special needs students, 221–247
bilingual, 257–262. *See also* Negotiated language experience
ESL, 237–247. *See also* ESL instruction
LD, 224–229. *See also* Learning disabled students
reading clinic, 110–117. *See also* Reading clinic profile

reading instruction, ZPD and, 230–236
assessment in, 234
conversation and, 232–233
expectations, 231, 234–235
theoretical base for, 231
writing experiences, 233
Spelling skills/strategies
assessing in middle grades, 206
of at-risk student, 113
of beginning writers, 95–99
DSTA, 161–173. *See also* Directed Spelling Thinking Activity
Stahl, Steven, 9
Stauffer, Russell, 6, 14, 30–32, 255, 265–266
basal readers, 29, 31
death, 39
DR-TA and, 31–32
LESIG and, 32, 37, 38
reading processes, 3, 4, 30
teaching skills in isolation, 7
Story
play as, 73–80. *See also* Play-story connections
sense of. *See* Sense of story
using nursery rhymes with, 83–85
Story discourse. *See* Sense of story
Story sense. *See* Sense of story
Storytelling unit, 189–194
collecting family stories, 191
generating story ideas, 190–191
sense of story and, 189–190
storytelling preparation and presentation, 191–193, 193f
writing process and samples, 191, 192f
Strategy instruction, 6–7
Student(s)
beginning readers. *See* Beginning readers
bilingual, 257–262
as builders of learning community, 131–132
as decision makers, 130–131, 133–134
female, 216, 218–220
goal-setting, 135–136
independence of, 6
middle grade. *See* Middle grades
primary grade. *See* Primary grades
with special needs. *See* Special needs students
teacher as watcher of, 134–135
Sulzby, E., 267

Taylor, N. E., 15
Teacher-directed activities for preschoolers, 56–57

Teachers
  of beginning readers, role, 45
  as builders of learning community, 131–132
  as decision makers, 127–128, 130–131
  goal-setting, 127–128, 135–136
  as kid watchers, 134–135
  as learners, 129
  as models, 135
  organizational role, 129–130
  partnering with parents, 132–133
  profiles, 123–125, 126–136
  as reflective practitioners, 128–129
  writing workshop role, defining, 217–218
Teaching, language experience learning and. *See* Language experience learning and teaching
Teale, W. H., 267
Tests
  essay, 205–206, 205f
  primary literacy instruction and, 102–103
Theater presentations, 197
Thematic instruction, for ESL students, 237–247. *See also* ESL instruction
Thinking skills/strategies, 148–149
  DR-TA, 149–155
  DSTA, 161–173
  Group Mapping Activity, 142–147, 143f–145f
  higher-level, assessing in middle grades, 199–207. *See also* Middle grades
Third International Math and Science Study, 174
Time
  for books, 78
  for writing workshop, 215
Transcript, of DR-TA history lesson, 151, 151t–153t

United Kingdom (U.K.). *See* Britain
United States
  DOE. *See* Department of Education
  National Assessment of Education Progress, 175
  National Institute of Education, 225
  National Standards, 140
  reading instruction, historical overview, 14, 25–34

Vacca, Richard T., 38
Valsiner, J., 231
Van Allen, Roach, 14, 38, 264, 266
Van Der Veer, R., 231
Vanishing Word Pictures, 57

Veatch, J., 4, 5–6
Vocabulary development
  at-risk student, 113–114, 117
  beginning readers, 46, 89
Voice, in written work, 208–213
  discerning, 209–210
  employing, across curriculum, 212–213
  nurturing, 208–209
  strategies for developing, 210–211
  student ownership of, 211–212
Vygotsky, Lev, 80, 164, 231, 233, 235, 259

Webbing, 57
Wells, G., 64
West Virginia University
  Child Development Laboratory, 54–57
  Nursery School, scrapbook project, 59–63
Whole language, 156–157
  LEA and, 1, 7–8, 33–34, 266
  tenets, 33
  word sorting and, 156–157
Wigginton, Elliot, 211–212
Williamsville simulation, 183–188
  assessment in, 187
  budget preparation, 184
  citizenship activities, 184
  community projects, 187
  problems with, 187–188
  professional impact, 188
  town centers, 184–186
The Winston Basic Readers Communication Program, 29
Woodward, V. A., 15
Word bank
  at-risk student, 113–114, 117
  word sorts using. *See* Word sorting
Word boundaries, 49
Word hunting, 166
Word method, 26
Word sorting
  in DR-TA, 157, 158–160
  in DSTA, 166–168, 167f
Word Wondering and Wandering, 243, 243f
Words
  boundaries of, 49
  formation by beginning writers, 95–97, 97f
  learned in DSTA, documentation, 168–169k168f
  sorting. *See* Word sorting
  word bank, for at-risk student, 113–114, 117
Work charts, 30
Writing process, 267
  assessing. *See* Assessment

of beginning writers. *See* Beginning writers
  computer composition, in ESL instruction, 250–251
  Individualized Reading and, 28
  integrating into curriculum, 16
  negotiated language experience, 259–261
  reading clinic profile, 117–119
  samples. *See* Writing samples
  scrapbook projects. *See* Scrapbook projects
  in social studies unit, 196, 197
  song picture books and, 89–90
  for special needs students, 117–119, 226–227, 233, 259–261
  for storytelling unit, 190–191, 192f
  voice in, 208–213. *See also* Voice, in written work
Writing samples
  from beginning writers
    letters, 95f, 96f
    play-based story, 77f
    preschooler stories, 61f, 63f
    stories, 99f, 100f
    words, 93f, 97f, 98f
  from DSTA, 170–171, 171f, 172f
  from fourth grade storytelling unit, 192f
  from middle grades
    journal writing, DSTA and, 170–171, 170f, 171f
    mapping activities, 143f–145f
    poetry, 219f
Writing workshop
  in bilingual classroom, 259–261
  in middle grades, 214–220
    classroom roles, defining, 217–218
    female students and, 216, 218–220
    LEA parallels, 214–215
    scheduling issues, 217
    students, unique needs of, 216–217
Written language, 48–58
  basic concepts, 49–50
  environmental print activities, 50–51, 54–57
  literacy development and, 15, 42, 48, 53–54

Zone of Proximal Development (ZPD), 164
  play and, 80
  reading by special needs students and, 230–236. *See also under* Special needs students